ENCYCLOPEDIA OF
SERIAL KILLERS

ENCYCLOPEDIA OF
SERIAL KILLERS

Colour
Library
Direct

CONTENTS

INTRODUCTION

AN IMPELLING FORCE SETS ONE TYPE OF murderer apart from the rest — the chilling, sinister desire to kill again and again.

Often the crimes are so sickening and evil that it is hard to accept the perpetrator could share any place at all among human beings in a supposedly civilised world. Yet these butchering beasts are capable of leading seemingly ordinary lives, while secretly carrying out murders whose horror sometimes defies belief. Add to their personality a peculiar cunning and a twisted track of thinking that even psychologists cannot unravel . . . and you are inside the mind of the serial killer.

He (and very occasionally she) is a psychopathic reaper of repugnant deeds, more sickening in their reality than ever could be created from the most shocking horror fiction. Quite simply, one act of murder is not enough for them. And each that follows is performed with equally satisfying, sadistic ritual.

The United States is a natural home for serial killers. In the 'peak' year of 1983 they accounted for 5,000 deaths. One estimate had it that as many as 35 murdering maniacs were on the loose at any one time.

The serial killer is a bizarre breed of murderer. In 1984 a 48-year-old vagrant, Henry Lee Lucas, made hundreds of confessions to rape, torture, kidnapping and mutilating victims before finally killing them. A total of 157 murders was eventually agreed between Lucas and police, making him a record-breaker in the annals of infamy. There have been other notorious killers both before and since Lucas. But perhaps his words best sum up what goes on inside the head of a serial killer, many of whom are included here in *The Encyclopedia of Serial Killers*.

'I was bitter at the world. I had nothing but pure hatred. Killing someone is just like walking outdoors. If I wanted a victim I'd just go out and get one.'

In a book of this size it is impossible to record the evil deeds of every person who has killed serially: indeed, it is only really in this century that society has been in a position to record the deeds. On top of this, the distinction between serial killer and mass murderer is a difficult one to make in many cases. I have therefore taken a cross-section of killers — including some from earlier centuries — and tried to cover as broad a spectrum of types of crime as possible.

ANN ARBOR HOSPITAL MURDERS

In just six weeks of 1975, no fewer than 56 patients died at the Ann Arbor Veterans' Administration Hospital in Michigan. There were eight deaths on one night alone in only three hours.

A muscle relaxant drug called Pavulon, derived from a South American poison, was revealed as the cause of the deaths. It was likely large doses had been given intravenously. The FBI was called in to investigate the massive increase in people who simply stopped breathing. The deaths of yet another eight patients virtually closed the hospital.

Suspicions fell upon two Filipino nurses, 30-year-old Filipina Narcissco and 31-year-old Leonora Perez. Both had always been on duty when the deaths occurred. Despite the written confession of a hospital supervisor who committed suicide in 1976, Narcissco and Perez went on trial the following year charged with eight murders, poisoning and conspiracy.

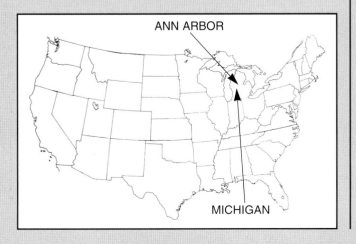

ANN ARBOR

MICHIGAN

NAME: Unknown, or not proved

PREFERRED MURDER METHOD: Drug causing respiratory arrest

NUMBER OF VICTIMS: 8 confirmed – likelihood of a total of 40

MURDER LOCALE: Ann Arbor Hospital

SPAN OF MURDER CAREER: months leading up to August 1975

DATE OF ARREST: June 1976 – two nurses charged – all charges dropped at second trial, February 1978

The case collapsed when it was revealed that although patients had stopped dying in large numbers once the nurses had been removed from duty, no one had actually seen them adding anything to the intravenous drips. Perez was discharged on instructions of the judge and Narcissco was found not guilty of murder. Both were convicted of poisoning and conspiracy, but the convictions were set aside when an appeal was lodged.

Awaiting a retrial, the two women underwent psychiatric testing but were pronounced sane and normal. All charges against them were dismissed at a second trial in February 1978. What exactly happened at the Ann Arbor Veterans' Administration Hospital was to remain a mystery.

THE BENDER FAMILY

NAME: Mr and Mrs Bender

BORN: 1813

DIED: Disappeared 1873 presumed dead

PREFERRED MURDER METHOD: Hammer

NUMBER OF VICTIMS: At least 8

NAMES OF VICTIMS: Unknown other than Dr W. York

MURDER LOCALE: Cherryvale, Kansas

SPAN OF MURDER CAREER: 1872-3

DATE OF CONVICTION: n/a

As owners of the fly-swept Wayside Inn, the villainous Bender family was always on the lookout for the easy touch, the passing stranger who appeared to have some money. Guests would be invited to the dinner table and seated with their backs to a curtained-off sleeping area. One of the family would be waiting behind the curtain to smash the victim's skull with a heavy hammer and finish him or her off with a knife to the throat.

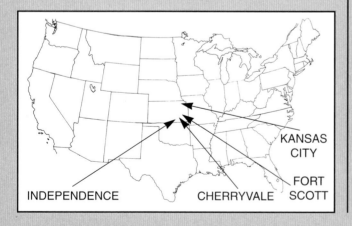

KANSAS CITY

FORT SCOTT

INDEPENDENCE   CHERRYVALE

After searching the body for valuables, it would be dropped through a trapdoor into the revolting cellar below. Then after nightfall, it would be buried in a shallow grave.

No one knows when the murderous reign of the Bender family began, but the end came after Dr William York left his brother's house at Fort Scott, Kansas, on 9 March 1873 to ride home to the town of Independence. He did not arrive. The doctor's brother, Colonel York of the US Cavalry, organised groups to search the area between Independence and Fort Scott. But there was no trace. So, after several weeks without news, the colonel set out himself to scour the trail.

Arriving at the hamlet of Cherryvale, Colonel York stopped at the Wayside Inn, a dirty, dingy, 16ft by 20ft cabin surrounded by farmland, where the Benders offered food and shelter. The colonel knew his brother had intended breaking his journey there, and that night he too got to know the unsavoury Bender family.

Locals knew little about the family except that they spoke in thick, guttural accents. But there had been strange stories about the Benders. One suggested that the family had something to do with the body of a man found with his skull smashed under the ice of a frozen creek.

A Mr Wetzell recalled visiting the inn after seeing a newspaper advertisement offering mystic healing. He called with a friend and was greeted by a smiling Kate Bender, the daughter of the house. It was her advert and yes, she told Mr Wetzell, her skills as a spiritualist and psychic healer would soon cure his facial neuralgia. The guests were invited to stay for supper — but as they sat down, could not but help notice the girl's father and brother disappear behind the curtain. Something worried Mr Wetzell and his companion enough to make them eat their dinner standing up. This enraged Kate who became abusive and the two startled guests quickly left.

Now entering that same inn himself, Colonel York soon realised he had come across a sinister household. There was old man Bender, a 60-year-old surly East European immigrant, his shrewish wife, a half-witted son and the ugly, unmarried daughter. They all denied any knowledge of Dr York, blaming bandits or indians for the brother's

disappearance. They even offered to help in the search by dredging the nearby river for any trace of a corpse.

The colonel was convinced and rode on to search further down the trail. A few days later another search party arrived to make enquiries at the inn. Again the Benders denied that they had ever seen the missing doctor and, again, the searchers were satisfied and rode away. The Benders, however, panicked and, hurriedly packing their meagre belongings onto a cart, they fled.

On 9 May another search party on the trail of Dr York found the Wayside Inn abandoned. First of all, the party heard sounds of distress coming from cattle at the back of the inn. Approaching the pen they found many of the creatures, together with a small flock of sheep, were either dead or dying from obvious hunger and thirst. Then one of the party spotted a freshly dug grave exposed by recent heavy rains, and a few minutes' spadework revealed the body of Dr York.

His skull was smashed and his throat had been cut from ear to ear. Further digging revealed the remains of no fewer than seven other victims. One of them, a small girl, had, to judge from her position, been thrown into the shallow grave while still alive. Yet another body had been badly and deliberately mutilated either before or after death.

Meanwhile, other members of the search party were investigating the source of a foul smell that permeated the cabin. Beneath a trapdoor in the floor they found a roughly-dug pit, its floor and walls stained with blood.

Following these grisly discoveries, posses were formed to hunt down the Benders. The family was distinctive, both because of their appearance and because one of the wheels on their cart had a fault that left a zig-zag trail. But they were never discovered — officially.

However, it is believed that one of the several local vigilante patrols may have caught up with the Benders. One local lawman later reported that a wagon with a badly skewed wheel had been found, completely riddled with bullets. Another sheriff advised an official search party that said it would be unnecessary for anyone to search further for the vile Bender family.

DAVID BERKOWITZ

NAME: David Berkowitz

A.K.A.: 'Son of Sam'; the '.44 Caliber Killer'

BORN: June 1953

DIED: Sentenced to 30 years, to be served at the Attica Correctional facility

PREFERRED MURDER METHOD: Shooting

NUMBER OF VICTIMS: 6

NAMES OF VICTIMS: Donna Lauria, Christine Freund, Virginia Voskerichian, Valentina Suriani, Alexander Esau, Stacy Moskowitz

MURDER LOCALE: Brooklyn, Bronx and Queens

SPAN OF MURDER CAREER: 29 July 1976 to 31 July 1977

DATE OF CONVICTION: 23 August 1977

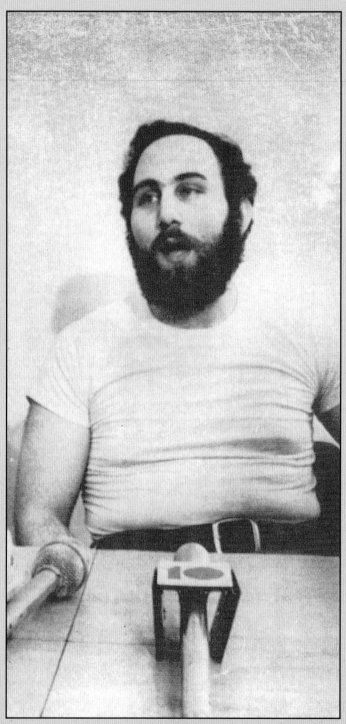

Michael Berkowitz was a sick stalker of young women. By night he prowled the streets of New York's Bronx and Queens seeking his prey. By day he was a soft-spoken employee of the US Mail, and no one who worked alongside him ever guessed at the deadly double-life he was leading.

For a year the plump, angel-faced bachelor brought terror to the streets. From 29 July 1976 to 1 August 1977, Berkowitz killed six women and viciously wounded another seven. And throughout his reign of terror, he taunted police with a series of letters, bragging about his deeds and giving tantalising clues to one of America's most wanted serial killers.

'I'll be back — I love to hunt,' he wrote to police after one vile killing. Determined to achieve the most notoriety, curly-haired Berkowitz also penned notes to the *New York Post* and the *New York Daily News*. And he gave himself an eerie nickname: 'Son Of Sam'.

His first victim had been Donna Lauria, a pretty 18-year-old who was entering her parents' Bronx apartment late one July night in 1976 when a man ran from the shadows, pulled a .44 calibre gun from a paper bag and fired three shots. Donna died and her friend Jody was wounded. As far as the cops were concerned, it was just another random crime in a city whose murder rate stood at 30 a week.

The police opened their murder files again in October when a young couple were seriously wounded by gunshots at Flushing, Queens. Even when two other young women were seriously wounded a month later, no one contemplated that New York was in the grip of a serial killer. It took the murders of secretary Christine Wheeler in January 1977 and of Bulgarian-born emigre Virginia Voskerichian in March for police to realise that a maniac with a .44 and a grudge against pretty girls was on the loose.

In April police examining the bodies of student Valentina Suriani and boyfriend Alexander Esau found that the killer had left more than death in his wake. David Berkowitz had left the first of a series of callously teasing letters, complaining that

From left: Victims Valentina Suriani, Christine Freund, Virginia Voskerichian and Stacy Moskowitz.

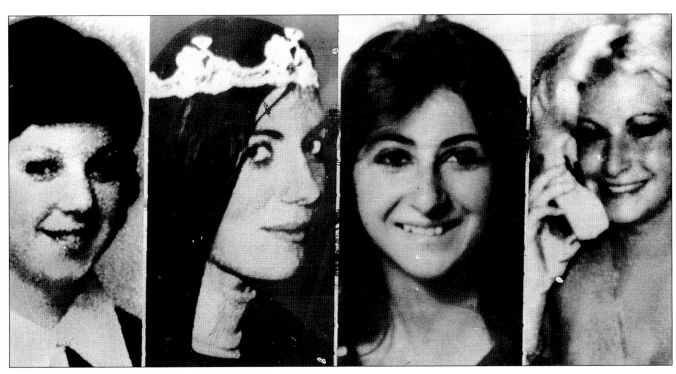

he was 'deeply hurt' that newspapers were calling him a woman-hater.

'I am not,' wrote Berkowitz. 'But I am a monster. I am the "Son of Sam". I am a little brat. Sam loves to drink blood. "Go out and kill," commands father Sam . . . I am on a different wavelength to everybody else — programmed to kill. However, to stop me you must kill me. Attention all police: Shoot me first — shoot to kill or else. Keep out of my way or you will die! I am the monster — "Beelzebub, the Chubby Behemoth". I love to hunt. Prowling the streets looking for fair game — tasty meat. I live for the hunt — it's my life. I don't belong on earth.'

Then came the words that filled the police with fear: 'I'll be back! I'll be back!' The letter was signed: 'Yours in murder, Mr Monster.'

Just who was this 'Mr Monster'? David Berkowitz was born in Brooklyn on 1 June 1953. Illegitimate, he knew little or nothing of his real parents but was raised by caring, adoptive parents Nathan and Pearl Berkowitz. Of above-average intelligence, David was popular at school and was good at sport. At 18, he enlisted in the Army, serving in Korea. Before he left three years later, he converted from Judaism to fundamentalist Christianity. Off duty, he would preach from street-corners in Louisville, Kentucky, where he was stationed, warning of 'the burning fires of Hell that lie in wait for all sinners'.

King's County Hospital, Brooklyn: Survivor Robert Violante is stretchered away.

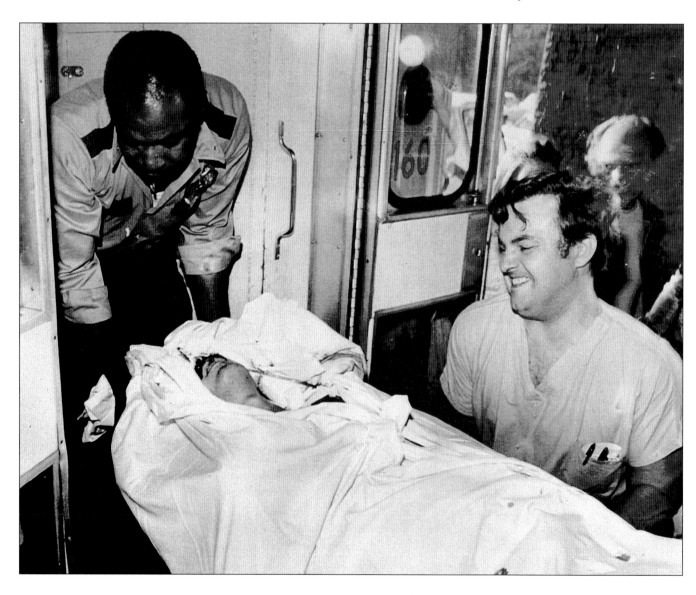

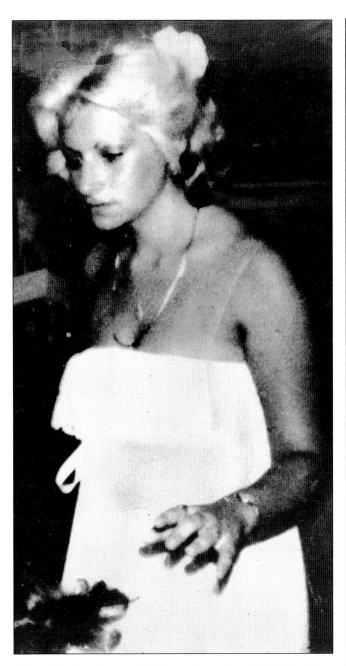

Stacy Moskowitz was killed as she sat by date Robert Violante, who survived the shooting.

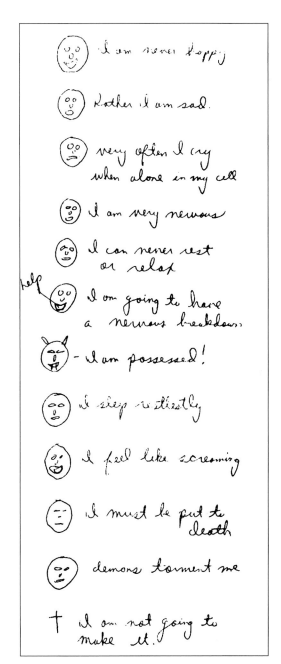

The scribblings of 'Son of Sam'.

In the spring of 1974 he returned to New York and rented an apartment in the Bronx. After a spell as a security guard, he joined the postal service. And as he sorted mail, his perverted fantasies grew — until he put them into bloody practice.

Ironically, Berkowitz may well have sorted the mailbags that contained his own letters taunting the New York Police Department and to the newspapers. *New York Daily News* columnist Jimmy Breslin began writing letters back to 'Son Of Sam'

in his column, hoping to draw the killer out from under his anonymous veil.

Though horrified about a murdering psychopath in their midst, New Yorkers could not help but be fascinated by the bizarre communications between Breslin and 'Son of Sam'. Written on 30 May 1977, one letter to the columnist said:

'Hello from the gutters of NYC which are filled with dog manure, vomit, stale wine, urine and blood. Hello from the sewers of NYC which swal-

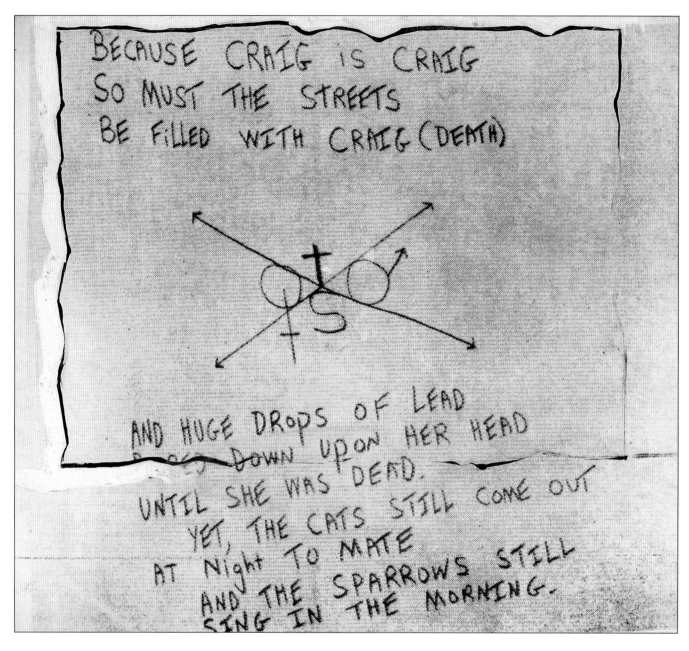

BECAUSE CRAIG IS CRAIG
SO MUST THE STREETS
BE FILLED WITH CRAIG (DEATH)

AND HUGE DROPS OF LEAD
POURED DOWN UPON HER HEAD
UNTIL SHE WAS DEAD.
YET, THE CATS STILL COME OUT
AT Night TO MATE
AND THE SPARROWS STILL
SING IN THE MORNING.

The note found by police in Berkowitz's car in front of his Yonkers apartment building: it led to the arrest of 'Son of Sam' late on 10 August 1976 .

low up these delicacies when they are washed away by the sweeper trucks. Hello from the cracks in the sidewalks of NYC and from the ants that dwell in these cracks and feed on the dried blood of the dead that has seeped into these cracks.'

Breslin was warned by the killer that he was by no means finished. 'Mr Breslin, sir, don't think that because you haven't heard from (me) for a while that I went to sleep. No, rather, I am still here. Like a spirit roaming the night. Thirsty, hungry, seldom stopping to rest.'

It was, Breslin thought, a letter from Hell. Circulation of Breslin's newspaper soared.

'Will you kill again?' Breslin wrote to 'Son Of

Sam' a year after the first murder. His reply was awaited.

Berkowitz was still sorting mail on 29 July 1976, the anniversary of his first attack, and the date passed uneventfully.

Instead, Berkowitz chose the very next night to strike, killing Stacy Moskowitz and injuring her date, Robert Violante, as they sat in their car in a Brooklyn street. The reign of terror of 'Son of Sam' was, however, coming to an end.

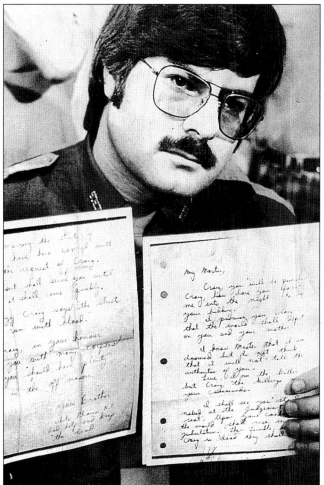

TOP: New York City Police sketch of the 'Son of Sam' published as the anniversary of his first killing – 29 July 1976 – approached.

LEFT: County Deputy Sheriff Craig Glassman – who lived in the apartment above the killer – shows threatening letters he received from Berkowitz. He noticed the similarity between these letters and the writings of 'Son of Sam' published in the press.

ABOVE: The .44 Charter Arms Bulldog revolver that gave David Berkowitz one of his sobriquets.

A few days after the murder, police were routinely checking out cars which had been given parking tickets in the vicinity of the Moskowitz slaying. One, a 1970 cream Galaxie, had been ticketed for parking too close to a fire hydrant just 30 minutes before the murder. When repeated telephone calls to the owner went unanswered, detectives Ed Zigo and John Longo were sent to his address, an apartment building in suburban Yonkers.

As they approached the Pine Street apartments, the detectives noticed the Galaxie, licence plate 561XLB, parked outside. Through the windows, they saw a rifle butt protruding from a duffel bag in the back seat. They broke into the car and, in the glove box, found an envelope addressed to Timothy Dowd, a deputy inspector leading the 'Son Of Sam' Task Force.

Zigo opened it and, in shocked amazement, read the enclosed letter — which Berkowitz had intended leaving at the side of his next victim. It promised more attacks, including a planned massacre at a Long Island nightclub where Berkowitz planned to 'go out in a blaze of glory'.

A call was made for a search warrant to allow the detectives to enter Berkowitz's apartment. It was not needed. For at 10pm the night stalker himself, dressed in jeans, brown boots and a white short-sleeved shirt, walked out of the building. In his hand was a brown paper bag, and inside was a .44-calibre gun. Berkowitz sauntered casually to his car, so confident that he didn't bother to look around. He switched on the ignition but got no

David Berkowitz was found guilty of murder on 23 August 1977 and sentenced to life imprisonment.

Sketches of 'Son of Sam' appeared in the Press but in the end it was chance that led to his arrest.

further. The barrels of 15 guns were suddenly levelled through the car windows directly at his head.

Berkowitz merely smiled. 'Okay,' he said, 'you've got me. What took you so long?'

Back at HQ, the suspect was grilled for two hours, confessing to all of 'Son Of Sam's crimes. When he was arraigned at Brooklyn courthouse the following morning, the press and public expected to see a chained, wild-eyed monster. Instead they encountered a meek, smiling David Berkowitz. He looked as dangerous as a lamb.

Nevertheless, a mob of several hundred angry citizens chanted, 'Kill him! Kill him! Kill him!', and there were numerous telephoned death threats to the switchboard of the King's County Hospital where he was taken for psychiatric evaluation. It was during his enforced stay at the heavily-guarded hospital that Berkowitz responded to a letter smuggled to him from Steve Dunleavy, a columnist with the New York Post. The reply to Dunleavy was

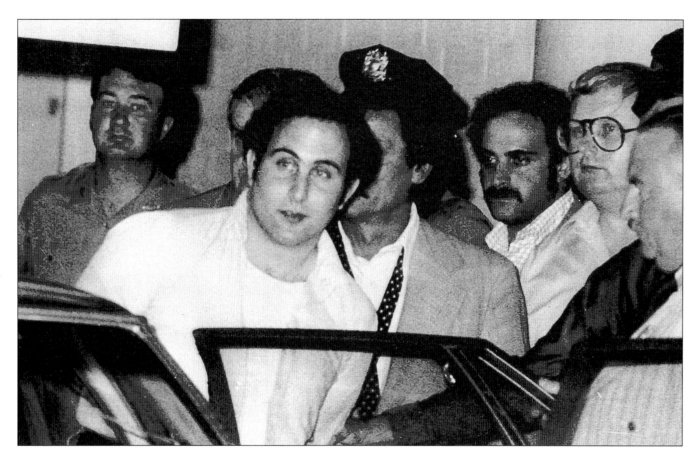

chilling. It spoke of Sam as 'one of the devils of Satan, a force beyond the wildest imaginations of people. He is not human.'

It continued: 'When I killed, I really saved many lives. You will understand later. People want my blood but they don't want to listen to what I have to say. There are other Sons out there. God help the world.'

At his subsequent trial, Berkowitz admitted all guilt and was given a cumulative sentence that was limited by law to 30 years.

Psychiatrist Dr David Abrahamsen, who examined Berkowitz and judged him sane, said after the trial: 'He found sexual gratification in killing women. He could not approach a woman as a man would do and date her or have sex with her. That was not for him. I think he developed a great deal of contempt for women. He is very dangerous.'

Abrahamsen quoted Berkowitz as saying in a 1977 interview: 'The tension, the desire to kill a woman had built up in me to such explosive proportions that when I finally pulled the trigger, all the pressures, all the tensions, hatred, had just vanished, disappeared.'

ABOVE: Berkowitz is taken away for booking.

BELOW: Doodlings while being evaluated at King's County Hospital.

'Son Of Sam' added that, after killing one young woman, 'I was literally singing to myself on the way home.'

KENNETH BIANCHI
AND ANGELO BUONO

NAME: Kenneth Bianci

A.K.A.: The 'Hillside Strangler'

BORN: 1952

DIED: Still serving life sentence

NAME: Angelo Buono

A.K.A.: The 'Hillside Strangler'

BORN: 1935

DIED: Still serving life sentence

PREFERRED MURDER METHOD: Raped, bound and strangled.

NUMBER OF VICTIMS: 12

NAMES OF VICTIMS: Elissa Kastin, Yolanda Washington, Judith Miller, Kristina Weckler, Dolores Cepeda, Sonja Johnson, Jane King, Lauren Wagner, Kimberley Martin, Cindy Hudspeth, *Karen Mandic, Diane Wilder*
(italics = Bianchi only)

MURDER LOCALE: Los Angeles and Washington State

SPAN OF MURDER CAREER: 6 October 1978 to January 1979

DATE OF CONVICTION: 9 January 1984

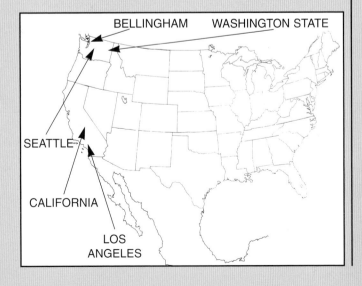

It started as a discussion over a beer. What would it be like to kill someone? The question was posed by Kenneth Bianchi and his cousin Angelo Buono Jr. Both were users of prostitutes, who were regular visitors to Buono's home in Glendale, California. It would be these girls who would become the victims of the evil duo . . . and their murderous activities would give rise to the hunt for what police and press labelled the 'Hillside Strangler'.

Bianchi, born 1952, was raised by foster parents in Rochester, New York State. In 1977 he arrived in Los Angeles to stay with his cousin, 17 years his elder, and immediately got sucked into a life of perversion. The subnormal but streetwise Buono introduced a parade of prostitutes through the Glendale house, from where he ran an upholstery business. Within months of Bianchi's arrival in California, the two cousins had launched themselves on a mindless murder spree that claimed the lives of 10 young women.

Between 6 October and 17 February 1978, the bodies of naked girls were found dumped on hillsides around Los Angeles. All had been raped and, from sperm samples, police knew that two men had been involved. This was information they kept secret, however, and they allowed the nickname 'Hillside Strangler' to be applied to the case.

The first victim was 21-year-old Elissa Kastin. Like those that were to follow, she had been lured to Buono's home where she had been savagely raped and killed. Her body was found on nearby Chevy Chase Drive.

As other bodies turned up, a pattern emerged. The girls were mainly part-time prostitutes; their wrists and ankles bore the marks of ropes that had bound them; they had been stripped naked, raped and sometimes sodomised; they had been carefully cleaned by the killers so as to leave no clues; they had finally been dumped by roadsides where they were certain to be discovered.

Often the bodies were displayed in lascivious postures. And, to the fury of the detectives on the case, the corpses were generally found near to police stations. It was if the killers were taunting them. In fact, Bianchi had even applied for a job with the Los Angeles Police Department — and had actually been taken for several rides with officers while the Hillside Strangler was being sought.

The killers' method of trapping their victims was to cruise Los Angeles in Buono's car, using fake badges to persuade girls that they were undercover cops. Ordered into the 'unmarked police car', the girls were driven to Buono's home, where they were tortured. After being abused by both men, the girls were strangled. Other methods of killing, such as lethal injection, had been tried by the murderers but rejected.

The slaying of 19-year-old Yolanda Washington, the couple's second victim, was typical of their murder pattern. Her body was found beside the famous Forest Lawn cemetery on the night of 18 October 1977. Grotesquely posed in a parody of lasciviousness, her naked body had been meticulously cleansed to remove all clues — apart from the marks of the ropes that had bound her in her final tormented moments. Two weeks later, petite Judith Miller, just 15 years of age, was found dead on a hillside above a Glendale roadway. Her neck, wrists and ankles bore rope marks, and she had been raped violently before being strangled.

On 20 November 1977 Bianchi and Buono murdered three girls — one of them only 12 years of age. She was Dolores Cepeda, whose body was found along with that of 14-year-old Sonja Johnson in Elysian Park. The body of 20-year-old Kristina Weckler was found on a hillside in Highland Park the same night. Three days later the body of Jane King, 28, was found in the most visible location: the exit ramp of the Golden State Freeway.

The pace of the killings briefly slackened. But on 17 February 1978 the naked body of Cindy Hudspeth was found in the trunk of a car. The LAPD believed that at last there must be a breakthrough. But the body had been immaculately cleaned and, despite a public outcry at its inability to hunt down the 'Hillside Strangler', the special police squad was no nearer making an arrest. Then the killings stopped . . .

The LAPD was baffled. But the reason for the cessation of the serial murders could not have been simpler — Bianchi had become sickened because of the filthy conditions in Buono's home. He had left his cousin and moved to Bellingham, Washington State, where he took a job as a security guard while again applying for a post with the local police force. Back in Los Angeles, the special murder squad had been disbanded. In Washington, however, the nightmare was to begin again.

In January 1979 the bodies of two girls were found in the back of a car in Bellingham. Bianchi had been seen with one of them shortly before her disappearance and he was immediately arrested. Forensic evidence proved him to be the killer. He was also grilled over the Los Angeles murders.

Bianchi now played mind games with the police. He tried to fool psychiatrists that he had split personalities — that he was a Jekyll and Hyde figure who had committed murder only after blacking out and assuming a temporarily bestial role. When a hypnotist was called in, Bianchi even faked a trance, in which his puported 'other identities' became apparent. In fact, the he had studied psychiatry himself and had long planned this form of defence in anticipation of the inevitable day he would be caught.

Bianchi did, however, manage to persuade six Washington State psychiatrists into labelling him insane. This saved him from the death penalty in Washington, where he would have faced hanging for the two murders. Instead he did a deal with police prosecutors to plead guilty in return for a life sentence and removal to California. There, he pledged, he would nail his accomplice Buono.

Back in Los Angeles, however, the ruling of the six Washington psychiatrists that Bianchi was insane prevented his evidence against Buono from being used in a trial. Instead two years were spent in court, during which more than 400 witnesses were heard, before Buono was finally convicted.

One of the most important of those witnesses was 27-year-old Catherine Lorre, daughter of actor Peter Lorre. She identified Bianchi and Buono as two men who had stopped her on a Hollywood street claiming to be police officers. She had shown them her identification, including a photograph of herself as a child alongside her famous father. That photo saved her life. It transpired that the killers had decided not to abduct Catherine for fear that murdering a celebrity's daughter would increase the manhunt for them.

On 9 January 1984 Angelo Buono Jr was given a life sentence. Despite his various ploys, Kenneth Bianchi was sent back to Washington to serve out his life sentence. Judge Ronald George ended the two-year trial by telling the pair: 'I am sure, Mr Buono and Mr Bianchi, that you will only get your thrills by reliving over and over the tortures and murders of your victims, being incapable as I believe you to be of ever feeling any remorse.'

Kenneth Bianchi (left) and his cousin and partner in crime Angelo Buono.

Victims of the 'Hillside Strangler' found in the Los Angeles area.

BIBLE JOHN

NAME: Unknown

A.K.A.: 'Bible John'

PREFERRED MURDER METHOD: Strangulation

NUMBER OF VICTIMS: 3 known

NAMES OF VICTIMS: Patricia Docker, Jemima McDonald, Helen Puttock

MURDER LOCALE: Glasgow

SPAN OF MURDER CAREER: 22/23 February 1968 to 30 October 1969

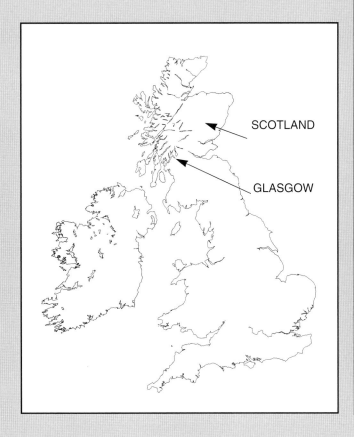

SCOTLAND

GLASGOW

No one ever discovered the real name of 'Bible John' for, despite strangling three young women in the 1960s, he was never caught.

So-called because the sister of his last victim recalled him quoting from the Bible and condemning adultery, Bible John's haunt was Glasgow's Barrowland Dance Hall. His first victim was Patricia Docker, aged 29, murdered in February 1968. A year later, Jemina McDonald, 32, was found dead in derelict flats. Helen Puttock, 29, was murdered on 30 October.

Each murder bore remarkable similarities. All the women had been strangled, all had had their handbags stolen, and all were menstruating at the time of their deaths.

Helen Puttock's sister, Jeannie Williams, gave a full description of the man Helen had danced with on the night she died. But despite a massive police hunt, the interviewing of 5,000 people, a televised documentary about the crime and a good response from the public, 'Bible John' was never traced.

In February 1996, 28 years after the death of 'Bible John's first victim, detectives gathered in a frozen cemetery to resume the hunt for the killer. They exhumed the body of John Irvine McInnes from a family grave at Stonehouse Cemetery, Lanarkshire, where he was buried after committing suicide in 1980 at the age of 41. In the years since his death genetic fingerprinting has become commonplace — and DNA taken from his remains were thought by scientists to link him with fluid found on the tights used to strangle Helen Puttock. But after 3 months of tests, police scientists announced that they could still not prove a link, and the file was again closed.

DAVID AND CATHERINE BIRNIE

NAME: David and Catherine Birnie

BORN: Both 1951

DIED: Still in jail serving life sentences

PREFERRED MURDER METHOD: Strangulation

NUMBER OF VICTIMS: 4

NAMES OF VICTIMS: Mary Neilson, Susannah Candy, Noelene Patterson, Denise Brown

MURDER LOCALE: Near Freemantle, Western Australia

SPAN OF MURDER CAREER: 6 October to 10 November 1986

DATE OF CONVICTION: 3 March 1987

Deprived of happy childhoods, David and Catherine Birnie turned sadistic killers in adult life. In 1986, they launched a five-week reign of terror in Western Australia.

The two became lovers when Catherine was 15. She was pregnant when they became small-time burglars. David had been sacked from his stables job after harassing a young, female colleague. After a spell in detention, the two went their separate ways, Catherine enjoying a happy marriage.

But the two met up again in 1983, resuming their affair. In February 1985 they set up home together in Willagee, Freemantle, where David worked in a car wrecker's yard. Their talk turned to kidnapping girls for Birnie to rape.

Psychology student Mary Neilson, 22, was raped and strangled in October 1986. Susannah Candy, 15, suffered the same fate two weeks later, as did air hostess Noelene Patterson, 31, a few days after. Hitchhiker Denise Brown, 21, was raped, stabbed and axed to death in November. Their final victim, a teenage girl, managed to escape.

The two were arrested and confessed to the murders, even taking police to their victims' graves — three at Glen Eagle National Park, Willagee, and the fourth in a pine tree plantation near Wanneroo. Both received life sentences. The judge said that David Birnie should never be released.

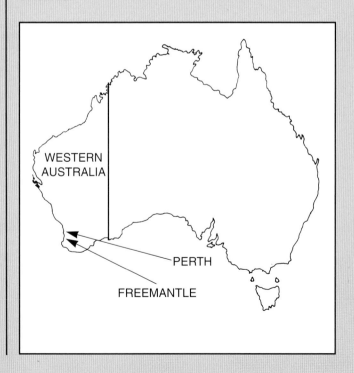

LAWRENCE BITTAKER

NAME: Lawrence Sigmund Bittaker

ACCOMPLICE: Roy Norris

BORN: 1941

DIED: Awaiting execution in San Quentin

PREFERRED MURDER METHOD: Strangulation

NUMBER OF VICTIMS: 5

NAMES OF VICTIMS: Jacqueline Lamp, Jackie Gillam, Shirley Ledford, Lucinda Schafer, Andrea Hall

MURDER LOCALE: Los Angeles

SPAN OF MURDER CAREER: June to October 1979

DATE OF CONVICTION: 17 February 1981

Lawrence Bittaker tortured and raped five teenage girls before murdering them. His killing spree lasted between June and October 1979 and his victims all came from the suburbs of Los Angeles. They were Jacqueline Leah Lamp, 13, Jackie Gillam, 15, Shirley Ledford and Lucinda Schafer, both 16, and Andrea Hall, 18.

Bittaker's trial in January 1981 made history as the first-ever televised court proceedings. He was charged with five murders, ten rapes, three other sex crimes and one count of conspiracy to commit murder, rape and kidnapping. Further charges concerned 40-year-old Bittaker's illegal possession of tear gas and an alleged attempt to coerce two prison inmates to commit murder. Bittaker was sentenced to death and was taken to San Quentin to await the gas chamber

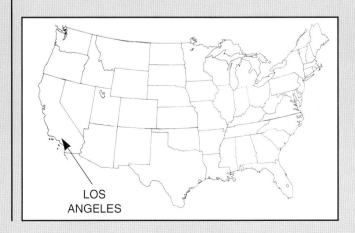

LOS
ANGELES

WAYNE BODEN

NAME: Wayne Boden

A.K.A.: The 'Vampire Rapist'

BORN: Unknown

DIED: Still serving life sentence

PREFERRED MURDER METHOD: Strangulation

NUMBER OF VICTIMS: 5

NAMES OF VICTIMS: Norma Vaillancourt, Shirley Andett, Marielle Archambault, Jean Way, Elizabeth Porteous

MURDER LOCALE: Montreal and Calgary

SPAN OF MURDER CAREER: 1968-71

DATE OF CONVICTION: 1972

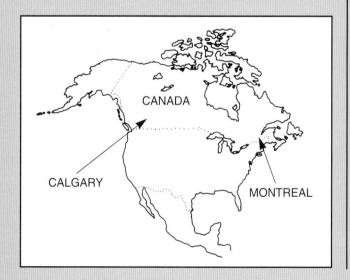

Canadian killer Wayne Boden was known as the 'Vampire Rapist' after a string of murders in which the strangled female victims were left with deep bite marks on their breasts.

Boden carried out his murders in Montreal and Calgary between 1968 and 1971. His victims were 21-year-old teacher Norma Vaillancourt, Shirley Audette, jewellery store clerk Marielle Archambault, 24-year-old Jean Way and schoolteacher Elizabeth Porteous.

In only two cases were there signs of a struggle by his victims. In the others, the girls seemed serene in death — one even having a faint smile on her lips. Detectives speculated that the killer, who was attractive to women, had targeted girls who had masochistic inclinations. They may have agreed to certain sexual experimentation before the fierce urges of the 'Vampire Rapist' caused him to lose control and probably asphyxiate the victims in the height of their lovemaking. He would then bestially abuse their bodies.

Boden was eventually captured when the blue Mercedes in which he and Jean Way had been seen on the day of her murder was tracked down by police. They also identified Boden from a crumpled photograph found at Marielle Archambault's apartment. Dental experts matched a cast of Boden's teeth with bite marks found on his victims' bodies.

Boden was sentenced in Calgary to life imprisonment for the murder of Elizabeth Porteous. He was then returned to Montreal to be found guilty of three other murders and receive three life sentences. Boden always protested his innocence over the murder of Norma Vaillancourt.

MORRIS BOLBER

A bogus doctor specialising in potions to curb husbands' sexual urges, Dr Bolber was well known in the Italian community of Philadelphia in the 1930s. It was the visit by a grocer's wife, seeking such a potion, that turned the charlatan doctor into a murderer. He reputedly killed some 30 people over five years.

He helped kill the wife's husband with poison after persuading her to take out life insurance on him. Bolber decided there were riches to be had in relieving unhappy wives of their husbands. He recruited an Italian tailor Paul Petrillo and Petrillo's cousin Herman to help him in his insurance 'claims'.

Bolber also teamed up with Carino Favato, who had already poisoned three husbands and who had plenty of contacts in the murky world of contract crime.

NAME: Morris Bolber

ACCOMPLICES: Paul Petrillo, Herman Petrillo, Carino Favato

BORN: Unknown

DIED: Unknown

PREFERRED MURDER METHOD: Heavy blow with sandbag to allow insurance claim

NUMBER OF VICTIMS: Over 30

MURDER LOCALE: Philadelphia, Pa

SPAN OF MURDER CAREER: 1932-37

DATE OF CONVICTION: 1937

One of their victims was pushed off a building site roof. Another, a fisherman, was completely unaware that one of the gang had impersonated him to take out a policy on his life — leaving his widow a handsome sum to share with her evil partners in crime. Bolber changed his method to dealing victims heavy blows with canvas bags full of sand so that there would be no signs of violence.

Bolber was finally arrested after Herman Petrillo bragged about his life of crime. Every member of his gang tried to avoid justice by blaming another. But by doing so, they helped police build up a dossier on their entire murderous operation.

Bolber and Favato escaped the death penalty and were sentenced to life imprisonment. The Petrillos met their deaths in the electric chair.

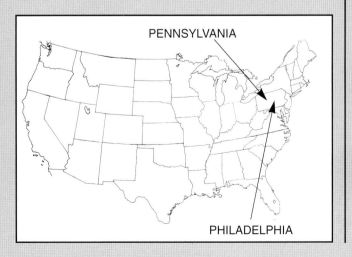

PENNSYLVANIA

PHILADELPHIA

WERNER BOOST

NAME: Werner Boost

A.K.A.: The 'Doubles Killer'

ACCOMPLICE: Franz Lorbach

BORN: 1928

DIED: Still serving life sentence

PREFERRED MURDER METHOD: Sedation of victim, rape and murder

NUMBER OF VICTIMS: 5

NAMES OF VICTIMS: Dr Serve, Thear Kuttmann, Friedhelm Behte, Peter Fallenberg, Hildegard Wassing

MURDER LOCALE: Düsseldorf

SPAN OF MURDER CAREER: 7 January 1953 to October 1956

DATE OF CONVICTION: 14 December 1959

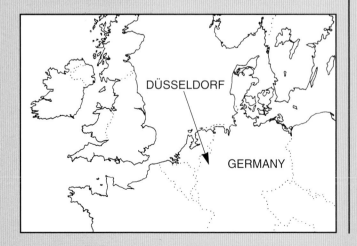

Werner Boost originally made a living transporting refugees across the East German border. Three years after moving to Düsseldorf in 1950, he became a murderer who preyed on courting couples.

With accomplice Franz Lorbach, Boost shot lawyer Dr Serve as he sat in his car with a male lover on 7 January 1953. The lover was beaten and robbed. Again accompanied by Lorbach, Boost battered to death Thear Kurmann and Friedhelm Behre as they left a Düsseldorf restaurant on 31 October 1955. Their bodies were dumped in a gravel pit.

Now labelled the 'Doubles Killer', Boost carried out his final double killing in October 1956. The charred bodies of Peter Falkenberg and Hildegard Wassing were discovered in a smouldering haystack.

Shortly afterwards, Lorbach was arrested. He told police he had been 'hypnotised' into committing the crimes. He also said Boost's method was to sedate the couples then rape the women before killing them.

Boost was caught on 10 June 1956 as he was about to pounce on a couple parked in woods on the outskirts of Düsseldorf. He was sentenced to life on 14 December 1959 for the murder of Dr Serve. Lorbach was jailed for six years. Evidence linking the two men to the other murders could not be proved.

MARIE DE BRINVILLIERS

NAME: Marie Marguerite de Brinvilliers

ACCOMPLICE: Chevalier Jean-Baptiste de Sante-Croix

BORN: 1630

DIED: Tortured and executed in 1676

PREFERRED MURDER METHOD: Poisoning

NUMBER OF VICTIMS: over 50

MURDER LOCALE: Paris

SPAN OF MURDER CAREER: 1666-76

DATE OF CONVICTION: 1676

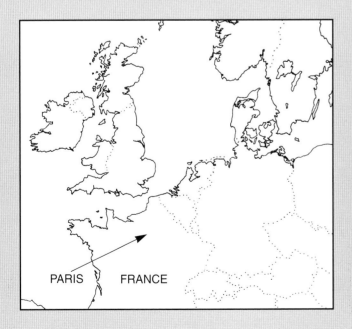

PARIS   FRANCE

Marie de Brinvilliers was the eldest of five children in the French aristocratic 17th century family of d'Aubray. She was married at 21 to a gambling womaniser who paid her little attention — and that was to lead her to murder.

Marie took a lover, Chevalier Jean-Baptiste de Sainte-Croix. Their affair outraged her father, who had Sainte-Croix thrown into the Bastille. It was here he learned the art of poisoning, which he passed on to Marie upon his release.

Viscount d'Aubray, Marie's father, was her first victim in 1666. But when her share of his inheritance ran out, she turned her attention to the rest of the family. Her elder brother died in June 1670, followed by her younger brother and then her sister and sister-in-law. Former lovers suffered the same fate. Marie's husband was allowed to live but was prone to mysterious illnesses.

Ruthlessly, Marie perfected her poison techniques on as many as 50 people during 'mercy missions' visiting the sick in hospital. She was exposed when her lover Sainte-Croix died. He left instructions that a box should be delivered to his mistress. But his wife opened it and saw a variety of poisons and incriminating papers.

The serial poisoner was tried in Paris in 1676 and found guilty. She was tortured before being executed, her body and severed head then thrown onto a fire.

JERRY BRUDOS

Jerry Brudos was a murdering rapist with a fetish for women's clothes and shoes. He first came to police attention when he was 17. He forced a woman to pose for naked pictures at knifepoint. Brudos was confined to a mental hospital for nine months with a personality disorder.

After his release, he continued stealing underwear from washing lines. By the time he was 28 and committed his first murder, Brudos had accumulated a large collection of women's attire.

The first victim was a 19-year-old encyclopaedia salesmen called Linda Slawson who happened to knock on the door of the Brudos home in Portland, Oregon, one day in January 1968. With his mother and child upstairs, Brudos knocked the young woman unconscious then strangled her. Then he abused the corpse, dressing it with clothes from his collection and photographing his handiwork. Finally, he chopped off the left foot and, with a newly fitted shoe, put it in his refrigerator. The body was disposed of in the Willamette River.

Three other murders followed: in November 1968 Jan Whitney, whose right breast Brudos kept; in March 1969 19-year-old student Karen Sprinkler, whose body was similarly abused; and Linda Salee, a month later. All were photographed shortly after death.

After quizzing fellow students of Karen Sprinkler, police discovered several girls had received phone calls from a man asking to meet them. A trap was set with one of the girls arranging a date with Brudos and he was arrested.

He pleaded insanity at his trial but psychiatric reports declared him sane. He was sentenced to life imprisonment at Oregon State Penitentiary.

NAME: Jerome Henry Brudos

BORN: 1940

DIED: Still serving life in Oregon State Penitentiary

PREFERRED MURDER METHOD: Strangulation followed by necrophilia

NUMBER OF VICTIMS: 4

NAMES OF VICTIMS: Linda Slawson, Jan Whitney, Karen Sprinkler, Linda Salee

MURDER LOCALE: Portland, Oregon

SPAN OF MURDER CAREER: 26 January 1968 to 23 April 1969

DATE OF CONVICTION: 1969

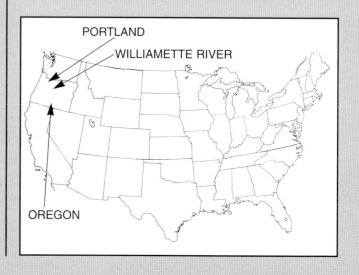

TED BUNDY

NAME: Theodore Robert Bundy

A.K.A.: The 'Campus Killer'

BORN: 1947

DIED: Went to electric chair on 24 January 1989 in Starke Prison, Florida

PREFERRED MURDER METHOD: Strangulation

NUMBER OF VICTIMS: At least 19 possibly 40

NAMES OF VICTIMS: Lynda Healy, Donna Manson, Susan Rancourt, Roberta Parks, Brenda Ball, Georgann Hawkins, Janice Ott, Denise Naslund, Carol Valenzuela, Nancy Wilcox, Melissa Smith, Laura Aime, Debra Kent, Carolyn Campbell, Julie Cunningham, Denise Olverson, Lisa Levy, Margaret Bowman, Kimberly Leach

MURDER LOCALE: All over USA

SPAN OF MURDER CAREER: 31 January 1974 to 15 February 1977

DATE OF CONVICTION: 24 July 1979

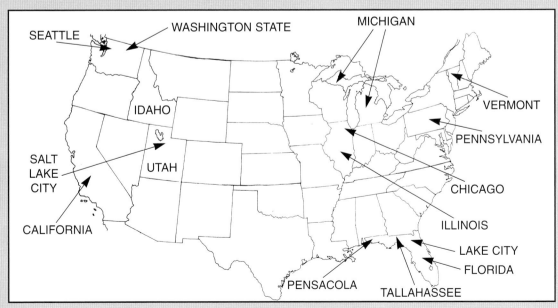

Ted Bundy was the all-American boy. As a youngster, he was a Boy Scout, he did a paper round and he started his own lawnmowing business. A high school athlete and then a graduate of the University of Washington, the handsome young man was never short of a date. He was a campaign worker both for the Republican Party and for the Crime Commission in Washington State. He also became a counsellor at a Seattle rape crisis centre after being screened for 'maturity and balance'.

This was Ted Bundy, one of the most feared serial killers in American history. And these were some of his victims . . .

Lynda Ann Healy, a 21-year-old law student at Seattle's University of Washington State, set her alarm for 7am on the morning of 31 January 1974. It rang for two hours until at 9am her room-mate found her gone, leaving a mysterious bloodstain on her pillow.

Six weeks later, on 12 March, student Donna Manson walked across the campus to attend a music recital and was never seen again. On 17 April, Susan Rancourt, aged 18, left campus to walk to a movie theatre only 400 yards away. She too vanished — as did 22-year-old Roberta Parks on 6 May, Brenda Ball, also 22, on 6 June, and Georgina Hawkins, 18, on 16 June.

On 14 July, Janice Orr, aged 23, was sunbathing at Lake Sammamish State Park, near Seattle, when she was approached by a young man with his arm in a sling. He asked: 'Would you help me put my sailboat on top of my car?' Janice walked with him to his car and was never seen alive again.

That same day, Denise Naslund swam with a party in a nearby stream, leaving them only to walk to nearby toilets. She became the eighth victim.

Two months later a team of grouse beaters found the remains of both Denise and Janice under a copse of trees. They had both been murdered in a sexual frenzy Their bodies had also been stripped bare and their jewellery stolen.

When detectives began their murder hunt, they found several women who had been approached that day by a handsome young man with his arm in a sling. He had told them all: 'Hi, I'm Ted.'

'Ted' was indeed the killer's name: Ted Bundy, 28 years of age — and about to move on to his next killing fields.

On 30 August Bundy quit his job at the Washington State Office of Emergency Services and moved to Utah, where he enrolled at the University of Utah law school in Salt Lake City. Two months later the killings began again. On 18 October, 18-year-old Melissa Smith was raped and murdered. On 31 October, 17-year-old Laura Aime was battered and strangled. Debra Kent, aged 17, died on 8 November.

An attempt on the life of Carol Da Ronch, aged 18, failed after Bundy approached her, posing as a police officer and saying: 'Hi, I'm Ted.' He handcuffed her and dragged her into his Volkswagen

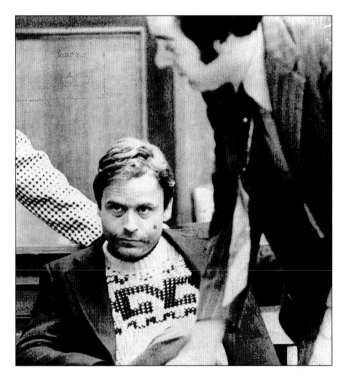

Ted Bundy — who had earlier in the 1970s escaped twice from capture — sits in court in Pensacola, Florida on 17 February 1978. He would not escape again.

The many faces of a monster . . . this was how Ted Bundy altered his appearance over the years he evaded capture.

Ted Bundy leaving Leon County Court on 10 March 1978.

but she escaped by rolling out of the vehicle as it slowed at a bend.

The slaughter spread from Utah to Colorado. Between January and April 1975 Bundy murdered four Colorado women but police still had no clues as to his identity.

Then police got a lucky break. On the evening of 16 August 1975 a highway patrolman in Granger, Utah, saw a VW pull out from the kerb without any lights. The cop pulled the VW over and asked Bundy what he had inside his car. The killer replied: 'Just some junk.' The 'junk' turned out to be a pair of handcuffs, a crowbar, a ski mask and a nylon stocking.

Incredibly, Bundy was booked only for a traffic offence and released on bail. It was not until the following day that he was arrested in his apartment at 565 First Avenue, Salt Lake City — and then only on a charge of possessing tools for burglary.

The case began to build, however, when police reinterviewed Carol Da Ronch, the girl who had escaped from Bundy's car the year before. Bundy, still out on bail, was put in an identification parade and was immediately picked out by Da Ronch. Frustratingly, the police still had no evidence to link him to the murders but he was at last charged with kidnapping. Again, he was allowed bail.

The mass-murderer faced trial — but only for kidnapping — on 23 February 1976. Bundy, then aged 29, made a great impression on the Utah court. He was polite, well-spoken and utterly charming. The jury obviously wondered why such a man needed to kidnap a girl when he could date the prettiest. The case almost went his way.

After months of legal arguments, however, he was found guilty of kidnapping and sentenced to between one and 15 years. Bundy was then moved from Utah to Colorado to stand trial for the murder of a 20-year-old student, Carolyn Campbell, who had been abducted from a ski resort.

Sadly, security was not as tight in Colorado. During a break in a court session in Aspen, Bundy leaped from a courtroom window. He was recaptured eight days later. Then, on 30 December, using a stack of books as a stepladder, Bundy cut through a ceiling panel of his Colorado Springs cell with a hacksaw blade. He stole a police car and headed first for Chicago, then south to Florida.

Wherever he stopped, Bundy took on a different identity. The killer was on top of the list of America's most wanted criminals, yet he went unrecognised when he rented a room near the University of Florida, Tallahassee. The mass-murderer was free to kill again.

On 15 January 1977, carrying a heavy wooden club, he crept into a girls' dormitory at the university. He battered 21-year-old Margaret Bowman and strangled her with her own tights before taking bites out of her buttocks. In the same way, he murdered Lisa Levy, aged 20. He savagely beat two others, Karen Chandler and Kathy Keiner, scarring both of them for life, before fleeing.

Bundy's next monstrous attack was in Lake City, Florida, on 8 February. There he killed his youngest known victim, 10-year-old Kimberly Leach. He strangled her, sexually violated her and left her body decomposing in a pig shed.

Luck finally ran out for Bundy a week later

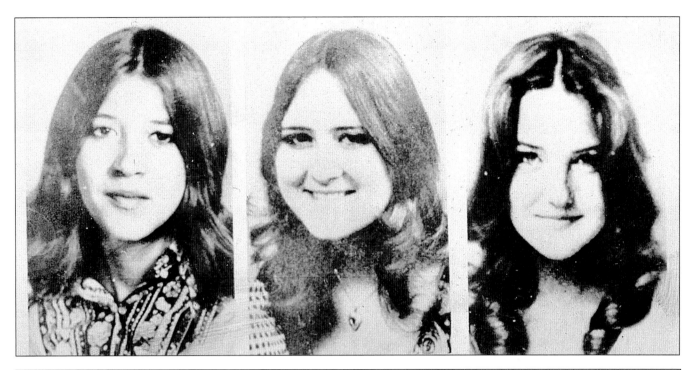

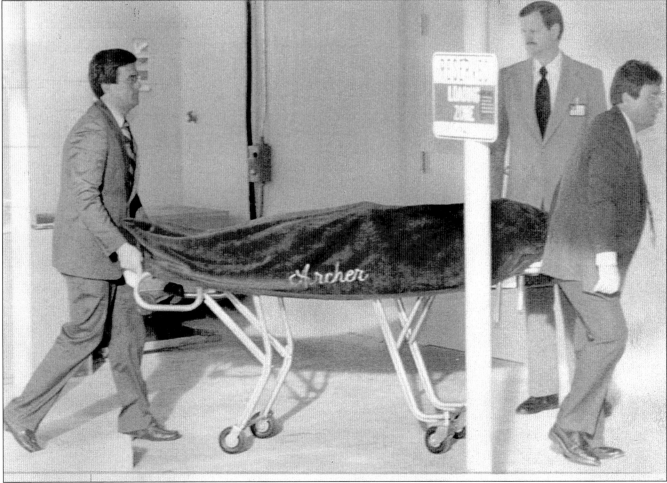

TOP: Laura Aime, Debra Kent and Melissa Smith — three of Bundy's victims.

ABOVE: Bundy's body is taken away following execution, 24 January 1989.

when, in the early hours of 15 February, a Pensacola policeman checked the numberplate of a VW in a restaurant car park and found that it had been stolen. The driver identified himself as Ken Misner — just one of 21 identities that Bundy had assumed, complete with credit cards, cheque books, passports and company IDs. When questioned further, Bundy attacked Patrolman David Lee and tried to escape. The officer was swifter than the killer, however, and he tackled him and clubbed him unconscious.

When Bundy came round, he told Lee: 'I wish you would have killed me.'

The mass-murderer was charged with the single murder of 10-year-old Kimberly. At his trial, jurors were shocked by evidence that confirmed that bite marks on the child's body could only have been made by his teeth. There was a nationwide sigh of relief as Bundy was sentenced to death.

Bundy lived in the shadow of the electric chair for almost 10 years, still protesting his innocence. Then, when he saw there was no way out, he broke down and confessed to almost 40 murders and admitted: 'I deserve to die for them.' He had killed girls in Idaho, California, Michigan, Pennsylvania and Vermont. Some were committed as 'day trips' with Bundy jetting into a city, selecting his victim, killing her and flying out again.

Time finally ran out for the serial killer at Starke Prison, Florida, on 24 January 1989. Bundy refused his condemned man's last meal and wept openly as the hour of his execution approached; but there were no tears for him. As he was strapped into the electric chair, a local DJ told listeners: 'Turn down your coffee makers, folks, because they're gonna need all the juice they can get there today!'

The last thing Ted Bundy felt was the cold metal of Old Sparkey's electrodes clamped to his leg in the death chamber. Three thousand volts of electricity coursed through his body.

His epitaph was the chant of protesters outside the jail, who whooped: 'On top of Old Sparkey, all loaded with juice, goodbye to old Bundy, no more on the loose!'

ABOVE: Ted Bundy shows no emotion as he is found guilty of first degree murder on 24 July 1979.

BELOW: Bundy during his trial.

BURKE AND HARE

NAME: William Burke

BORN: Unknown

DIED: Hanged 28 January 1829

ACTUAL NAME: William Hare

BORN: Unknown

DIED: Said to have died in poverty in London

PREFERRED MURDER METHOD: Suffocation

NUMBER OF VICTIMS: At least 16

MURDER LOCALE: Edinburgh

SPAN OF MURDER CAREER: December 1827 to 31 October 1928

DATE OF CONVICTION: 23 August 1977

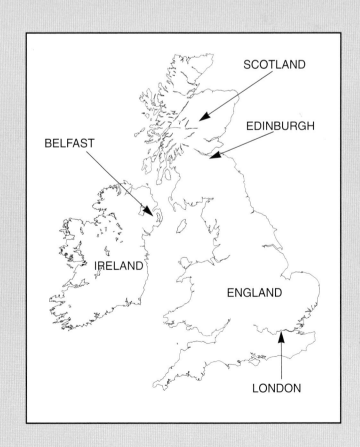

One night shortly before Christmas 1827, two furtive strangers presented themselves at the door of No 10 Surgeons' Square, the Edinburgh establishment of the brilliant anatomist Dr Robert Knox. The doorman knew enough of the kind of tradesmen with whom his master did business, and asked them inside.

The strangers had something to sell, merchandise that was good and fresh, and delivery could be guaranteed that night. The men were told to return close to midnight. They arrived with the goods in a sack which Dr Knox himself inspected and pronounced acceptable. The price was struck at £7 10s, and all sides left well satisfied with the night's work.

William Burke and his accomplice William Hare had just sold their first corpse. It was the opening chapter in the case of Scotland's most celebrated and gruesome serial murderers.

Surgeons' Square, Edinburgh, was a place where the frontiers of medicine were advancing at an inexorable rate. Yet there was one vital ingredient lacking in this exploration of the human body. In the early 19th century, dissecting human corpses was prohibited by law, and it was unheard of for anyone to donate their body for research. A supply of corpses had to be provided — and the fresher the better. William Burke and William Hare were the men to do it.

Burke and Hare came together when the former, who had deserted his wife and young family in Ireland, knocked on the door of Hare's lodging house in 1827. Burke, who was accompanied by a girlfriend, Helen M'Dougal, whom he had acquired in his travels, found he had much in common with his landlord. William Hare was also Irish born and had just moved in with a widow who had inherited the threepence-a-night 'tramp hostel' upon the sudden death of her husband.

Burke and Hare went into the 'body business' together upon the death of a lodger known as Old Donald, who succumbed to a long illness, owing £4 in rent. To recoup his loss, landlord Hare hit upon the plan of selling the corpse to the doctors at Surgeons' Square. With his fellow countryman and fellow whisky-lover Burke, they removed Old Donald's body from the coffin that lay in the backyard and made their fateful visit to Dr Knox.

It was easy money but Burke and Hare realised they would have difficulty in continually restocking the merchandise they required for their new unholy trade. Churchyards were now well guarded at night because of previous raids by grave robbers, and many tombs even had iron bars around them. The only solution was to 'make' corpses to sell to their distinguished customer at No 10.

The first of 16 victims was an old man called Joe the Mumper, who fell ill of a high fever and was too weak to offer resistance as Burke and Hare laid a pillow over his face and held him down until he suffocated. His body fetched £10 at Surgeons' Square.

The second victim was despatched in what became the hallmark of Burke and Hare's murder technique. A lodger, whose name they did not even know, was confined to his bed with jaundice. While the man was asleep, his landlord, together with Burke, held his mouth and nose until there was no sign of breathing. Third to die was an old woman tramp whom Hare and his wife met in a city bar, lured to their lodging house and suffocated. In the spring of 1828 the killers saw off two more lodgers, both destitute women. Then came the murder of a prostitute, Mary Paterson.

Mary was sold for the usual £10 and the sight of her naked body, barely six hours into death, aroused great excitement among the medical students, one of whom claimed to recognise her. Mary's shapely figure and good looks were even remarked upon in the popular newspapers. Dr Knox gladly revelled in the publicity for his research efforts. Rather than take the body straight onto the dissecting table, he had it preserved in whisky for three months, allowing it to become almost a tourist attraction.

His junior assistant, a Dr Lonsdale, later wrote: 'The body of the girl Paterson could not fail to attract attention by its voluptuous form and beauty; students crowded around the table on which she lay and artists came to study a model worthy of the best Greek painters. Here was publicity beyond the professional walk.'

Burke and Hare, meanwhile, were already back at their business, becoming increasingly audacious. On one occasion, Burke encountered a drunken woman being escorted along the street by a policeman. He intervened, convinced the officer that he was a Good Samaritan — and the hapless wretch was released into Burke's care. She was delivered to Surgeons' Square that very night.

In June 1828 the partners committed their vilest crime. Burke was stopped in the street by an Irish woman, leading by the hand a young boy who was deaf and dumb. She said she had come to Edinburgh to seek a relative, and asked Burke for directions. He told her he knew the person she was looking for, then led her to his home where she was murdered in the usual way.

Burke and Hare were unsure what to do with the boy, however. They considered turning him out onto the streets, in the hope that he could tell no tales against them. Instead, Burke took the boy over his knee and, as he later told police, 'broke his back' while the terrified youngster stared piteously into his face. The two victims were then stuffed into a barrel and sold for £16 the pair.

As the gruesome trade continued, Dr Knox never once questioned the source of these fresh bodies. By the time of the 15th murder — a hapless idiot well known to the folk of Edinburgh as Daft Jamie — he must surely have had the gravest suspicion, yet said nothing. In the end, Burke and Hare were trapped by the enemies of all serial murderers: over-confidence and carelessness.

On 31 October 1828, a female lodger turned up the corner of her straw mattress and was horrified to discover the body of a naked crone, her face horribly bloodstained. She went to the police.

Burke and Hare, along with their women, were arrested. Because all of them denied murder, and because medical evidence was insubstantial, charges could not immediately be brought. After weeks of unsuccessful interrogation, William Hare was given an opportunity to turn King's Evidence and thereby obtain immunity. He immediately denounced his former partner.

The trial began on Christmas Eve 1828 and continued without pause until the final guilty verdict was returned against Burke on Christmas morning. The court's sentence was a piece of poetic justice. Burke would be hanged and his body would be used for medical science . . . to be publicly dissected by the anatomists.

On 28 January 1829 William Burke died on the gallows, watched by a crowd of around 25,000, the largest then seen in the city. Among them was the poet Sir Walter Scott, having rented one of the prime seats. The body was then removed to the medical rooms, where guests were admitted in batches of 50 to watch it being dissected. The following day, the general public was admitted, 30,000 people filing past Burke's remains. His body was then salted and put into barrels for use in future experiments.

What of the other players in the vile pantomime? Hare was freed but is said to have lived out a miserable existence, dying a poverty-stricken blind beggar in London. Helen Burke was a victim of mob hate wherever she went, though she later found anonymity in the West Country. Mrs Hare fled to Belfast, where her fate is unknown.

The infamous Dr Knox found his career in ruins. He died in disgrace on 20 December 1862. The few mourners at his funeral would have recalled the rhyme chanted the length of mid-19th century Britain:

'Burke's the murderer, Hare's the thief.
And Knox the boy who buys the beef.'

DAVID CARPENTER

David Carpenter was the man responsible for a series of murders known as the 'Trailside Killings' in San Francisco between 1979 and 1980. His reign of terror began in August 1979 with the murder of 44-year-old Edda Kane in Mount Tamalpais State Park. She had been raped and then shot through the head while kneeling.

Seven months later, 23-year-old Barbara Swartz was stabbed while on her knees. Then came Anne Alderson, found dead in the park with three bullets in her head. She, too, had been in the kneeling position at the time of her death.

The grisly pattern continued. In November 1980, Shauna May's body was found alongside that of her friend 22-year-old Diane O'Connell. Yet another girl, Heather Skaggs, 22, was found dead in Big Basin Redwood State Park near San Francisco. The following March, hitchhikers Gene Blake and Ellen Hansen were threatened at gunpoint by Carpenter. She was shot dead, but he managed to crawl for help, bleeding heavily from his wounds.

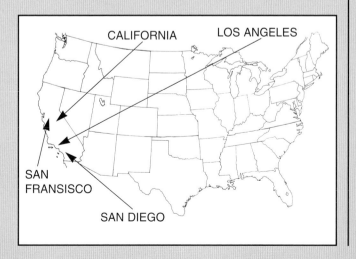

NAME: David Carpenter

A.K.A.: The 'Trailside Killer'

DIED: Sentenced to death (for murder of Hansen and Skaggs)

PREFERRED MURDER METHOD: Raped followed by shot in head

NUMBER OF VICTIMS: 10

NAMES OF VICTIMS: Edda Kane, Barbara Swartz, Anne Alderson, Shauna May, Diane O'Connell, Heather Skaggs, Richard Stowers, Cynthia Moreland, Ellen Hansen

MURDER LOCALE: San Fransisco

SPAN OF MURDER CAREER: August 1979 to 1980

DATE OF CONVICTION: 10 May 1988 (judgement set aside; awaiting retrial)

Blake's description led police to Carpenter, who had some years earlier been prime suspect in the slaughter of five people. He had been cleared when fingerprints did not match up.

Now, however, Carpenter's luck ran out. Helen Scaggs had worked in the same print shop as him. Bullets used to kill her matched those fired at Gene Blake and Ellen Hansen. More proof came with the discovery of the body of Anna Menjivas, who had been a friend of Carpenter's.

Carpenter was found guilty in Los Angeles of the murders of Heather Scaggs and Ellen Hansen. He was sentenced to death in the gas chamber of San Quentin. At a second trial in San Diego, Carpenter was convicted of five more murders and two rapes and again sentenced to death. Following an appeal, however, a new trial was set because of a legal technicality.

ANDREI CHIKATILO

NAME: Andrei Chikatilo

A.K.A.: The 'Rostov Ripper'

BORN: 1936

DIED: Shot dead in prison on 14 February 1994

PREFERRED MURDER METHOD: Torture, murder and cannibalism

NUMBER OF VICTIMS: At least 53

MURDER LOCALE: Rostov and the rest of Russia

SPAN OF MURDER CAREER: December 1978 to 1992

DATE OF CONVICTION: 15 October 1992

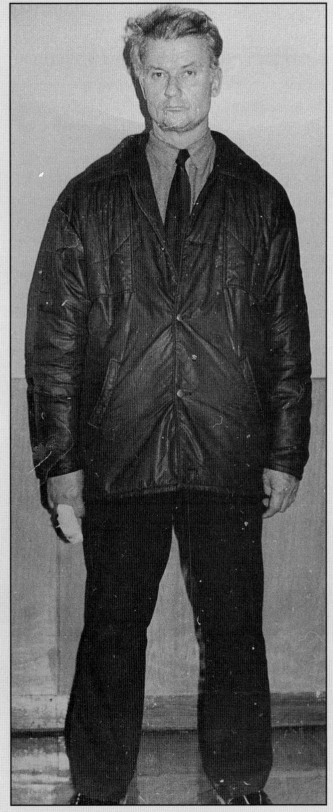

Russian cannibal killer Andrei Chikatilo was dubbed the 'Rostov Ripper'. To his family he was a mild-mannered grandfather but in reality he tortured, murdered, mutilated and ate as many as 53 victims.

To those around him, Chikatilo, a former school-teacher, was a happily married man. Some might have said he was henpecked at home. Others found his habit of sleeping in the bathroom a little bizarre. Even if they knew Chikatilo was haunted by the memory of a cousin being eaten during the 1934 Ukrainian famine, no one could have believed Chikatilo was the perpetrator of a catalogue of sickening crimes, many involving children.

Incredibly, Chikatilo, 56, was arrested and questioned twice during his 12-year reign of slaughter and cannibalism. Both times, he convinced police he was innocent of any wrongdoing. The murder investigations, in which half a million people were questioned, were further hampered by the disappearance of some victims going unreported.

Chikatilo's first victim was was pretty, nine-year-old Lena Zakotno. In December 1978 he lured the girl back to the shack he had bought for the sole purpose of taking prostitutes for sex. He tried to rape Lena but failed. Chikatilo's wife Fayina was later to admit that her husband was unable to make love to her properly. This inability seemed to be a crucial factor in Chikatilo's attacks on his victims. He would become enraged at his impotence, being able to have sexual intercourse only when his victims were dead.

Chikatilo dropped Lena's body into a river. After neighbours reported a light had been on at the shack that night, Chikatilo was interviewed about the murder nine times. Strangely, enquiries then switched to another suspect man living nearby. Even more bizarre was the fact that this man confessed to the horrific crime — and was found guilty and executed.

Chikatilo was free to continue his secret, murdering life. Neither age nor sex mattered to him. His victims were raped and mutilated, sometimes

disembowelled, and had organs cut out or bitten off. Chikatilo would also remove the eyes, fearing the lifeless gaze as he set about his mutilation. Sometimes he bit off nipples in a sexual frenzy.

Lt-Col Viktor Burakov, who led the murder hunt, said: 'In our search for the criminal, we just couldn't imagine what sort of person we were dealing with. This was the height of sadism, the like of which we had never seen.'

Eleven bodies were found in 1984 alone. Chikatilo did not see children as innocents. Instead he believed their simple walks through the forest would turn them into 'rootless elements'.

Although Chikatilo seemed well settled in the teaching job he took in 1971, he gave it up 10 years later. It baffled his wife and others around him when he took on the job of a humble supply clerk. Little did they suspect that this gave Chikatilo, whose existence now revolved around his bloodlust, the splendid opportunity to travel. He went to St Petersburg in the north-west and Tashkent in Uzbekistan. But his favourite killing fields were home-based. He would hang around bus stops and railway stations, stalk possible victims on buses and trains, or simply target them on the streets or out walking.

Chikatilo's victims seemed prepared to go off with him on the promise of small gifts: chewing gum or to watch a video or the offer of a meal. But bearing in mind that most of them were runaways or prostitutes, it is less difficult to understand how they would be tempted by such treats from the kindly grandfather figure. Chikatilo was later to tell police:

'As soon as I saw a lonely person I would have to drag them off to the woods. I paid no attention to age or sex. We would walk for a couple of miles or so through the woods and then I would be possessed by a terrible shaking sensation.'

At the height of the murders, police kept regular surveillance in woods around Rostov. But still the cannibal killer eluded them. He was even apprehended near the scene of one murder carrying an attache case containing a knife. But he talked his way out of suspicion.

At one point, Chikatilo was forced to take a break from his devil's work. In the summer of 1984 he was arrested for the 'theft of state property' —

three rolls of linoleum — and was jailed for three months. He quickly caught up with those missing murdering moments by slaughtering eight people in a single month after his release.

In the end, it was simple, down-to-earth police work which led to the arrest of the 'Rostov Ripper'. After the body of Chikatilo's final victim, a young boy, was discovered, police gathered evidence from

A cage was built in court for the trial of the 'Rostov Ripper' which started on 14 April 1992.

the site of the murder and painstakingly cross-checked it against an index containing around 25,000 possible suspects. Witnesses had also reported a middle-aged man hanging around as the boy bought a rail ticket. Police attention now cen-

tred on the railway station and 600 men were deployed on the forest path along the rail line. They were getting closer to Chikatilo.

The 'Rostov Ripper' was arrested as he approached his latest potential teenage victim on a street. Realising her husband was the beast responsible for the series of unspeakable crimes, his wife went into hiding, taking the couple's two grown-up children with her.

Chikatilo admitted murdering 11 boys and 42 girls during his reign of terror but there may have been many more. Of the cannibal killer's known victims, the youngest was seven-year-old Igor Gudkov, who died because he strayed from home, and the oldest was 44-year-old prostitute Marta Ryabyenko.

When the monster went on trial in Rostov, he did so chained in an iron cage which stood in the courtroom. Relatives of his victims bayed for justice, and on the first day of the trial, proceedings were delayed for half an hour as the hysterical crowd demanded Chikatilo be handed to them as

Andrei Chikatilo swayed behind the bars of his courtroom cage, eyes rolling and mouthing abuse.

a human sacrifice. Ambulance men gave spectators sedatives. Chikatilo cut a chilling figure as from within the cage he rolled his eyes, swung his head and waved pornographic magazines at the 'audience' in front of him.

Chikatilo's trial started on 14 April 1992. On 15 October that year, he was found guilty. The judge was fiercely critical of the police and said: 'If they had done their job in 1978 after the first killing, 51 lives could have been saved. Or if they had not released him after questioning in 1984, at least 20 people would not have died.'

Andrei Chikatilo was sentenced to die with a bullet in the back of the neck. The 58-year-old schoolteacher, labelled by the press as 'the world's most sadistic and perverted killer', was finally shot dead in prison on 14 February 1994 after President Boris Yeltsin rejected an appeal for clemency.

JOHN CHRISTIE

NAME: John Reginald Halliday Christie

A.K.A.: Reg

BORN: 8 April 1898

DIED: Hanged at Pentonville Prison 15 July 1953

PREFERRED MURDER METHOD: Strangulation

NUMBER OF VICTIMS: 8

NAMES OF VICTIMS: Ruth Fuerst, Muriel Eady, Beryl Evans, Geraldine Evans, Ethel Christie, Kathleen Maloney, Rita Nelson, Hectorina MacLennan

MURDER LOCALE: 10 Rillington Place, London

SPAN OF MURDER CAREER: August 1939 to February 1951

DATE OF CONVICTION: 25 June 1953

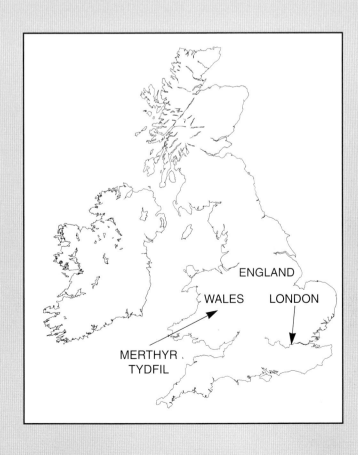

Few addresses are more enduringly spine-chilling than 10 Rillington Place, the home of woman-slayer John Christie. It was in the shabby surroundings of the rented ground-floor flat in London's Notting Hill that Christie, gaunt, bespectacled and balding, killed seven times. He buried the bodies around the house leaving a gruesome legacy for the next tenant to find. Among the victims, he claimed, was a woman whose husband had already been sent to the gallows for her murder.

John Reginald Halliday Christie, known as Reg, was one of seven children born to a carpet designer from Halifax and his wife, an amateur actress. The insipid child, who preferred to scamper in cemeteries instead of local playgrounds, was a choirboy and later a Scout master, but remained aloof, unpopular and unpleasant.

Later in life, he claimed that, as an eight-year-old, the sight of his dead grandfather, waxy and impassive, had had a vital influence on him.

Christie enlisted in the British Army to fight in World War 1 but his service came to an abrupt end when a mustard gas shell exploded and injured his eyes and larynx. He was demobbed in 1919 with a small disability pension.

Back home in Halifax, he began to date Ethel Waddington, a local girl he had known for years. They married when they were 22. If Ethel thought she was in for a cosy, routine marriage, she was sorely mistaken. On the outside, John Christie appeared a respectable Post Office worker. In fact, he was stealing postal orders in an attempt to bring thrills to his humdrum life. His felony was discovered and he was sent to jail, the first of several spells behind bars for petty crimes. Worse than that, from Ethel's point of view, Christie was consorting with prostitutes — he had been since his

army days — and showed no enthusiasm for giving up his sexual adventures.

Following a series of rows, job-hopping Christie finally left and moved to London alone. There followed more crimes and a conviction for violence against a prostitute. Pondering his predicament in a prison cell, Christie wrote to his typist wife for the first time in nine years to ask for a reconciliation. She agreed and on his release they set up home together, choosing the then seedy West London area of Notting Hill. In 1938 they moved to Rillington Place, one of three apartments in a rundown house with a tiny garden and Wheaties which contained the communal lavatory.

Astonishing though it seems, when World War 2 broke out in 1939, Christie was accepted as a special constable in the War Reserve Police, no checks having been made for previous convictions. Soon after, when Ethel was visiting relatives in Sheffield, Christie, dapper in his uniform, picked up 17-year-old Ruth Fuerst, an Austrian refugee, ex-nurse and probably part-time prostitute. Back at 10 Rillington Place, Christie took a rope and strangled her.

Christie first hid the body beneath the floorboards. Then he dragged it into the toilet, concealed it behind some rubbish and dug a grave in his garden, in full view of the neighbours. Finally, under cover of darkness, he buried Ruth's body, where it lay undisturbed for a decade.

Before the end of the war, Christie was sacked from the police and went to work in a radio factory where he met attractive 31-year-old Muriel Eady. Although she already had a regular boyfriend, Muriel was enticed back to Christie's home when he knew his wife was out. Reclining in an armchair, she was tricked into inhaling coal-gas fumes. As she slipped into unconsciousness, he raped her and strangled her with a stocking.

In his confession, Christie said: 'I gazed down at her body and felt a quiet, peaceful thrill. I had no regrets.' He buried her alongside his first victim.

In 1948 Christie had a new neighbour in the rooms above him: lorry driver Timothy Evans, his wife Beryl and their baby Geraldine had moved in, and when Beryl found herself pregnant with an unwanted baby, Christie persuaded her to allow him to carry out an abortion. That same day Beryl died, although at whose hands to this day no one really knows.

Events took a bizarre turn when Timothy Evans walked into a police station in distant Merthyr Tydfil, South Wales, claiming to have killed his wife. Police searched Rillington Place but failed to find the body of Beryl Evans down the drain where her husband said it would be. They also failed to uncover the bodies buried in the garden. Finally, after several visits, they found Beryl Evans's body stashed in the washroom next to that of 14-month-old Geraldine.

On hearing that his daughter had also been killed, Evans seemed shocked and dramatically changed his story. He was innocent, he insisted; his neighbour Christie was the killer. Evans, who had an extremely low IQ, said Christie told him that an abortion on his wife had gone wrong and that the baby was being adopted.

Christie cut a much finer figure in court than Evans ever could. He convinced the judge and jury that he was an innocent bystander, and his damning words sealed Evans's miserable fate. Evans was convicted of murdering his daughter and sentenced to the gallows. He was executed in March 1950.

Christie and Ethel continued to live together, although the secret killer's behaviour became increasingly odd. He was not at all plagued by guilt but suffered instead a variety of minor ailments including headaches, backache and amnesia for which he consulted a doctor.

The urge to kill came upon Christie again in 1952. This time his victim was the unfortunate Ethel. She was strangled in bed and buried under the floorboards. Her dead body was not violated by Christie, unlike the majority of his other victims.

Now the neurotic killer's existence became even more squalid than before. An habitual shirker, he was jobless and had to sell almost every stick of furniture to raise some cash. His straightened circumstances did not stop him seeing prostitutes, however. Kathleen Maloney, 26, a happy drunk, agreed to go home with him in January 1951. She was gassed, abused and her body stowed behind a kitchen cupboard. Days later the same fate awaited another prostitute, 25-year-old Rita Nelson. Christie claimed his last victim, Hectorina

Timothy Evans, who lived in the same house as Christie, confessed to murdering his wife — then recanted and blamed Christie when he found his daughter dead too.

Maclennan, 26, a month later. Then Christie moved out, took his mongrel dog to the vet to be destroyed and hit the road.

It was not until a new tenant moved in and noticed the unbearable stench which pervaded the house that Christie was unmasked. Believing a rat may have died under the floorboards, the tenant poked about in a newly-wallpapered alcove and exposed a woman's legs. His frantic call to police resulted in the unearthing of all the bodies. In the yard they found a tobacco tin containing four sets of pubic hair. Christie, once a prime prosecution witness, was now the subject of one of the biggest manhunts ever. Homeless and alone, he was arrested after being recognised by a policeman as he leaned over Putney Bridge.

Despite a physical and mental breakdown, the glib manner which served him so well did not fail him as he faced horrified detectives. He denied all the sexual aspects of his crimes. The killings were all accidental, he claimed — caused by the victims themselves in their struggles. The referred to the murders as 'those regrettable happenings'. There seemed no end to his suffocating hypocrisy.

On 22 June 1953 Christie's trial began at London's Old Bailey. He pleaded insanity but just three days later he was sentenced to death for four murders, including that of Ethel. The judge described the case as 'a horrible one and a horrifying one'. Christie was hanged at Pentonville Prison on 15 July 1953.

On the eve of Christie's execution, a government tribunal had failed to find a miscarriage of justice in the case of Timothy John Evans. John Scott Henderson QC decided Christie had confessed to the murder of Beryl Evans only to help his own case by adding weight to his plea of madness. Many Members of Parliament and the Howard League for Penal Reform refused to accept the findings.

Public disquiet about the possible miscarriage of justice rumbled on until 1966 when an inquiry under Mr Justice Barbin ruled: 'It is more probable than not that Evans killed Beryl Evans and it is more probable than not that Evans did not kill Geraldine.' It was not satisfactory as far as campaigners were concerned — but it was enough to get Evans a posthumous royal pardon. His body was exhumed from Pentonville Prison and reburied in consecrated ground.

ABOVE: John Christie poses with wife Ethel in their garden. In 1952 he strangled her and buried her under the floorboards: she was his fifth victim.
BELOW: The back of 10 Rillington Place; the Evans' family lived in the top flat.

10 Rillington Place.

ADOLFO DE JESUS CONSTANZO

NAME: Adolfo de Jesus Constanzo

BORN: 1962

DIED: Killed by gang member 5 May 1989

PREFERRED MURDER METHOD: Various after torture

NUMBER OF VICTIMS: at least 15

MURDER LOCALE: Mexico City and Matamoros

SPAN OF MURDER CAREER: 1983-89

DATE OF CONVICTION: Died before capture

Adolfo de Jesus Constanzo was a practitioner of voodoo for the power it gave him over others. He was also a devotee of the strange religion because it allowed him to satiate his bloodlust with regular torture and human sacrifices.

Born in Miami of Cuban extraction, Constanzo studied the black magic arts of Palo Mayombe, a vicious and violent sect imported from the Congo. The cult believes the spirits of the dead exist in limbo and can be harnessed if the gods are regularly appeased with the fresh blood of human sacrifices. Constanzo would keep a cauldron constantly filled with blood and, most importantly, the skull of a human who had died a violent death. The more painful and horrific the death, the more potent the spell that the high priest could cast.

At the age of 21, Constanzo moved to Mexico City where in 1983 he launched himself as a Palo Mayombe priest. Superstitious drugs-family godfathers turned to him for magical protection at $50,000 a spell. As a consequence, his cauldron needed constant replenishment with fresh blood and skulls, and decapitated corpses were regularly fished out of rivers and lakes.

In 1987 Constanzo fell out with one drugs family, led by godfather Guillermo Calzada. Shortly afterwards the drugs baron, his wife, his mother, his partner, his secretary, his maid and his bodyguard were all dragged from a river. All seven had been dreadfully mutilated before being killed. Their fingers and toes and, in the case of the men, their genitals, had been sliced off. Their heads were also missing — gone to feed the cauldron.

Constanzo moved his voodoo circle to Matamoros, near the Texan border, where between May 1988 and March 1989 the gang tortured and ritually sacrificed at least 13 people. All male, they were were often rival drug dealers, but they also included innocent strangers picked up at random. On one occasion, the victim was a police undercover agent who had infiltrated the gang but had been uncovered.

Constanzo's normal method of sacrifice was to have the victim soundly beaten, then dragged into the shed containing the sacred cauldron. Here he would cut off the nose, ears, fingers, toes and genitals of the hapless wretch and partially flay him. Then the others would be ordered out while Constanzo sodomised him. Only then would there be a merciful release through death.

It was essential to the success of the ceremony that there should be as much pain as possible and the victim should die screaming. The spirit had to be confused and terrified as it left the body, making it easier to subjugate. And it was this particular evil that was to bring about Constanzo's downfall.

In March 1989 the selected victim was a small-time Mexican drugs dealer. Every torture was applied to him, but the tough little man would not cry out, even when his upper body was skinned. He endured every torture, even castration, but died silently. Constanzo declared the ceremony a failure and sent his men out to kidnap a softer touch. He was easy to find.

On 14 March 1987 a group of students was celebrating the end of term at their university by crossing the border for a night of cheap alcohol, perhaps a woman or two and possibly a session of pot smoking or cocaine sniffing. When one became separated from his colleagues, he was pushed into the back of a truck and driven to Constanzo's remote Santa Elena ranch.

His name was Mark Kilroy, a 21-year-old medical student at the University of Texas, and he must have screamed sufficiently to satisfy Constanzo before his brains were tipped into the cauldron, for the leader declared the ceremony a great success.

This time, however, the cultists had overreached themselves. Kilroy's parents were devout and loving people who would not rest until they had found their son. They were aided by the boy's uncle, who happened to be a US Customs official. The manhunt that ensued stretched across both sides of the border.

Success came swiftly. Mexican police set up a road block near Matamoros. One of Constanzo's gang came upon it by truck but, since he had been told by his leader that he was invisible, he simply drove straight through it. The cops followed him at a discreet distance as he led them to Constanzo's ranch — and to the shallow graves around the slaughtering shed.

As well as finding a Palo Mayombe altar, goat's head and traces of blood and brains, disgusted police unearthed bodies, including that of student Mark Kilroy. The grave was marked by a length of wire sticking out of the ground. Subsequent examination revealed that a strip of thin but strong wire had been pushed through the length of the boy's spine. Once the body had decomposed sufficiently, it had been Constanzo's intention to pull out the backbone and add it to the revolting mix in his bloody cauldron.

Constanzo and his favoured inner circle — which included the High Priestess of the gang, Sara Maria Aldrete, were tracked to Mexico City — by a chance discovery on 5 May 1989. The apartment he was hiding in was in a poor part of town but the Satanic cult leader left his luxury limousine in the street nearby. Two policemen spotted it and strolled over to investigate, thinking it might have been stolen.

When Constanzo saw them, he assumed the game was up. Suddenly the cops found themselves under fire from a nearby apartment building and radioed for back-up. Soon a heavily armed riot team had surrounded the gang's apartment where, as Constanzo's cultist gunmen exchanged fire with the police, the padrino himself stuffed armful after armful of cash into a furnace, or ripped it up and threw it out of the windows.

Almost out of ammunition, determined not to be taken alive, Constanzo huddled in a wardrobe with his current male lover, bodyguard Martin Rodriguez, and ordered gang member Alvaro de Leo Valdez to shoot them both. When the gunman simply stared aghast, Constanzo smacked him hard across the face and ordered brutally: 'Do it or I'll make things tough for you in hell. And don't worry, I'll be back.'

They were his last words. He and his lover died in a hail of lead as they huddled together in a final despairing clinch. The rest — including Sara Aldrete and Valdez — were taken alive. Their detailed confessions allowed police to close the files on at least 15 unsolved killings of boys and men whose graves had been found at Rancho Santa Elena.

Sara Maria Aldrete was acquitted of Constanzo's murder but was sentenced to six years' imprisonment for 'criminal association'. Constanzo's lieutenant Alvaro de Leo Valdez was sentenced to 30 years for murder.

The sinister and sickening Palo Mayombe cult did not die with him. Voodoo practices are still rife in Mexico and among the immigrant populations of Florida. The Miami River is nicknamed the

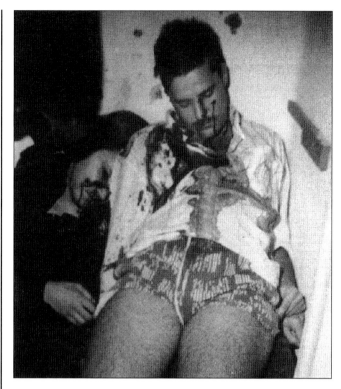

Adolfo Constanzo and his homosexual lover lie in a final embrace after having been shot by gang members.

'River Of Chickens' by the sanitation crews who, in one three-day period alone, dredged up the headless bodies of 200 chickens — all the remains of sacrifices to the spirits of the 'living dead'.

DEAN CORLL

NAME: Dean Corll (above left)

ACCOMPLICES: Elmer Henley (above right) and David Brooks

BORN: 1939

DIED: August 1973 shot by Elmer Henley

PREFERRED MURDER METHOD: Strangulation and shooting

NUMBER OF VICTIMS: At least 32

MURDER LOCALE: Houston

SPAN OF MURDER CAREER: 1970-73

DATE OF CONVICTION: Killed before capture

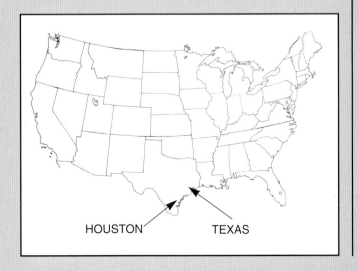

HOUSTON   TEXAS

Dean Corll, a Houston electrician, killed at least 27 teenage boys, burying them under a boathouse between 1970 and 1973.

Dean Corll, born in 1939, had two accomplices, Elmer Henley and David Brooks, who helped him procure boys. Homosexual Corll would organise glue-sniffing parties at which boys — usually aged between 13 and 17, but one of only nine — would be plied with drink and drugs. Afterwards the chosen victim, usually by now unconscious, would be taken to Corll's 'torture room'.

There the victim would be stripped and handcuffed to a plank of wood. Corll would then sexually assault, torture and murder them — but sometimes only after several days of his perverted 'sex games'.

When the killing spree approached 30, Henley cracked and, in a showdown, shot Corll dead in August 1973. The breaking point had been reached when Henley unusually brought a 15-year-old girl to the apartment. When Corll returned home, he angrily confronted Henley who seized a gun. Corll mocked him with the words: 'Go on, kill me if you dare.' Henley fired all six bullets into Corll and then called the police.

Following Henley's directions police investigated a boathouse in Houston where they quickly discovered the first of 17 bodies. Henley next led them to Lake Sam Rayburn where more corpses were discovered.

He and Brooks were subsequently found guilty of six murders and sentenced to life imprisonment.

JUAN VALLEJO CORONA

NAME: Juan Vallejo Corona

BORN: 1933

DIED: Still serving 25 life sentences

PREFERRED MURDER METHOD: Knifed and hacked to death by machete

NUMBER OF VICTIMS: 25

MURDER LOCALE: Near Yuba City, California

SPAN OF MURDER CAREER: February-May 1971

DATE OF CONVICTION: July 1971

An itinerant Mexican fruit picker, Juan Vallejo Corona crossed the border into California in the 1950s and steadily worked his way up the social ladder to become a successful businessman in Yuba City. His book-keeping was meticulous — as police discovered when they followed up an anonymous tip-off and raided Corona's farm near Feather River in 1971.

There they found 25 names carefully listed in a ledger. They corresponded with Mexican migrants who had disappeared in the previous few months. Their bodies were found secreted around the farmstead. All had been hacked to death with a knife or a machete.

A jury found Corona guilty of 25 counts of homicide and the judge sentenced him to no fewer than 25 life sentences — to be served consecutively.

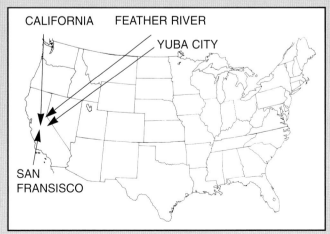

CALIFORNIA   FEATHER RIVER
YUBA CITY
SAN FRANSISCO

MARY ANN COTTON

Mary Ann Cotton was not like most serial killers. She knew her victims . . . for all of them were members of her immediate family.

BORN: 1832

DIED: Hanged in Durham Prison on 24 March 1873

PREFERRED MURDER METHOD: Poison

NUMBER OF VICTIMS: At least 21

LOCALE: Low Moorsley, Co Durham

SPAN OF MURDER CAREER: 1852-72

DATE OF CONVICTION: March 1873

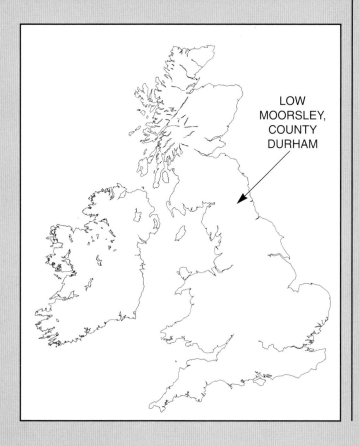

LOW MOORSLEY, COUNTY DURHAM

Mary, raised in the County Durham mining village of Low Moorsley, was married in 1852 to William Mowbray. They had eight children. But only one daughter, Isabella, survived. She had been sent to live with her grandmother while those remaining at home all died of gastric fever.

After her husband's death, Mary married George Ward. Yet after only 13 months he too was dead. The merry widow even murdered her own mother, who became ill at the same time as her third husband, James Robinson, asked Mary to marry him. Rather conveniently, mother was dead within 10 days. Mary herself became mother to James Robinson's five children, taking with her the surviving daughter Isabella. Within months Isabella and four of the Robinson children had died. Robinson left Mary, taking with him the remainder of his children.

Even though she was still legally married, Mary next wed Frederick Cotton, who had two children from a previous marriage. His bride soon fell pregnant and had another child. After a year Frederick too was dead. Gastric fever was blamed.

It was at this stage of her killing spree that Mary met up with a former lover, Joseph Nattrass. The resumed romance was ill-fated as the greedy widow found yet another way of improving her lifestyle. This time her heart was set on a customs officer by the name of Mr Quick-Manning — and everyone else became no more than millstones around her neck. Mary killed Nattrass, along with 10-year-old Frederick Cotton and her 14-month-old baby.

It was this final murder that doomed her. Charlie had been fine one day and dead the next. His tiny body was subjected to an autopsy . . . and the cause of all the deaths became apparent. Mary was a poisoner, using arsenic to kill her victims.

After the bodies of family members were exhumed, Mary was tried. It will never be known how many people she killed but it is though to be 21 — giving her the infamous title of Britain's greatest mass-murderer.

DR THOMAS NEILL CREAM

NAME: Dr Thomas Neill Cream

A.K.A.: The 'Lambeth Poisoner'

BORN: 27 May 1850

DIED: Hanged at Newgate Prison 15 November 1892

PREFERRED MURDER METHOD: Poison

NUMBER OF VICTIMS: 7

NAMES OF VICTIMS: Kate Gardener, Julia Faulkener, Daniel Stott, Ellen Donworth, Matilda Clover, Alice Marsh, Emma Shrivell

MURDER LOCALE: Chicago, Canada and London

SPAN OF MURDER CAREER: 1880 to 12 April 1892

DATE OF CONVICTION: 20 October 1892

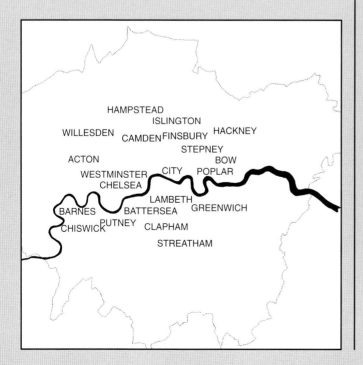

The hooded figure of convicted killer Dr Thomas Neill Cream stood with a noose around his neck on the scaffold at Newgate Prison and declared 'I am Jack the . . .'

Cream's astonishing last words were silenced when the trap door burst open beneath his feet and he was hanged. Cream, tagged the 'Lambeth Poisoner', was indeed a suspect in the relentless search for Jack the Ripper, the slaughterer of five women in London at the close of the last century. Yet he was apparently in jail across the Atlantic at the time the Ripper was in action. Cream certainly had the medical know-how displayed by the Ripper, who savagely disembowelled his victims. There is even a faint chance that he was part of a murderous double act. More probably, however, it was a final flight of fancy by a man who appeared to be rapidly losing his his hold on reality.

Cream was born in Glasgow on 27 May 1850, one of eight children of William and Mary Cream. Before he celebrated his sixth birthday, he had emigrated with his family to Canada, where his father became the manager of a Quebec shipbuilding firm.

At first, young Thomas was a shipbuilder's apprentice but his heart was set on a career in the medical profession. He studied at McGill University and emerged with an American MD qualification. This bright, eligible young man became engaged to one Flora Eliza Brooks but before they could be married Flora fell pregnant. Obligingly, Cream carried out an illegal abortion, leaving her seriously ill.

When her parents realised what had occurred, they were furious. Her father confronted Cream and insisted that he marry Flora or face the consequences. This was to be a genuine shotgun wedding and it duly took place in September 1876. The next day, Cream cynically fled the country. He arrived in England, where he studied at St Thomas's Hospital, London, and the Royal College of Physicians and Surgeons in Edinburgh.

Cream lived quietly, apart from one strange incident later recalled by a prominent lawyer of the day. Marshall Hall was asked to defend a man accused of bigamy with a string of women. After advising him to plead guilty, the lawyer was surprised to hear the man declare himself innocent. Not only that, he had an alibi. He was in jail in Australia, at the time of the offences. A cable from the jail 'down under' confirmed his innocence. When Hall attended the trial of Dr Cream much later, he recognised the errant doctor as being the same man charged with bigamy. There must have been collusion with a double, Hall concluded, although no one knows how long or to what extent this continued.

With his new qualifications, Cream returned to Canada — safe from the wrath of his wife, as he was by now a widower — and set up a practice in London, Ontario. Soon afterwards the body of chambermaid Kate Gardener was found in the water closet behind his rooms. She had been killed by chloroform. Although it was known she was visiting him for an abortion, no action was taken against Cream.

He moved to Chicago where another woman seeking an abortion, Julia Faulkener, died in August 1880. This time he was taken into custody but once again slipped through the net — in time to kill off another woman patient. His luck ran out, however, with his next murderous fling.

Cream took up with an attractive married woman, Julia Stott. She had visited him to buy a medicine he marketed for epilepsy in the hope it would help her ailing and ageing husband. After eventually taking his medicine from Cream, Daniel Stott died in agony. The death would have remained unremarkable if Cream himself had not written an anonymous letter to the coroner and district attorney accusing the chemist of meddling with the medicine. Stott's body was exhumed and the poison strychnine was discovered in his stomach. Cream tried to flee but was captured, brought to book and sentenced to life for murder in November 1891.

With remission, Cream was released a little under a decade later. He returned to Canada to collect cash left to him by his father and then went on to England. His mind was clearly unbalanced, as companions noticed, possibly addled by an addiction to morphia. His conversation was centred on poisons, pornography and money.

Cream's next chosen victim was prostitute Ellen Donworth, 19, who was found in the road suffering violent convulsions. Before her death, she was able to tell her landlady that she took a mystery drink from a cross-eyed stranger who had bushy whiskers and wore a silk hat. The description was that of Cream, who wore a false beard beneath his moustache when he was up to no good. An inquest found that Ellen had died from strychnine poisoning.

A letter written in Cream's hand found its way to the coroner's office, pledging help in the search for the killer in exchange for a huge sum of cash. It was signed 'A. O'Brien, detective'. Another letter was sent to Frederick Smith, of the stationery company W. H. Smith, claiming that he knew Ellen Donworth and demanding cash. Cream also printed 500 leaflets claiming that the killer of Ellen was on the staff of the Metropole Hotel. All the residents, he alleged, were in danger. These letters baffled police and have perplexed historians, who are still unable to establish his motives.

A week later another prostitute, Matilda Clover, died the same agonising death, but this was put down to alcoholic poisoning. Cream wrote yet another of his crackpot letters, this time trying to blackmail a doctor over the death. Police were alerted but when the blackmail attempt fizzled out, they failed to pursue the case.

London was saved from more of his lunatic behaviour when Cream met and fell in love with Laura Sabbatini. The pair became engaged, although their wedding plans were delayed by a business trip Cream made to the United States in 1892. Nine days after his return, two prostitutes in lodgings woke in the early hours writhing and screaming in pain. Alice Marsh, aged 21, and Emma Shrivell, 18, had spent the evening in the company of a stout man with whiskers, wearing glasses to correct a squint. It was, of course, Cream — although unknown to him, he had been spotted leaving them in the early hours by sharp-eyed PC George Cumley.

Cream next tried to extort money from Dr Joseph Harper, father of a fellow lodger, in a letter which claimed his son Walter had been responsible for the prostitutes' murders. In the letter, he also mentioned the killing of Matilda Clover, who at that time was still thought to have been a victim of alcohol poisoning.

Police at last seriously concerned themselves with the suspicious deaths occurring in the seedy slums of London. Their breakthrough came when PC Cumley again saw Cream and followed him home. Two undercover men were put on the case: Patrick McIntyre, a police sergeant, and John Haynes, a covert government agent. Cream condemned himself in confidences to them both. His knowledge of the deaths were too detailed to have been gained from newspaper reports.

Finally a prostitute who had narrowly escaped being poisoned came forward, and the police persuaded Dr Harper to press charges for blackmail. On 3 June 1892, Cream was arrested in London's Lambeth Palace Road. He pompously told the police inspector: 'You have got the wrong man, but fire away!'

The body of Matilda Clover was exhumed and strychnine was discovered in her stomach. A jury which sat at the delayed inquest into her death decided she had died of strychnine poisoning at the hand of Thomas Neill Cream.

In the dock at the Old Bailey, Cream was faced with several charges of murder and two counts of blackmail. He pleaded not guilty to all the charges. Finally, the Crown proceeded with the murder of Clover alone.

Cream was confident he would be freed. He might have been, too, if Mr Justice Hawkins had not ruled that he would hear evidence in the other cases, not just that gathered by the police relating to the death of Clover. His barrister's defence was so eloquent and stirring that Cream sang and danced in his cell, sure that acquittal was only

Dr Thomas Neill Cream: his last words on the gallows were, 'I am Jack the . . .'

hours away. The judge thought otherwise. His summing-up of the case was damning, and the jury took just 10 minutes to decide Cream was guilty.

As he strutted out of the dock, Cream muttered defiantly: 'They shall never hang me.' Less than a month later, he died on the gallows.

GORDON CUMMINS

Gordon Cummins earned the name the 'Blackout Ripper' for his series of murders carried out in the London blackouts of 1942.

His four victims were a schoolteacher, two prostitutes and the wife of a hotel manager. Three were strangled and the other had her throat cut. All were mutilated with a variety of instruments.

RAF airman Cummins's reign of terror lasted just seven days, between 9 February and 15 February, before he was arrested. He had tried to kill Mrs Margaret Mulcahy in her flat in Paddington, but the woman managed to fight him off. Cummins left behind a damning clue: his gas mask stencilled with his RAF number 525987.

The 28-year-old airman was quickly tracked down to his London billet in St John's Wood. His fingerprints matched those at the murder scenes and several items belonging to his victims were found in his quarters.

As was the custom of the time, Cummins was charged with only one murder: that of Mrs Oatley. However, apart from his other three killings in 1942, Cummins was also suspected of two previous murders of young women in North London in 1941. The wartime 'Jack the Ripper' was hanged on 25 June 1942.

NAME: Gordon Cummins

A.K.A.: The 'Blackout Ripper'; the 'Wartime Jack the Ripper'

BORN: 1914

DIED: Hanged at Wandsworth Prison on 25 June 1942

PREFERRED MURDER METHOD: Strangulation

NUMBER OF VICTIMS: 4

NAMES OF VICTIMS: Eveyln Hamilton, Evelyn Oatley, Margaret Lowe, Doris Jouannet

MURDER LOCALE: London

SPAN OF MURDER CAREER: 9-15 February 1942

DATE OF CONVICTION: 1942

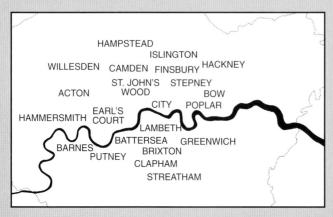

JEFFREY DAHMER

NAME: Jeffrey L. Dahmer

BORN: 1960

DIED: Murdered in prison while serving 1,070 years

PREFERRED MURDER METHOD: Various followed by necrophilia and cannibalism

NUMBER OF VICTIMS: 17 (15 in Wisconsin, 2 in Ohio).

NAMES OF VICTIMS: Steven Tuomi, Stephen Hicks, James Doxator, Donald Montrell, Jeremiah Weinberger, Oliver Lacy, Joseph Bradehoft, Anthony Sears, Richard Guerrero, Ernest Miller, Raymond Smith, Edward Smith, David Thomas, Curtis Straughter, Errol Lindsey, Tony Hughes, Konerak Sinthasomphone

MURDER LOCALE: Wisconsin and Ohio

SPAN OF MURDER CAREER: January 1988 to July 1991 (proven — but also confessed to killings from 1978).

DATE OF CONVICTION: June 1992

Jeffrey Dahmer was everybody's nightmare. An ordinary, insignificant little man, the kind who blends in to any background, melds in to any crowd. No one passing him in the street would have looked at him twice. He was Mr Ordinary. Mr Average. Mr Invisible.

It was not until 1991 that Jeffrey Dahmer was unmasked as the monster he was.

Yet this was the monster who held a city in the grip of terror for two long years as he kidnapped, drugged, killed, sexually molested and finally ate his victims.

Dahmer was a homosexual, a pervert, a serial killer, a necrophiliac. Dahmer was a real-life Hannibal the Cannibal. And like Hannibal Lecter, Dahmer's fearsome counterpart in the film *The Silence of the Lambs*, he had to be caged up like a dangerous beast, completely cut off from even his jailers. Even then, his fellow inmates managed to get to the hated prisoner. So hated was he that he was murdered within the jail that caged him. Only then was the city in which he once operated able to breathe freely again.

As is so often the case with serial killers, Dahmer's reign of terror was ended by accident.

Just an 'ordinary' high school kid in 1978 — in 1995 his mother asked that his brain be preserved for medical research, saying that 'science can be aided' by studying the mind of her monstrous son.

Two cops were in the right place at the right time. Cops who followed their instincts and uncovered a house of horrors that was to shake Milwaukee to its foundations.

Dahmer's insane, perverted lusts drove him to kill because only with corpses could he achieve sexual gratification. His flat became an abattoir, a brothel, a gourmet restaurant and a shrine — in which he could keep grotesque trophies like hands, skulls or genitals cut from his murdered and sodomised victims. Choice cuts from the bodies went into his fridge for later consumption, the rest went into an acid bath he set up in his kitchen.

It was on a warm July night in 1991 that Dahmer was finally captured. Patrolmen Robert Rauth and Rolf Mueller were sitting in their car in a seedy section of town when a young black man ran up to them, handcuffs dangling from his wrists. His story was one that even seasoned beat cops found hard to believe. The man, Tracy Edwards, said someone in a nearby block of flats had threatened to cut out his heart and eat it. Edwards had taken to his heels — having narrowly avoided becoming Dahmer's 18th victim.

The patrolmen took Edwards back to the flats and rang the bell of one of Dahmer's neighbours, John Batchelor. 'Police . . . open up,' they ordered through the intercom. Batchelor pressed his door release mechanism and the policemen charged in.

The two veteran cops called their headquarters from Batchelor's apartment to 'run a make' on Dahmer and discovered he was on probation for a sexual assault on a 13-year-old boy. It was shortly

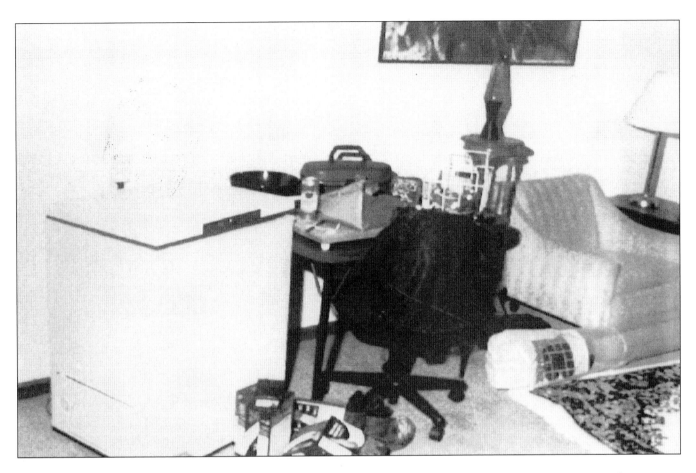

In Dahmer's Milwaukee apartment stands the freezer where he kept human flesh.

before midnight that Rauth and Mueller finally hammered on Dahmer's door. They were surprised by the nauseous stench that attacked their nostrils when the door opened.

The policemen read Dahmer his rights and started looking round the apartment. They found not just kinky videos, not just pornographic pictures of other homosexuals. They found hands, heads and fingers stored in lobster pots. In the fridge was a man's head — along with tenderised strips of meat that were later identified as human flesh.

Dahmer seemed almost relieved to have been caught. He immediately volunteered the information that he had killed 15 young men in Wisconsin and two more in Ohio. Yet there had to be a very public trial because he decided to plead insanity.

Scenes of white-coated forensic scientists entering Dahmer's flat and leaving with black plastic bags full of human remains became commonplace on American TV. Next came the trial at which family after family turned out to curse the monster.

Towards the end of the trial, Dahmer made a statement — an apology composed in his prison cell. Declaring that he would rather have faced the death penalty, he said: 'This was not about hate. I never hated anyone. I knew I was sick or evil, or both. I can't undo the harm I have caused, but I know I will be in prison for the rest of my life. I will turn back to God. I will cooperate with psychologists and become a human guinea pig so that they can study this bizarre mind and perhaps discover what turned a human being into a ghastly killer and cannibal.'

The diatribe fooled no one. Least of all the jury who returned verdicts of guilty and sane. The judge sentenced him to 1,070 years in jail.

After sentence was passed, he was taken to Wisconsin's toughest jail, the Columbia Correctional Institution where he had no contact with other prisoners. Perhaps the strangest thing was that, until his death at the hands of a fellow prisoner, around two dozen letters arrived for him every week — from women who wanted to meet him and fall in love.

ALBERT DE SALVO

NAME: Albert Henry De Salvo

A.K.A.: The 'Boston Strangler'

BORN: 1937

DIED: Murdered in prison on 26 November 1973 while serving life

PREFERRED MURDER METHOD: Strangulation

NUMBER OF VICTIMS: 13

NAMES OF VICTIMS: Anna Slesers, Mary Mullen, Nina Nichols, Helen Blake, Ida Irga, Jane Sullivan, Sophie Clark, Patricia Bissette, Mary Brown, Beverly Samans, Evelyn Corbin, Joann Graff, Mary Sullivan

MURDER LOCALE: Boston, Massachusetts

SPAN OF MURDER CAREER: 14 June 1962 to 4 January 1964

DATE OF CONVICTION: Sentenced to life for lesser offences, being judged unfit to stand trial

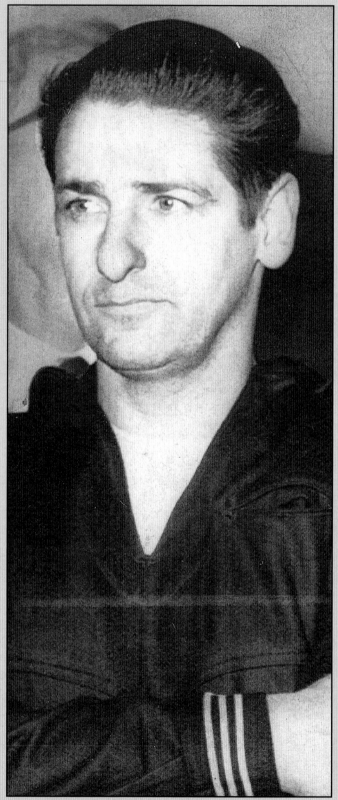

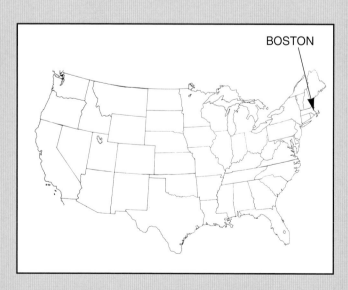

BOSTON

Better known as the 'Boston Strangler', Albert De Salvo attacked women in their own homes, stripping them naked and tying them up before he raped and killed them. Almost all were strangled with their own clothing — usually stockings or tights — which he tied in a neat bow underneath their chins.

Albert Henry De Salvo came from an unpleasant background. His father had battered the young Albert, his brothers and sisters and his wife. The children had also been taught how to steal from an early age. Even more unsavoury was that De Salvo Sr had sex with prostitutes in front of his family. It was no wonder that Albert left home as soon as he could and joined the army.

He married a girl he met in Germany but they divorced after she complained of his unreasonable sexual demands. De Salvo was arrested in 1960 for the bizarre crime of taking girls' measurements while pretending to be a model agency scout. He seduced some of the girls and assaulted others. But strangely, bearing in mind his future reign of terror, none of the young models ever complained about the actual assaults.

His 13 murder victims were all slain between 14 June 1962 and 4 January 1964. During this time he was also known as the 'Green Man' because he generally wore green work trousers. He broke into the homes of women, forcing them to strip, then often raping them. Most of his early victims were either middle-aged or elderly, giving rise to psychologists' predictions that he hated his mother.

De Salvo was finally arrested in 1965, then charged only with a single rape. It was not until he was undergoing psychiatric examination in the Boston State Hospital that he suddenly admitted the true extent of his crimes. He told detectives that he had no idea why he had killed and that indeed he was deeply ashamed that he had hurt a single woman.

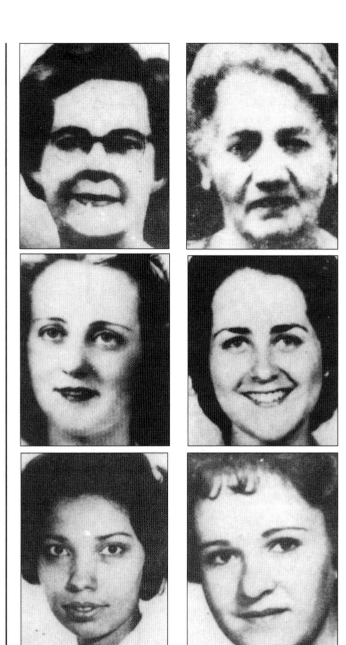

Six of De Salvo's victims: from top to bottom and left to right — Helen Blake, Ida Irga, Joann Graff, Patricia Bissette, Sophie Clark and Mary Sullivan.

He confessed to the 13 killings and was able to provide such precise detail that police were left in no doubt of the veracity of his account. Nonetheless, there was not an iota of supporting evidence to back his story and De Salvo never stood trial for the 'Strangler' murders. His astute lawyer ensured that he was only arraigned on a number of separate sexual offences and a robbery.

De Salvo got a life sentence but it ended on 26 November 1973 when he was 36. He was found in his cell, his heart punctured by a single stab wound.

NANNIE DOSS

NAME: Nannie Doss

BORN: 1905

DIED: In prison of leukemia in 1965

PREFERRED MURDER METHOD: Poison

NUMBER OF VICTIMS: 11

NAMES OF VICTIMS: Four of her five husbands (Frank Harrelson, Arlie Lanning, Richard Morton, Samuel Doss), her mother, two sisters, her own children, a nephew of one husband

MURDER LOCALE: Tulsa, Oklahoma

SPAN OF MURDER CAREER: 1920-54

DATE OF CONVICTION: 1964

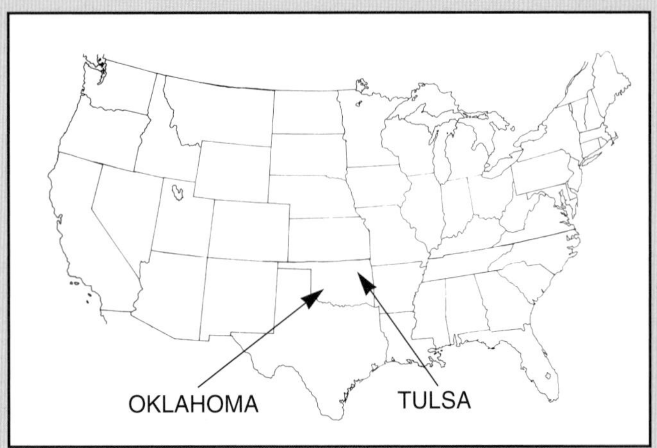

OKLAHOMA   TULSA

Nannie Doss was a compulsive reader of pulp fiction. She claimed she was just a born romantic looking for the perfect love. Having married in 1920 at the age of 15 and having failed to find love, she turned to other means of finding fulfilment — murder.

When first husband George Frazer returned to their home in Tulsa, Oklahoma, one day to find his two children dying on the floor, allegedly poisoned, he walked out. Her second mate, Frank Harelson, died of stomach trouble that same year. Husband number three, Arlie Lanning, survived until 1952 before succumbing to the same affliction. Number four, Richard Morton, left a healthy insurance policy. Her mother, her two sisters and the nephew of one of her deceased husbands were added to the list of deceased.

It was only upon the admission to hospital of her fifth husband, 58-year-old Samuel Doss, with stomach problems, that her criminal activities were recognised. For, after his discharge, she again served him his favourite dish, stewed prunes, and poisoned him. An autopsy was ordered and discovered that there was enough arsenic in him to kill 20 men.

At her trial, police estimated the total tally of her victims at 11. Nannie Doss explained that she had poisoned the last four of her five husbands because they were 'dullards'. She was sentenced to life imprisonment and died of leukemia in 1965. Copies of true-romance magazines were stacked in every corner of her cell.

ALBERT FISH

NAME: Albert Howard Fish

A.K.A.: The 'Moon Maniac'

BORN: 19 May 1870

DIED: Went to electric chair in Sing Sing prison on 16 January 1936

PREFERRED MURDER METHOD: Various and cannibalism

NUMBER OF VICTIMS: At least 15

NAMES OF VICTIMS: Grace Budd and other unidentified children

MURDER LOCALE: New York and all over USA

SPAN OF MURDER CAREER: 1928-34

DATE OF CONVICTION: March 1934

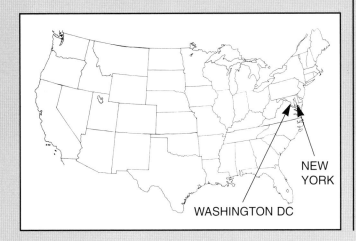

Albert Howard Fish has to be one of the most loathed murderers in American criminal history. His speciality was molesting, torturing and castrating children, occasionally eating his dozens of victims. Born in Washington DC in 1870 to a family with a history of mental illness, he attributed the root cause of his terrible crimes to the experience of watching boys being ruthlessly whipped at the orphanage where he grew up.

Fish was perhaps the oldest serial killer ever because he was not arrested until he was in his 60s — having spent an entire lifetime in pursuit of satisfaction of his sado-masochistic urges. He is believed to have murdered at least 15 children and devoured at least four. But in addition he subjected at least 100 other youngsters to torture and depraved acts without actually taking their lives.

Such was his penchant for pain that he drove 29 needles into his body, mostly around his genitals. He stuffed cotton wool balls soaked with lighter fuel into his rectum and set fire to them. Apart from consuming human flesh, he ate excrement and drank human urine and blood.

Fish was a painter and sometimes his overalls would be covered in suspicious red marks, although he pounced upon his victims in the nude. He once said that he had developed a taste for human flesh during a famine in China. The monstrous killer was not a reclusive bachelor, as is the case with many serial killers. In 1898 he married a woman who was nine years his younger; the couple had six children before his wife ran off with another man. It is believed that this was when Fish's behaviour changed. He heard voices, had hallucinations and became fascinated with evil, pain and sacrifice.

Fish even once said that he was carrying out 'God's work' — abusing girls and boys in every state of America. He was forever on the move, and the painting and decorating work he did meant that he had access to places like basements and attics which he always bore in mind as suitably secluded spots to take child victims. Most of them came from poor, black families. Fish said this was because they 'didn't make such a fuss' if their children disappeared or returned home in distress.

Hard-bitten detectives were sickened by Fish's description of the manner in which he had cooked the buttocks of one little boy:

'I put strips of bacon over each cheek and put in the oven. When the meat was roasted for about a quarter of an hour, I poured a pint of water over for gravy and put in the onions. At frequent intervals I basted with a wooden spoon so the meat would be nice and juicy. In two hours it was nice and brown. I never ate any turkey that tasted half as good as his sweet, fat little behind did. I ate every bit of the meat in about four days.'

Perverted Albert Fish became America's number one hate figure after the remains of 10-year-old victim Grace Budd were uncovered at his home, Wisteria Cottage, in White Plains, New York.

The fiend was finally tried for the murder of 10-year-old Grace Budd, a girl he lured to a children's party in 1928. Police tracked him down after he wrote to the little girl's parents: 'I took her up to Westchester County, Worthington, to an empty house up there, and I choked her to death. I cut her up and ate part of her flesh. I didn't fuck with her. She died a virgin.'

Fish, nicknamed the 'Moon Maniac' because of his tendency to strike around the night of a full moon, went to the electric chair at Sing Sing prison in January 1936. He spoke of the prospect of electrocution as 'the supreme thrill' and even helped his executioners fasten the straps that held him in place. Because of the needles in his body, which caused short-circuits, the first charge failed to kill him. Witnesses told how wisps of blue smoke floated over his head before the second, fatal charge coursed through him.

JOHN WAYNE GACY

NAME: John Wayne Gacy

A.K.A.: The 'Fat Man'

BORN: 17 March 1942

DIED: By lethal injection 10 May 1994

PREFERRED MURDER METHOD: Strangulation

NUMBER OF VICTIMS: 33

MURDER LOCALE: Chicago

SPAN OF MURDER CAREER: 1972-December 1978

DATE OF CONVICTION: 12 March 1980

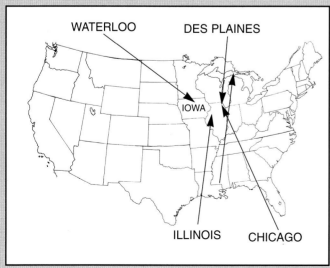

WATERLOO   DES PLAINES

IOWA

ILLINOIS   CHICAGO

Fifteen-year-old Robert Piest set out for his job interview full of hope. His appointment was with a local building contractor who had suggested that there might be some vacation work for him. As he stepped out of the family home in Des Plaines, Illinois, on the evening of 11 December 1978, his mother urged him to return speedily. It was her birthday and a family party was getting into full swing. When there was still no sign of Robert by midnight, his worried mother phoned the police to report that he had not returned. He never did.

Police soon established the identity of the builder Robert had been due to meet: 36-year-old John Wayne Gacy, a name well known to them. Gacy — or the 'Fat Man' as he later became known — has spent most of his life in and out of the correctional institutions. In 1968 he had been sentenced to a 10-year term at Waterloo, Iowa, after being found guilty of sexually assaulting a young male employee at his fried chicken restaurant business. The terrified boy had been handcuffed while 20-stone Gacy subjected him to a vicious attack.

Eighteen months later he was back on the streets, his reputation as a model prisoner convincing his parole board that he was no longer a risk to the public. The following year, 1971, he was questioned by police for trying to force a teenage boy into having sex, but the case was dropped after the boy failed to turn up for the preliminary hearings.

This criminal history was interesting enough for the detectives assigned to investigate the disappearance of Robert Piest. But there was another incident which focused their minds even more closely on Gacy.

Nine months earlier, on 21 March 1978, a 27-year-old Chicago man, Jeffrey Rignall, told police how he had been approached by a fat man driving a flashy Oldsmobile car. The man had invited him to sit in the passenger seat for a smoke of cannabis, but as he held the joint a handkerchief drenched in chloroform was stuffed into his face. He remembered regaining consciousness in his abductor's house where he was beaten with whips and repeatedly raped. The following morning he was driven to the city's Lincoln Park and dumped by the side of a lake, more dead than alive.

In hospital Rignall was found to have suffered permanent liver damage as a result of the huge dose of chloroform he had inhaled. He was bruised and bleeding and he was in severe mental trauma. Yet because he could give no accurate description of his assailant, and precious little information about the crime generally, police held out little hope of making an arrest.

Eventually Rignall decided to take matters into his own hands. He combed the city in search of the Oldsmobile car and presented the police with its location and registration mark. Yet even this was not enough. Rignall later claimed he almost had to beg detectives to pull Gacy in for questioning. When they finally did, it was to no avail. Gacy denied all knowledge of any homosexual rape and, as there were no witnesses to challenge his statements and alibi, senior officers felt that the case against him was wafer thin.

John Wayne Gacy was also known as the 'Fat Man' — and the 'Killer Clown'.

A check on his personal life also drew a blank. Detectives established that Chicago-born Gacy, the son of a Danish mother and Polish father, had completed a good education at business school, going on to become a top shoe salesman with the Nunn-Bush Shoe Company. He was a man who liked to be liked in his community. At one point he had become a leading light in the Junior Chamber of Commerce and he was much in demand as a children's entertainer. His character was Pogo the Clown.

A marriage to fellow employee Marlynn Myers in 1964 had ended during his first spell of imprisonment in 1968. His second marriage, to Carole Hoff in 1972, also ended in failure. Police were later to learn how Carole Hoff was puzzled by his lacklustre sexual performance and terrified of his violent temper. Also, she complained to him constantly about the fetid smell that seemed to hang around the house.

Unsurprisingly, the disappearance of Piest following his arrangement to meet 36-year-old Gacy brought about a transformation in the attitudes of detectives. They visited the builder's home at 8213 West Summerdale Avenue and began interrogating him about the missing youngster. His answers were unconvincing and police decided to undertake a methodical search of the house. The smell that hung around had an awful familiarity.

It was when they lifted the trapdoor that led to the crawl-space beneath the floorboards that they knew they had chanced upon one of America's worst serial killers. The stench of rotting flesh was unmistakable. Stored in the cramped void were seven corpses in different stages of decomposition. Later eight more were dug out of crude lime pits in the garden. In total, the remains of 28 teenage boys were accounted for in the house and grounds. Gacy confessed that he had run out of space to store any more corpses. Another five victims, including Robert Piest, had been thrown into the Des Plaines River.

During questioning it became clear that Gacy had used his building contracting business to attract young men seeking work. Yet although he bore all the signs of a closet homosexual, he always remained adamant that he was not gay. He justified his action by telling police that he hated

Democractic Party worker Gacy gets a handshake from President Jimmy Carter's wife, Rosalynn.

homosexuals and refused to accept the counter-argument that most, if not all, of his victims were in fact heterosexual. Once he had raped them, it was enough. He could convince himself they deserved to die for their 'homosexual' activities.

Gacy confessed his crimes to detectives on several occasions But he decided not to give evidence at his trial and sat stony-faced as the prosecution placed photographs of the 22 identified victims on a large board facing the jury. Gacy entered a plea of insanity to the charges against him. It cut little ice with the jury. On 12 March 1980 they convicted him of murder.

John Gacy survived on Death Row through a long string of appeals. The 'Fat Man' was finally executed by lethal injection at a prison near Chicago on 10 May 1994.

GERALD GALLEGO

It could be said that Gerald Gallego never stood a chance, given his difficult background. Born in 1947, he was the son of a three-times killer who was executed in a Mississippi gas chamber at the age of 28. Gallego Jr was first wed at 18, and by the age of 32 was marrying for the seventh time, twice to the same woman.

Gallego first came to the attention of California police in 1978 when his daughter complained to them that he had been abusing her from the age of six. They tried to interview him but he went on the run with his latest fiancée, Charlene Williams, who agreed to help fulfil his fantasy of finding the perfect sex slave. Driving a van, she would patrol the Sacramento area luring young girls with the promise of drugs. Once inside, Gallego would pounce on the girls, rape them and murder them while Charlene sat coolly in the front seat.

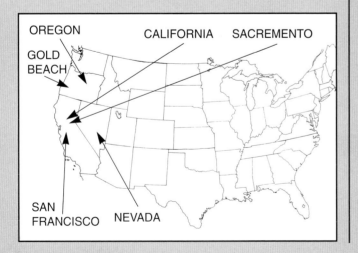

ACTUAL NAME: Gerald Armand Gallego

BORN: 17 July 1946

DIED: Still on death row, Nevada State Prison

PREFERRED MURDER METHOD: Shooting

NUMBER OF VICTIMS: 10

NAMES OF VICTIMS: Rhonda Scheffler, Kippi Vaught, Sandra Kaye Colley, Brenda Judd, Stacy-Ann Redican, Karen Chipman-Twiggs, Linda Teresa Aguila, Virginia Mochel, Beth Sowers, Craig Miller

MURDER LOCALE: California and Nevada

SPAN OF MURDER CAREER: 11 September 1978 to 2 November 1980

DATE OF CONVICTION: 21 June 1983 (California — sentenced to gas chamber); 17 June 1984 (Nevada — sentenced to lethal injection)

One of their most horrific crimes was the murder of 21-year-old Linda Aguilar who was four months pregnant when Charlene pulled up in a van at Gold Beach, Oregon, and offered her a lift. Her body was found with her skull shattered and her legs and hands tied. A post-mortem revealed that the injuries had not killed her — but that she had been buried alive.

Gallego and Charlene, now bigamously married, killed 10 people before finally being identified. On 2 November 1980 Craig Miller and Beth Sowers were leaving a dance near Sacramento when a woman brandishing a gun forced them into the back of a van. A friend tried to follow them and took down the registration number.

When arrested, Charlene Gallego cracked when she realised that she faced a death sentence. She turned state's evidence for a maximum of 16 years in jail. Gallego was tried in both California and Nevada and condemned to death — twice.

EDWARD GEIN

ACTUAL NAME: Edward Theodore Gein

BORN: 27 August 1906

DIED: 26 July 1984 in Mendota Mental Health Institute

PREFERRED MURDER METHOD: Shooting

NUMBER OF VICTIMS: At least 2

NAMES OF VICTIMS: Mary Hogan and Bernice Worden

MURDER LOCALE: Plainfield, Wisconsin

SPAN OF MURDER CAREER: 8 December 1954 to 16 November 1957

DATE OF CONVICTION: Never tried – committed indefinitely to State mental hospital, 6 January 1958.

Few murderers can claim their evil deeds were copied into two block-busting Hollywood movies. That dubious infamy belongs to Edward Gein, said to be the inspiration behind schizophrenic transvestite Norman Bates in Hitchcock's *Psycho* and, through his liking for wearing human skin, also resurfaced in *The Silence of the Lambs.*

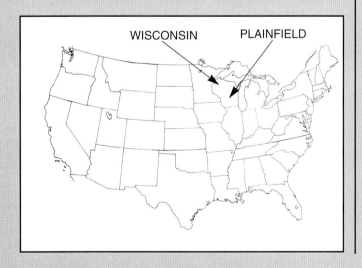

No film director, however, could ever hope to replicate the atrocities discovered at the lonely, ramshackle house that was Ed Gein's family home. For Gein created his very own House of Horror at a remote homestead near Plainfield, Wisconsin. Country boy Edward Gein had grown up dominated by his possessive, woman-hating mother — so much so that neither he nor his brother Henry ever got close to a member of the opposite sex. There were precious few pleasures in his life and gradually he retreated into a deviant fantasy world.

When his brother died in 1944 and his mother Augusta the following year, the lurking madman that lay within him took control. He kept his mother's corpse in her bedroom, the surroundings unchanged from the moment of her death.

Gein's interest in women's anatomy developed into an obsession, and soon he cast aside his medical text books to get a closer look at the real thing. At first, he satisfied his curiosity about women by digging up corpses from a local graveyard, aided by a simple-minded farmer. Gein would wear bits of the women's flesh and touch their sexual organs.

Gradually his fetishism grew more extreme and he would drape himself in the skin or arrange it over a tailor's dummy as though he were somehow trying to resurrect his mother. Eventually the stench of rotting corpses became too much even for Gein and he sought fresher flesh.

On 8 December 1954 Gein, then aged 48, committed his first murder, shooting a 51-year-old saloon bar owner, Mary Hogan, with a Mauser pistol, then dissecting and skinning her body. Between then and his final killing three years later, Gein put paid to an unknown number of victims.

It was not until 16 November 1957, however, that police caught up with the maniac in their midst. They were out looking for storekeeper Bernice Worden, and Gein's car had been seen parked near her Plainfield hardware shop. He was arrested after Mrs Worden's son, the local sheriff's deputy, recalled that Gein had mentioned 'calling by' her store to buy anti-freeze.

Police found Bernice's headless body hanging by its feet from the rafters of one of Gein's outbuildings. It had been gutted and dressed like a deer hunted from the surrounding woods.

Around the Gein farm police found a stomach-churning array of artifacts. There were lampshades made of human skin; a hollowed-out skull was used as a soup dish; skulls were stuck on bedposts; a belt had been made of nipples; a pair of slippers were of human skin; a blind-pull was adorned with a pair of lips; nine vulvas, one trimmed with red ribbon, were found in a shoe box; and the refrigerator was stocked with human organs.

They found the remains of Mrs Hogan — a death mask of skin and hair, alongside no fewer than nine others. Mrs Worden's head was discovered ready to go into a cookpot.

Edward Gein eventually explained to detectives what uses he made of these various human remains. He said he would dance by moonlight in his farmyard — with a woman's torso, tanned like leather, strapped around his body. He regularly oiled the skin to keep it supple.

Gein confessed to as many murders as he could remember. He admitted wearing skin from the dead women, eating their flesh and playing with other parts of their bodies. But inexplicably he was adamant in denying the relatively minor crime of stealing the cash register from Mrs Worden's store.

The discoveries of the bodies of Mrs Hogan and Mrs Worden were grisly enough. But Gein also refused to explain how he came to possess the preserved private parts of two teenage girls, aged approximately 12 and 18, which were found among his sickening collection. No girls of that age had been buried in the area during Gein's macabre activities. Detectives could only deduce that the remains were of live victims.

HARVEY GLATMAN

NAME: Harvey Murray Glatman

BORN: 1928

DIED: Gas chamber, San Quentin 18 September 1959

PREFERRED MURDER METHOD: Strangulation

NUMBER OF VICTIMS: 3

NAMES OF VICTIMS: Judy Ann van Horn Dull, Shirley Bridgeford, Ruth Mercado

MURDER LOCALE: California

SPAN OF MURDER CAREER: 1 August 1957 to 24 July 1958

DATE OF CONVICTION: November 1958

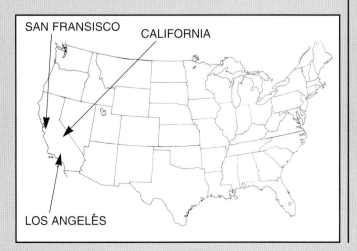

Harvey Glatman was an ugly, jug-eared, Los Angeles television repair man who posed as a professional photographer to get close to beautiful women.

Already having served time for robbery, Glatman's reign of terror was short-lived but vicious. On 1 August 1957 he abducted a model, Judy Ann Van Horn Dull, drove her into the desert, tied her up, raped and strangled her.

Shirley Bridgeford was the next to die. After meeting her through a lonely hearts advert, he drove her into the desert outside San Diego, and photographed her bound and gagged before finally strangling her. His photographic recoerd of her suffering was made right up until the moment of her death.

His next victim Ruth Mercado, a 23-year-old Los Angeles stripper, was attacked in her own apartment, bound and abducted by car into the desert. Glatman raped her, photographed her in her bondage and finally strangled her.

Glatman's last target, Lorraine Vigil, managed to turn the tables on Glatman by fighting back and wresting his gun away from him. As they struggled on the ground, they were spotted by a passing policeman.

When photographs of the dead girls were found at his home, Glatman confessed. He was sentenced to death and was led into the San Quentin gas chamber on 18 September 1959.

GREEN RIVER KILLER

NAME: Never established

PREFERRED MURDER METHOD: Strangulation

NUMBER OF VICTIMS: As many as 49

MURDER LOCALE: Bodies washed up in Green River, near Seattle

SPAN OF MURDER CAREER: 15 June 1982 until 1984

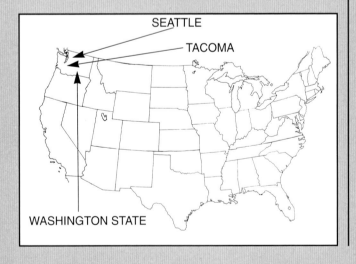

SEATTLE

TACOMA

WASHINGTON STATE

The 'Green River Killer' was credited with the murder of 49 people but left no clues to his identity and was never caught.

The murder spree was first noted when the naked body of Deborah Bonner was found on the bank of the Green River at Kent, in King County, Washington — only half a mile away from the spot where the body of Wendy Coffield had been found a month earlier. Most of the 49 victims were either prostitutes or runaway teenagers, picked up along the sleazy Sea-Tac highway running from Seattle to Tacoma. They were generally strangled and their bodies hidden in woodland, where decomposing remains were found up until March 1984.

The police did have a couple of suspects in mind. The first was Melvyn Wayne Foster, a 44-year-old taxi driver who seemed to possess too much information about the murders. He was arrested but cleared. The second suspect was William J. Stephens II, a 38-year-old law student. Stephens had pictures of naked women, a fascination for serial killer Ted Bundy and a collection of police uniforms and badges. However, detectives were eventually forced to announce that Stephens was 'no longer a viable suspect'.

There has been no arrest and, as far as police are concerned, the 'Green River Killer' is still at large.

BELLE GUNNESS

NAME: Bella Poulsdatter

A.K.A.: Belle Gunness

ACCOMPLICE: Ray Lamphere

BORN: 1859

DIED: Unknown; assumed 24 April 1908

PREFERRED MURDER METHOD: Various

NUMBER OF VICTIMS: At least 14

MURDER LOCALE: La Porte, Indiana

SPAN OF MURDER CAREER: Early 1900s to 28 April 1908

DATE OF CONVICTION: Not convicted, presumed dead

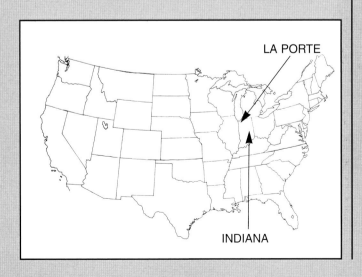

The murderous career of Belle Gunness not only requires a mention in every catalogue of serial killers, it also warrants an entry in the log of great criminal mysteries. For, although police closed their files after finding what they thought was the lady slaughterer's corpse, it is more than likely that widow Gunness got away with murder — at least 43 of them.

Belle Gunness was born in Norway and came to the United States in 1883. She married a Swede, Mads Sorenson, who died in suspicious circumstances. Although his body was later exhumed, no evidence of foul play was detected. Sorenson was insured — and so was the couple's house, which burned down shortly afterwards. Belle invested the insurance money in a bakery, which also burned down, although this time the insurance company refused to pay up.

Belle moved to Indiana, where she married widower Peter Gunness, and they settled on a lonely farm near the town of La Porte. He was persuaded to take out heavy life insurance — and was dead shortly afterwards. According to his widow, a sausage grinder fell from a shelf under which he was sitting and split his skull. It is far more likely that his brains were beaten out by his fat, ferocious wife. That was also the fate of their 14-year-old adopted daughter, Jennie, murdered after she had gone to the police to report Mr Gunness's slaying. They had not believed her.

As a widow in her 50s, Gunness found difficulty making the mortgage payments on her farm. So she advertised for suitors through the matrimonial advertisements of newspapers. This was a sample of the temptress's lure:

'Rich, good-looking woman, owner of a big farm, desires to correspond with a gentleman of wealth and refinement, object matrimony. No replies by letter will be considered unless the sender is willing to follow an answer with a personal visit. Triflers need not apply.'

Gunness would invite prospective suitors to stay at the farm to experience her country hospitality first-hand — first having persuaded them to bring along a suitable sum of money to prove their willingness to invest in the property. Belle would feed them royally, sleep with them, drug them, steal their savings and then hack them to death with a meat cleaver.

Her one-woman crimewave ended in 1908, although the circumstances surrounding the demise of widow Gunness are still shrouded in mystery. On the night of 28 April, the farmhouse was burned to the ground. Belle's hired handyman and lover, Ray Lamphere, was seen running from the scene. Since he had recently been fired by his employer, it was assumed that he had burned the farm in revenge. He was later jailed for a year for arson — after going to the police with a tale of 42 murders committed at the farm in four years.

However, it is more likely that Lamphere and Gunness were accomplices in the crimes. The murderess, learning that the brother of one of her victims was making inquiries about her, had panicked. The burning of the farmhouse was more in her interest than her handyman's.

Several bodies were found. Fourteen male corpses were discovered in a pigsty, and among the ashes in the basement of the house were the burned bodies of Gunness's four children. Alongside them lay the headless body of a woman — which police presumed to be that of Belle because her false teeth were recovered nearby.

Forensic experts, however, pointed out that the corpse was considerably shorter and lighter than the strapping widow. There were also traces of poison in it. It is likely that Belle Gunness had lured yet another victim to the farm, this time a vagrant woman, and had callously murdered her alongside her own children in order to conceal her escape. Belle Gunness may have continued quietly murdering elsewhere in America for many years afterwards.

FRITZ HAARMANN

NAME: Fritz Haarmann

A.K.A.: The 'Butcher of Hannover'; the 'Werewolf of Hannover'

ACCOMPLICE: Hans Grans

BORN: Unknown

DIED: Beheaded 20 December 1924

PREFERRED MURDER METHOD: Biting through the throat

NUMBER OF VICTIMS: Convicted of 27; confessed to 40 plus

NAMES OF VICTIMS: Fritz Franke, Wilhelm Schulze, Hans Keimes, Roland Huch, Hans Sennefeld, Ernst Ehrenberg, Heinrich Strauss, Paul Bronischewski, Richard Graf, Wilhelm Erdner, Hermann Wolf, Heinz Brinkmann, Adolf Hannappel, Adolf Hennies, Ernst Spiecker, Heinrich Koch, Willi Senger, Hermann Speichert, Alfred Hogrefe, Hermann Bock, Wilhelm Apel, Robert Witzel, Heinz Martin, Friedrich Abeling, Fritz Wittig, Freidrich Koch, Erich de Vries

MURDER LOCALE: Hannover

SPAN OF MURDER CAREER: 12 February 1923 to 14 June 1924

DATE OF CONVICTION: December 1924

In the spring of 1924 Germany found itself sucked into the kind of werewolf scare that should have died out in the Middle Ages. It started when housewives became suspicious about cuts of meat they had bought. The joints looked, smelled and tasted odd, the women said. Several turned up at the local police station asking if it could be human flesh. 'Nonsense,' senior officers announced publicly, blaming the rumours on 'public hysteria'.

And yet a monster was on the loose. His name was Peter Haarmann, his stalking ground was Hannover and his prey was young boys — especially if they were homeless with no family to report them missing. Over the years, his victims numbered at least 27 and possibly as many as 50.

On 17 May, children found a human skull on the banks of the River Leine. It was to be the first of many but, incredibly, detectives put out a statement to the press claiming the bones found had been placed near the river by medical students as a sick jape. In their haste to quell public anxiety, police chiefs were guilty of a huge misjudgment. But although they should have realised they were dealing with a ruthless sex killer, they could not have known the appalling depravity with which he committed his crimes. For Fritz Haarmann liked to seduce or rape his boy victims before dispatching them, vampire style, with a savage bite to their young throats.

Haarmann came from a difficult family background. He adored his mother, who became an invalid soon after he was born, but loathed his father, a mean and moody locomotive stoker nicknamed Sulky Olle. Olle Haarmann tried to get his boy committed to an asylum on the grounds that he had a feeble mind. The doctors refused, saying he was not mentally ill. Rejected by his father,

young Fritz soon found himself wandering around Germany getting involved in petty crime. He was seen by other crooks as something of a simpleton who tried hard to please. And he got a reputation among police for coming quietly when arrested, with a laugh on his lips.

In 1918, the chaos of postwar Germany, Haarmann, then aged 39, found a ready source of victims for his ultimate, perverted pleasures. He patrolled Hannover's central station to watch the drifters arrive, many of them young and vulnerable and desperate to see a friendly face. Haarmann was that face. He would be down there every night, offering cigarettes and chocolate to the new arrivals. The relief and gratitude would shine out from their eyes as he offered them shelter and a mattress for the night.

Soon even the welfare workers at the station began to regard Haarmann as one of their team. Police knew about his history of petty crime but Haarmann convinced detectives he could be a useful informer. His activities as a fence and petty thief were thereby undisturbed while he provided intelligence on planned robberies and hideouts. As his wealth increased, he set himself up as a meat and second-hand clothes salesman. Housewives appreciated his supply of keenly-priced joints in an economy still reeling from the war.

When, in September 1918, the parents of a 17-year-old youth reported that he had gone missing, detectives were forced to follow up a lead that he had been seen with Haarmann. They reluctantly questioned their informant, though finally clearing him from their inquiries. At his trial six years later, Haarmann was to boast: 'When the police examined my room, the head of the boy was lying wrapped in newspaper behind the oven.'

That close shave served only to convince Haarmann that he was unstoppable. The following year he teamed up with a homosexual accomplice, 20-year-old Hans Grans, who regarded himself as Haarmann's social superior. He wielded a terrible influence over Haarmann, picking out victims and once even instructing him to murder a boy 'because I like the clothes he's wearing'.

This disgusting pair grew amazingly lax, often carting around buckets of blood in front of neighbours in Rothe Reihe, near the River Leine, and chopping up bodies so that everyone could hear. But still Haarmann's cover as a butcher remained intact.

Yet the noose was closing. Newspapers wrote about the 'Werewolf of Hannover' and one writer claimed that 600 people had disappeared in the city inside a year. The findings of the skull and the bones by the river at last spurred the police into action. Underworld sources were questioned and increasingly the finger of suspicion pointed to Haarmann.

On the night of 22 June 1924, police raided Haarmann's apartment, with its blood-splattered walls and heaps of clothes, of varying sizes. 'Of course', he told his interrogators, 'what do you expect. I am a butcher and I trade in second-hand clothes.'

Parents of the missing children were invited to the flat to examine the clothes. One mother could find nothing she recognised — until she spotted the son of Haarmann's landlady, wearing a coat that used to belong to her boy. Haarmann broke down and confessed everything.

At their trial on 4 December 1924, Haarmann and Grans were jointly charged with the murders of 27 boys aged 12 to 18. Grans, who was eventually sentenced to life imprisonment, and Haarmann both reacted dismissively to most of the photographs of victims as they were held up by the prosecution. But when the picture of one young boy was produced, Haarmann revealed his uncompromising callousness. Turning on the youngster's distraught father, who was sitting in court, Haarmann told him scathingly:

'I should never have looked twice at such an ugly youngster as, according to his photograph, your son must have been. You say your boy had not even a shirt to his name and that his socks were tied on to his feet with string! Deuce take it, you should have been ashamed to let him go about like that. There's plenty of rubbish like him around. Think what you're saying man. Such a fellow would have been far beneath my notice.'

One newspaper account of the time records: 'Nearly 200 witnesses had to appear in the box, mostly parents of the unfortunate youths. There were scenes of painful intensity as a poor father or mother would recognise some fragment or other of the clothing or belongings of their murdered son. Here it was a handkerchief, there a pair of braces, and again a greasy coat, soiled almost beyond recognition, that was shown to the relatives and to Haarmann. And with the quivering nostrils of a hound snuffling his prey, as if he were scenting rather than seeing the things displayed, did he admit at once that he knew them.'

The exchanges between the prosecution counsel and Haarmann filled the courtroom with an atmosphere of undiluted tension:

Counsel: 'How many victims did you kill altogether?'
Haarmann: 'It might be 30, it might be 40. I really can't remember the exact number.'
Counsel: 'How did you kill your victims?'
Haarmann: 'I bit them through their throats.'

The 'Vampire of Hannover' was found guilty on 19 December 1924. His last words to the court were screamed at the judge and jury with an appalling, frightening ferocity:

'Do you think I enjoy killing people? I was ill for eight days after the first time. Condemn me to death. I ask only for justice I am not mad. It is true I often get into a state when I do not know what I am doing, but that is not madness. Make it short, make it soon. Deliver me from this life, which is a torment. I will not petition for mercy, nor will I appeal. I want to pass just one more merry evening in my cell, with coffee, cheese and cigars, after which I will curse my father and go to my execution as if it were a wedding.'

Fritz Haarmann's last wish was granted the very next day. He was beheaded.

JOHN GEORGE HAIGH

ACTUAL NAME: John George Haigh

A.K.A.: The 'Acid-Bath Murderer'; the 'Vampire Killer'

BORN: 24 July 1909

DIED: Hanged at Wandsworth prison 10 August 1949

PREFERRED MURDER METHOD: Shooting or coshing, followed by immersion of bodies in acid

NUMBER OF VICTIMS: 6

NAMES OF VICTIMS: William, Donald and Amy McSwan, Archie and Rosie Henderson, Olive Durand-Deacon

MURDER LOCALE: Crawley,Sussex, and London

SPAN OF MURDER CAREER: 9 September 1944 to 18 February 1949

DATE OF CONVICTION: 19 July 1949

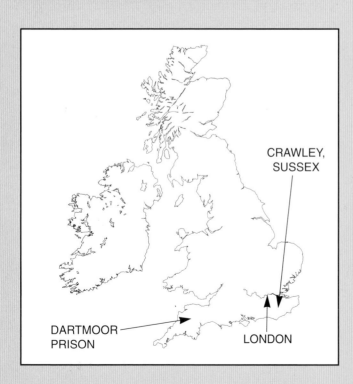

John George Haigh was not the first killer to realise the useful properties of acid in disposing of a body. He was, however, one of the most prolific 'dissolvers' and, but for one careless oversight, would almost certainly have gone on to claim the lives of many more unfortunates charmed by his plausibility. Right to the moment of his death on the gallows on 10 August 1949, Haigh relished the title bestowed on him by the press: the 'Acid Bath Murderer'.

Cherubic-faced choirboy John George Haigh grew up to become a handsome killer.

From his strict religious upbringing (his parents were both followers of the Plymouth Brethren sect) he grew up to be an intelligent, if socially backward, young man. He became a skilled forger and confidence trickster, specialising in fraudulent hire purchase deals and selling cars he didn't own. As the cash rolled in, Haigh acquired a gleaming sports car and a pretty wife. He lost both when he was jailed for fraud in 1934 and again in 1938.

Confined in the bleak fortress of Dartmoor prison, Haigh learned new skills. He studied chemistry and also worked in the tinsmith's shop where he had access to sulphuric acid. The idea of dissolving bodies in acid began to take shape. He would experiment on small animals brought in as pets by prisoners on outside work parties. He made careful notes about the time taken for acid to dissolve flesh and bone.

During World War 2, Haigh avoided military call-up by volunteering for fire-watching duties, while working for a Mr McSwann who ran a pin-table saloon empire from his home in Wimbledon. By 1944 Haigh had set up his own business repairing pin-tables. One of the regular callers at his basement in London's Gloucester Road was his former employer's son, Donald McSwann, who was seeking help in dodging the draft.

One night Donald failed to return from a visit to the flat. Haigh had staved his skull in with a pin-table leg and dissolved the body in a 40gal water butt filled with acid. The little that was left of Donald McSwann had been poured down a drain in Gloucester Road.

Haigh told the boy's parents that he had gone into hiding to avoid his call-up papers. He could explain the situation better, he assured them, if they would call and see him. They did — and never returned home. Their remains also went down the drain.

Using forged papers, Haigh managed to seize control of the couple's assets to the tune of £4,000, then a small fortune. He lived in comfort at the respectable Onslow Court Hotel nearby. With money came a passion for gambling, however, and Haigh's debts mounted. He decided that new victims were needed for his bubbling baths.

Haigh had got to know a Dr and Mrs Henderson after putting in a spurious offer to buy their house in London's Ladbroke Square. Although they eventually sold to another buyer, some of his infectious charm rubbed off and the Hendersons later invited him to join them for a short break in Brighton. One afternoon the doctor decided to accompany Haigh on the short drive to Crawley, in Sussex, where the killer's repair workshop was now based. The doctor was murdered at the first convenient moment and his body consigned to the acid vat.

Mrs Henderson was fetched on the pretext that her husband had fallen seriously ill. Haigh smashed her over the head and heaved her body into the bath. It was then absurdly straightforward for the couple's murderer to forge a letter giving authority over their assets. Later that year, 1948, he banked around £7,000.

Haigh's final victim was a fellow resident of the Onslow Court Hotel, 69-year-old colonel's widow Olive Durand-Deacon. Haigh had already had the audacity to sell her Mrs Henderson's crocodile-skin handbag for £10. Now he was hatching a plan to get his hands on her assets and £1,000-a-year income.

The charmer began ingratiating himself to Mrs Durand-Deacon, escorting her to literary lunches and presenting himself as the perfect dinner table companion. When invited to visit his business in Crawley, she agreed — but got only the briefest of inspections before Haigh shot her in the back. He then removed her jewels and Persian lamb coat, trussed her up and heaved her 14-stone bulk into one of his water butts. The acid was squirted in with a stirrup pump and all seemed to have gone according to plan.

Haigh had become over-confident, however. He forgot to allow for the long time that body fat can take to dissolve completely in sulphuric acid. False teeth are equally resistant. Police found the remains of both in soil at the back of the Crawley yard when they were called in by a friend of Mrs Durand-Deacon who knew of her appointment with Haigh.

The killer had also been careless. He had taken his victim's lamb coat to the cleaners and left the ticket lying around in his workshop. Police knew Mrs Durand-Deacon had been seen in a lamb coat

Haigh arrives at court, dapper and smiling as ever.

shortly before she went missing. They were also interested in the revolver, vats of acid, rubber gloves and other protective clothing they found lying around in Haigh's lair.

On 2 March 1949 John Haigh was charged with murder after making a full confession of all the acid bath killings. He spiced up the accounts with stories about how he drank the blood of his victims before dissolving them. He believed it would help him escape the gallows on the grounds that he was insane. He was wrong.

Hours before he was due to hang, Haigh made the most bizarre of several last requests. He told his jailers that he would soon be immortalised as a waxwork in Madame Tussaud's Chamber of Horrors — a venue close to his heart as it was a place he regularly visited with girlfriends. Could the owners of Tussaud's be presented with the clothes he wore throughout his trial: his green hopsack suit, green socks and red tie with green squares? He was also very keen that his suit trousers should be properly pressed. His wishes were granted a few days after his execution.

While in custody, Haigh faked insanity — but a jury took only 15 minutes to find him guilty. He was hanged in 1949 at Wandsworth Prison.

ARCHIBALD HALL

ACTUAL NAME: Archibald Thomson Hall

A.K.A.: Roy Fontaine; the 'Monster Butler'

BORN: 17 July 1924

DIED: Jailed for life 1 November 1978

PREFERRED MURDER METHOD: None — different in every case, but always violent

NUMBER OF VICTIMS: 5

NAMES OF VICTIMS: David Wright ,Dorothy and Walter Scott-Elliott, Mary Goggle, Donald Hall

MURDER LOCALE: London, Scotland and the Borders

SPAN OF MURDER CAREER: September 1977 to January 1978

DATE OF CONVICTION: 2 May 1978 (Scotland) 1 November 1978 (England)

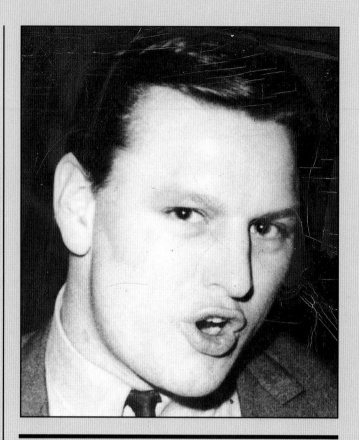

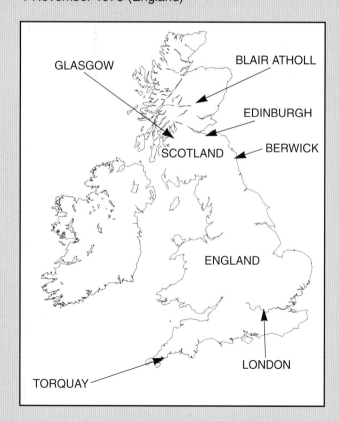

At first sight, Roy Fontaine seemed the perfect servant. Charming, attentive, witty, immaculately dressed and impeccably mannered, he was the epitome of the gentleman's personal gentleman. He might almost have modelled himself on P. G. Wodehouse's immortal manservant Jeeves. But bisexual womaniser Fontaine, born Archibald Hall in a Glasgow tenement in 1924, was a burglar, forger, conman, jewel thief, jailbird and mass murderer. He was the Butler from Hell.

The son of a Post Office sorting clerk, Hall, though he lacked for little, was never well off. He did, however, get a taste of the good life at the age of 16 when he was seduced by an older woman who took him to the best hotels and pampered him with presents, fine food and wine. He determined that this elegant lifestyle would be his from then on, whatever he had to do to get it.

His criminal career started in a small way, by cheating the Red Cross. He became a regular and successful collector for them, but when he went out on the streets, he always took two tins. Into one went the notes and the higher denomination coins, while he made sure that the tin he handed in was always full — albeit only with pennies. From this, it was a small step to outright theft, and in 1943 he embarked on a crime spree in Glasgow and London that saw him jailed on four separate occasions for burglary and forgery.

In 1951 he embarked on a new career as a 'gentleman's gentleman'. With forged references, he answered an advertisement placed by a shipping executive in Stirlingshire. He was turned down because the executive recognised one of the names among the referees . . . that of a blind man who could neither read nor write.

Undaunted, Hall, now calling himself Roy Fontaine, took his phony references to a neighbouring country home and started his career as a butler. It was a career that would give him many opportunities to exercise his true calling — thieving, which he now combined with confidence trickery. Eventually, it would lead to bloody and gruesome murder.

Among the less harmful conman's stunts over the following five years were standing in for his unwitting employer at a royal garden party, posing as a rich Arab in order to fool jewellers into parting with gems, and playing the part of a wealthy American while in Torquay to gain access to top-notch functions.

Justice caught up with the agile swindler in 1956 when he was sentenced to 30 years for a string of theft-related offences. Released on parole in 1963, he was back inside again the following year. He escaped and was on the run for two years before his recapture, when a further five years were added to the original ten of his sentence. He was

paroled again in 1972 and sent to Lancashire where he met Mary Coggle who was to become his accomplice. He was in jail again shortly afterwards until 1977.

That year, with forged references, Hall obtained a post as butler to Lady Peggy Hudson in Scotland's border country. On his recommendation, David Wright, a homosexual lover from prison, was taken on as gardener. Wright and Hall soon quarrelled, however, as Wright wanted to rob the property immediately, while Hall had far bigger plans. The disagreement was to lead to murder.

While Lady Peggy was absent, Wright stole an expensive ring. Hall immediately tracked it down to a girlfriend of Wright's and took it back. The following night he was awoken dramatically by a gunshot as a drunken Wright tried to kill him as he lay sleeping, missing him by only a fraction of an inch. Hall calmed the man down and disarmed him, but he realised that he would always be in danger of blackmail, exposure or worse as long as Wright lived.

The following day the two men went out shooting rabbits. Hall waited until his companion's gun was empty, then cold-bloodedly shot him, burying his body under a pile of stones in a stream. A week later, by great good fortune, his employer received an anonymous letter exposing Hall's criminal past and he was dismissed.

Hall's next post was with wealthy Walter Scott-Elliott and his wife Dorothy at their home in Chelsea. At 82, the former Member of Parliament for Accrington had to take a number of drugs, which left him vague and almost helpless. He was an easy mark for Hall, who persuaded the old man to sign blank cheques with which to pay the household bills.

Hall now called in two accomplices: Mary Coggle, his erstwhile lover who forged credit cards, and petty thief Michael Kitto. The three planned to rob and defraud the Scott-Elliotts, though at this stage it is unlikely that any of them had murder in mind.

Hall took Kitto to look round the house on 8 December 1977, while Mrs Scott-Elliott was in a nursing home. However, she returned a day early and surprised the pair in her bedroom. In a panic, Hall knocked her down and suffocated her to stop her screams. Her husband, who had been awoken by the noise of the struggle, was told she had had a nightmare, and returned to bed.

The murder of Dorothy Scott-Elliot was to launch Hall on a killing spree which was to end in death for himself and life imprisonment for his two accomplices.

The next day Hall and Kitto filled the boot of a hired car with Mrs Scott-Elliott's body, along with a haul of valuable antiques and jewellery. Mary Coggle put on the dead woman's furs and impersonated her well enough to fool the well-drugged Scott-Elliott. They drove to a cottage near Carlisle, which Hall had rented the month previously. The strangely assorted party then drove another 200 miles into Scotland, and at Glen Afric, near Blair Atholl, they murdered the old man and buried him in bushes.

Back at the cottage, Hall and Coggle disagreed over the mink coat, she wanting to keep it but Hall considering it too easily identified. In the course of the row, Hall attacked her with a poker, striking her several times across the head. The two men finished her off by suffocating her and dumping the body in a stream. They then returned to London to ransack the Chelsea house.

The following month Hall's brother Donald, 17 years his junior, appeared on the scene. Recently freed from jail where he had served three years for burglary — he had also spent time in jail for assaults on young girls — Donald became curious about his brother's new affluence and, after an argument, Hall and Kitto killed him with chloroform. Again, the two hired a car, put the body in the boot and, with false plates, drove into Scotland. Unbeknown to them, however, the body of Marry Coggle had been found on Christmas Day and when the two killers checked into a hotel at North Berwick, the manager became suspicious of them. While they ate, he telephoned the police, who ran a check on the car, discovered the false plates — Escort registration on a Granada — and arrested them.

Hall escaped, hailed a taxi but was apprehended at a road-block. Back at the police station, he was told that a body had been found in the boot of the car. He asked for a glass of water and tried to commit suicide with a pill secreted in his rectum. The bid was foiled after a dash to the Edinburgh Royal

Archibald Hall, also known as Roy Fontaine, the 'Monster Butler'.

Infirmary. Two days later Hall again tried to kill himself.

Hall and Kitto both cracked under interrogation. They were tried twice, in England and Scotland, and both received life sentences. Kitto was to serve a minimum of 15 years, but in Hall's case, there was to be no chance of parole.

His life of crime over, Hall languishes behind bars, unlikely ever to be released. One mystery remains, however . . . a secret he has sworn he will take with him to the grave. Hall has several times claimed that he was involved in two further killings — of an American helicopter pilot and a Preston garage worker — though he has steadfastly refused to give further details of the deaths. He has made a lengthy statement to a lawyer, a statement that will be released on the occasion of his death. Until then it remains, like Hall, securely under lock and key.

MYRA HINDLEY AND IAN BRADY

NAMES: Myra Hindley and Ian Brady

A.K.A.: The 'Moors Murderers'

BORN: Hindley — 23 July 1942;
Brady — 2 January 1938

DIED: Both still serving life imprisonment

PREFERRED MURDER METHOD: Various

NUMBER OF VICTIMS: At least 5

NAMES OF VICTIMS: Lesley Ann Downey, Pauline Reade, John Kilbride, Keith Bennett, Edward Evans

MURDER LOCALE: Saddleworth Moor and Manchester

SPAN OF MURDER CAREER: 23 November 1963 to 16 June 1964

DATE OF CONVICTION: 6 May 1966

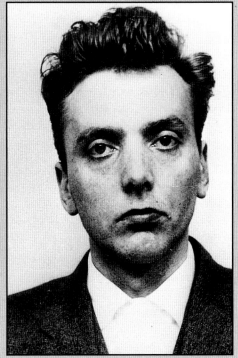

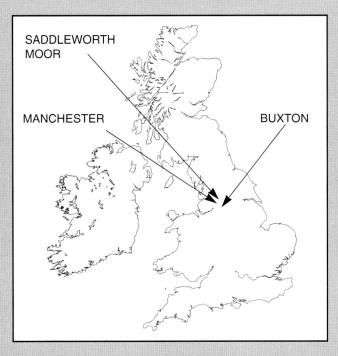

SADDLEWORTH MOOR

MANCHESTER

BUXTON

No one who sat in the courtroom at Chester Assizes that day would ever forget the harrowing tape recording played to them. It was of a little girl's voice, begging for her mother and pleading for mercy. The child's plaintive cries were accompanied by the horrific sounds of torture and sexual assault.

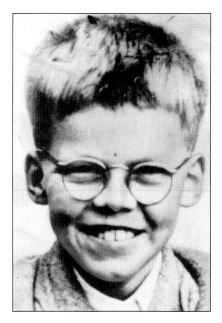

Keith Bennett and Pauline Reade.

The recording was of 10-year-old Lesley Ann Downey, the youngest victim of evil killers Myra Hindley and Ian Brady, destined to be forever known as the 'Moors Murderers'.

The recording, made by the sick couple themselves as little Lesley was put to death, was the most damning evidence of sickening crimes against youngsters. It also revealed Hindley to be a woman without mercy, a woman who could stand by and do nothing as her sadistic lover toyed with such innocent victims.

Hindley and Brady lived out their obscene fantasies in the Manchester area between 1962 and 1965. During that time, they abducted, tortured and murdered at least five, possibly eight, children or teenagers. Most of the bodies were buried on Saddleworth Moor on the outskirts of the city.

It was if Brady and Hindley met through some dark destiny. Brady, born in 1938, was the illegitimate son of a Glasgow waitress. A sullen, moody boy, his first court appearance was for burglary in 1951 when he was 13. He was put on probation twice. Brady moved to Manchester in 1954 to live with his mother and her new husband. He took a job in a brewery but was caught stealing lead and served a year in Borstal.

After his release, it seemed Brady had finished with his criminal ways and he settled into a job as a clerk. But his mind was becoming more and more twisted. And as his obsession with sadism grew, typist Myra Hindley walked into his life.

Hindley and Brady worked for the same company, a chemical supply firm. Their paths first crossed in 1961 when she was 19. Hindley meticulously kept a diary after making Brady's acquaintance. One entry read: 'Ian wore a black shirt and looked smashing. I love him.' Their affair began a year later.

The satanic hold Brady had over Hindley has never been understood. But right from the start, she eagerly participated in his fetishes. They both wore leather and acted out Nazi crimes together. They took pictures of themselves having sex and with whips. But this was not enough for Brady. He wanted to inflict his perversions on innocent victims. And Hindley was a willing partner.

In July 1963, 16-year-old Pauline Reade from the Gorton area of Manchester disappeared. She

lived a few doors away from Hindley's brother-in-law David Smith. Four months later, 12-year-old John Kilbride went missing. As with all of their victims, Hindley was the one who lured the children into Brady's clutches. John Kilbride was said to have gone with the couple 'like a lamb to the slaughter'. Another 12-year-old, Keith Bennett, vanished in June 1964.

Lesley Ann Downey disappeared while attend-

The searches on Saddlewott Moor spanned the decades: TOP LEFT Detectives in 1968; TOP RIGHT Keith Bennett's mother in 1988; ABOVE Pauline Reade's body is found in 1987.

ing a Christmas fair on 26 December. She was taken to Brady's home and forced to pose nude for pornographic photographs. The song Little Drummer Boy played in the background as Lesley was strangled.

It was 10 months before Brady and Hindley

struck again. In October 1965, Brady met 17-year-old Edward Evans, believed to be a homosexual.

There was a special reason why Brady wanted to entice this victim to his home — where he had also invited David Smith. Brady had confessed the previous murders to Smith but then became fearful that his confidante would go to the police. So it was vital that Smith was present at the murder of Evans, so that he too would be implicated.

In front of the horrified Smith, Brady then launched his fatal, bloody attack on Evans with a hatchet. Brady also ensured that Smith's fingerprints were on the hatchet. After the murder, Brady boasted to Smith: 'It's the messiest yet. It normally only takes one blow.' Edward's body was wrapped in plastic and taken upstairs.

But Brady's attempt to involve Smith was a fatal mistake. What he had witnessed so disturbed him that Smith went to the police.

When Brady's house was searched, a book with John Kilbride's name in it was found, together with nine pornographic pictures of Lesley Ann Downey. A ticket led police to a luggage locker at Manchester Central railway station. The two suit-cases found there contained sex and torture books, whips, coshes and other items used for perverted activities. Yet another photograph, of Hindley posing next to John Kilbride's shallow grave on Saddleworth Moor, enabled police to locate not only his grave but that of Lesley Ann Downey.

The trial of Hindley and Brady began on 19 April 1966 at Chester Assizes. According to Hindley's confession, Brady told her that he had strangled John Kilbride with a thin piece of string and had cut Pauline Reade's throat. Together with the notorious tape recording, the case against Brady and Hindley was the most horrific to have ever come before a British court.

On 6 May the couple were found guilty of killing Edward Evans and Lesley Ann Downey. In the cases of Pauline Reade and Keith Bennett, the Department of Public Prosecutions decided against a new trial, although both Brady and Hindley had implicated themselves by their statements. Both were given life sentences.

The 1965 search on Saddleworth Moor.

Pauline's Reade's body was found on the moors in July 1987. Keith Bennett's body still lies there.

During his time in prison, Brady 'confessed' to five other murders, including 'bricking' a man on wasteland behind Manchester's Piccadilly railway station, stabbing a man under railway arches in Glasgow, throwing a woman into a canal in Manchester, shooting and burying an 18-year-old youth on Saddleworth Moor and shooting a hiker at Loch Long, Scotland. But it was difficult to give too much credence to this information from Brady, diagnosed as suffering from a paranoid psychosis.

Despite campaigns to have Myra Hindley released, the killer, who had many lesbian affairs during her imprisonment, has remained firmly in jail. Brady has said he never wants to be released. But there are many who feel a lifetime in jail is inadequate punishment for the evil perpetrators of the 'Moors Murders'.

ABOVE: A body leaves the Moor.

BELOW: Myra Hindley in 1990.

Despite continued attempts to locate it, Keith Bennett's
body still lies somewhere on the Moor.

COLIN IRELAND

NAME: Colin Ireland

BORN: 1954

PREFERRED MURDER METHOD: Strangulation

NUMBER OF VICTIMS: 5

NAMES OF VICTIMS: Peter Walker, Chris Dunn, Perry Bradley III, Andrew Collier, Emmanuel Spiteri

MURDER LOCALE: Pick up at the Colherne pub, Earl's Court

SPAN OF MURDER CAREER: 9 March 1993 to 13 June 1993

DATE OF CONVICTION: December 1993

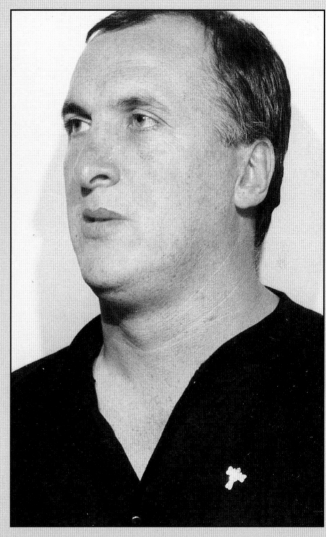

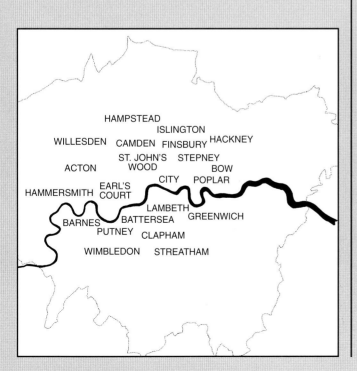

As London gay slayer Colin Ireland's hideous acts were reported week by week in the newspapers, he would telephone detectives to taunt them. 'I've got the book,' he would say. 'I know how many you have to do.' After the fifth victim was found, he boasted: 'I've done another one.'

The 'book' was the FBI handbook by Robert Ressler. It stated that only someone who had murdered 'one over four' could count as a serial killer. Ireland wanted nothing more than that notoriety. Later, after he confessed to his five murders, he told police he had just wanted the thrill of fame.

Ireland, a 6ft, 15-stone survival enthusiast with two failed marriages behind him, launched his reign of terror in spring 1993. His stalking ground was the Coleherne pub in London's cosmopolitan Earl's Court district. On 9 March he met 45-year-old theatre director Peter Walker there and was invited back to his flat for a sado-masochistic sex session. Ireland, aged 39, had come equipped with his own cord, knife and a pair of gloves.

At Walker's flat he told his victim to lie naked on his bed and then tied him firmly down before whipping him, placing a plastic bag over the man's head and suffocating him. Two days later he rang the Samaritans and a newspaper asking if someone could go round to the address to free Walker's two pet dogs trapped inside.

In his confession to detectives, Ireland said: 'I had gone there [the Coleherne pub] with the idea that if someone approached me something would happen. It would be some sort of trigger — a stepping over the line in a way.'

Now that line was crossed and Ireland soon struck again. On 29 May he picked up a 37-year-old librarian, Chris Dunn. At Dunn's flat, Ireland handcuffed him to the bed, beat him with a belt and held a cigarette lighter to his testicles before strangling him.

Third to die was Perry Bradley III, a 35-year-old businessman whose father was a US congressman. Friends later insisted he was not gay, though the facts suggest he was certainly bisexual in his tastes. Bradley was also picked up at the Coleherne and again Ireland was invited home, this time to a smart flat in Kensington. That night, 4 June, Bradley eventually fell asleep. Ireland admitted in his statement: 'I sat there in the room and thought about it and at one point I was thinking of letting him go. Then I thought, "it's easier to kill him". I walked round and pulled the noose.'

Ireland's next pick-up four days later followed a similar pattern. Andrew Collier, a 33-year-old warden at an old people's home, ended up being spread-eagled on his own bed, beaten black and blue and strangled. In an additional twist, Ireland broke the neck of his victim's cat Millie.

The killer said later that he had been outraged to discover from papers he read at the flat that Collier was HIV positive. He had not, he said righteously, even been offered a condom by the man. He told police: 'I wanted him to have no dignity in death. It was a way of saying to the police, "what do you think of that?" It was like a signature to let them know I'd been there. I was reaching a point where I was just accelerating. It was just speeding up, getting far worse.'

After the Collier killing, Ireland phoned police and asked them: 'Are you still interested in the death of Peter Walker? Why have you stopped the investigation? Doesn't the death of a homosexual man mean anything? I will do another. I have always dreamed of doing the perfect murder.'

Ireland then referred to the call he had made about Walker's dogs. 'I pissed myself when I read I was an animal lover. I thought I would give you lot something to think about, so I killed the cat.'

On 13 June, Collier killed for the last time. Emmanuel Spiteri, a 42-year-old chef, was tied up and tortured in an attempt to make him disclose his cash card number. Spiteri screamed back: 'You will just have to kill me.' Ireland said later: 'He was a very brave man, but I couldn't allow him to stick around.'

Within days, police knew the face of the killer. Checks on Spiteri's usual haunts took them to Charing Cross station where a security video had caught him and Ireland walking together. Ireland went to police admitting he had been with Spiteri but said that a third man had also been at the flat.

The story was quickly demolished. Police recognised Ireland's voice from the anonymous phone calls and, more damning, his fingerprints matched ones left on the grille on Collier's window. The game was up. On his way to a magistrates court, he confessed to all five murders.

In December 1993 an Old Bailey judge told him: 'You expressed a desire to be a serial killer. That must be matched by your detention for life.' Colin Ireland was given five life sentences and told he would never be released from prison.

'JACK THE RIPPER'

NAME: Unknown

A.K.A.: The 'Whitechapel Murderer'

PREFERRED MURDER METHOD: Throat-cutting, followed by mutilation of body

NUMBER OF VICTIMS: 5

NAMES OF VICTIMS: Mary Anne Nichols, Eliza Smith ('Annie Chapman'), Elizabeth ('Long Liz') Stride, Catherine Eddowes, Mary Jane Kelly

MURDER LOCALE: East London

SPAN OF MURDER CAREER: 31 August 1888 to 9 November 1888

CONVICTION: Never caught

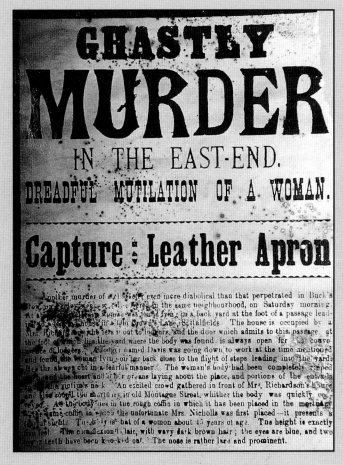

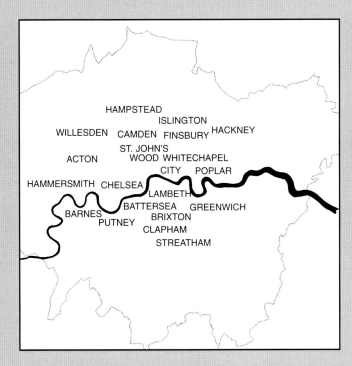

'Jack the Ripper' is hardly the most prolific murderer in the annals of crime. This minor Victorian killer put paid to no more than five humble prostitutes. Yet his brief reign of terror in 1888 has become perhaps the most tantalising murder mystery of all time. In fact, the story of 'Jack the Ripper' raises two mysteries — the first being his identity, the second being why his notoriety has continued to fascinate us for more than a century.

To historians, forensic experts and amateur sleuths worldwide, the dastardly deeds of 'Jack the Ripper' have become the greatest unsolved and intriguing series of bloody atrocities in criminal history. Since his skilled slayings shocked England in those few months of late summer in 1888, researchers have endlessly poured over the few, juicy clues that he left behind. And rather than interest in him waning, investigation is again intensifying, guaranteeing the vile perpetrator a place in history.

Although particularly gory (each killing was followed by mutilation with surgical precision) the 'Ripper's brief crime wave was quickly forgotten after the turn of the century. Yet in recent years books galore have been written about him. Speculation as to his identity is rife and often wildly wide of the mark — which has resulted in 'Jack' being credited with many more names than the number of his victims!

Was the murderer a self-styled purger of prostitutes who plied their sad trade under the gas-lights of London's East End? Was he a Jewish ritual slaughterman, as some clues suggested? Was he a surgeon who had turned his talents to butchery? Was he a mortician, skilled in the art of disembowelling? Was he a policeman, his nightly beat giving him the perfect alibi to be out on those dank, dark streets? Was 'he' in fact a 'she' — a midwife with a grudge? Or, most extraordinarily of all,

was the killer a deranged member of the British Royal Family?

Amid this endless debate, it is easy to forget that 'Jack the Ripper's' reign of terror was short and swift. It lasted less than three months. Between 31 August 1888 and 9 November 1888, five prostitutes were murdered. Then just as suddenly as the slayings started, they stopped.

Jack's first victim was Mary Ann Nichols, a 42-year-old prostitute who plied her trade in the Whitechapel area of the East End. 'Pretty Polly', as she was known, approached a tall stranger with the invitation: 'Looking for a good time, mister?' If the stranger had accepted, a sum of four pence would have exchanged hands. Mary would have spent it in one of the gin palaces that infested the area.

Instead, the man put his hands around her throat to stop her crying out, then dragged her into the darkness of an alleyway. Within seconds he had cut her from ear to ear.

A police surgeon who examined the body said: 'Only a madman could have done this. I have never seen so horrible a case. She was ripped about in the manner only a person skilled in the use of a knife could have achieved.'

The residents of Bucks Row, where Mary Ann Nichols's body was found, were so ashamed of their sudden notoriety — and so outraged by officials who dubbed the street 'Killer Row' — that they petitioned to have it renamed. It was duly retitled Durward Street and remained so until it was demolished many years later.

Police put Mary's murder down to one single, frenzied attack. Then a week a later, on 8 September, another prostitute, 47-year-old 'Dark Annie' Chapman was butchered in Hanbury Street, near Spitalfields Market. Her few pitiful possessions had been laid out neatly alongside her disembowelled corpse. Also alongside her were her entrails, slashed out of her in a sexual frenzy.

A witness who dashed to scene after hearing the cry 'Murder' said: 'I jumped off my cart, being a lad, and joined the crowd — and there she was, all her entrails steaming hot.'

Shortly afterwards a Fleet Street news agency received the following letter:

'Dear Boss, I keep on hearing that the police have caught me. But they won't fix me yet. I am down on

certain types of women and I won't stop ripping them until I do get buckled. Grand job that last job was. I gave the lady no time to squeal. I love my work and I want to start again. You will soon hear from me with my funny little game. I saved some of the proper stuff in a little ginger beer bottle after my last job to write with but it went thick like glue and I can't use it. Red ink is fit enough, I hope. Ha, ha. Next time I shall clip the ears off and send them to the police, just for jolly.'

The third victim was 44-year-old Elizabeth 'Long Liz' Stride. Her body was found in Berner Street, Whitechapel, on 30 September. Police believe the killer had been disturbed in his grisly work because, although the victim's throat had been cut, her body was otherwise untouched.

Victim number four was discovered on the same day not far away in Mitre Square. This time the 'Ripper' achieved the bestial satisfaction he seemed to crave. Catherine Eddowes, a drunkard in her 40s who had just been released from police cells after causing an affray, was disembowelled and her intestines draped across her right shoulder. Her face had been hacked off and her ears were missing.

A trail of blood led from Catherine's corpse to a torn part of her apron. And on a nearby wall was scrawled in chalk: 'The Jewes (sic) are not men to be blamed for nothing.'

The final victim was Mary Kelly, younger than her predecessors at just 25 years of age. Mary, also a prostitute, had accosted a man on the night of 9 November. He was described as being tall, dark, with a moustache and a deerstalker hat.

Poor Mary was butchered not in the street but in her own tiny apartment, where the 'Ripper' spent hours grotesquely mutilating her. The following morning her landlord knocked on her door to demand his rent. After discovering her remains, he told police: 'I shall be haunted by this sight for the rest of my life.'

Terror had by now gripped the East End. Vigilante groups were formed and a host of accusations were bandied about. Was the 'Ripper' a mad surgeon? Was he a Jewish ritual slaughterman, as the writing on the wall seemed to suggest? Was he, perhaps, a policeman on his nightly rounds, his job giving him the perfect alibi to be out on those dank, dark streets?

One suspect was revealed by Inspector Robert Sagar, who played a leading part in the Ripper investigation. Shortly before his death in 1924, Sagar said: 'We had good reason to suspect a man who lived in Butcher's Row, Aldgate. We watched him carefully. There was no doubt this man was insane. After a time his friends thought it was advisable to have him removed to a private asylum. Once he was removed, there were no more "Ripper" atrocities.'

After the slaying of poor Mary, London held its breath. Terror had by now gripped the East End and vigilantes patrolled the streets at night. The populace awaited news of another ' 'orrible murder'. But it never came. The killings had ended as suddenly as they had begun.

The 'Ripper' fever died down — for half a century. Then, for some reason, fascination with the case slowly began to grow again. The pursuit of the Ripper's identity became a fresh fascination for modern-day criminologists. Today, with most of the crumbling old workers' homes gone and the taverns replaced with office blocks, the East End is a lurid shrine for 'Ripper' enthusiasts. Americans are escorted on guided tours of the streets where the maniacal 'Jack' dispensed with his victims, and sip beer afterwards in a pub named after him. Books are churned out and TV documentaries made, all posing the same question: just who was 'Jack the Ripper'? And all coming up with different answers . . .

The suspect favoured by several authors of 'Ripper' investigations is Montagu (sometimes also spelled 'Montague') John Druitt. In their book *The Ripper Legacy*, authors Martin Howells and Keith Skinner say that Druitt, an impoverished barrister, had been trained in medical skills as a young man. He was unstable and his family had a history of mental illness. His body was found floating in the River Thames a few weeks after the murder of Mary Kelly.

Richard Gordon, famous for his *Doctor In The House* series of comic novels, was an anaesthetist before turning to writing. In 1980 he retraced 'Jack's' steps through the East End and observed: 'The victims died by having their throats cut. The vein in the neck is only three or four inches from the heart and, given that the victim is apprehensive, the heart would be pumping at enormous pressure. It always does when you're frightened. That meant the villain chloroformed his victims first, because that slows down the heartbeat.' For this reason, said Richard Gordon, the Ripper was not only a doctor but an anaesthetist like himself.

The most original theory, however, came from author William Stewart who suggested that 'Jack' was really 'Jill the Ripper', a midwife and abortionist who went mad after serving a jail sentence for prostitution.

Almost unbelievably, another suspect was a member of the British Royal Family. The finger of suspicion fell on Queen Victoria's grandson, Prince Eddy — or, to give him his full title, Albert Victor Christian Edward, Duke of Clarence and Avondale, heir to the throne and great-uncle of the present Queen.

Certainly the talk at the time was that the

prince was a bisexual who had turned criminally insane after contracting venereal disease. According to renowned forensic psychiatrist Dr Harold Abrahamsen in his book *Murder And Madness: The Secret Life Of Jack The Ripper*, the prince was supposedly aided and abetted in his dark deeds by his mentor, tutor and woman-hating homosexual lover James Stephen.

Prince Edward died in 1892 of brain damage brought on by syphilis, although the official announcement described his fatal ailment as 'pneumonia'.

Excitement among 'Ripper' hunters was rekindled in 1993 when a diary was said to have been discovered under floorboards of a house in Liverpool, proving that wealthy cotton broker James Maybrick was 'Jack the Ripper'. The discovery was enough to fire up one publishing house but the claims and the 'Ripper Diary' itself were derided by experts.

The principal expert contracted by one newspaper to disprove the diary's authenticity was author Melvin Harris, who himself wrote one of the best researched books on the subject. *In The True Face Of Jack The Ripper*, Harris named as his prime suspect Robert D'Onston Stephenson, born 20 April 1841, the son of a wealthy Hull mill owner.

As a youth, Stephenson became obsessed with witchcraft and, in his own word, the 'black arts'. He embarked on a tour of Europe, ending up in southern Italy, where in 1860 he joined Garibaldi's uprising as a medical officer. There he learned a further art — crude field surgery. He revelled in the adventure and particularly the butchery. Once the war was over, Stephenson sailed to West Africa where, he boasted later, he killed a black woman in cold blood because he believed she was a witch doctor.

Returning home to Hull in 1863, he took a post as a customs officer but began consorting with prostitutes, contracted venereal disease and was banished from home. He was sent away in disgrace ending up in London where, to spite his parents, he married their illiterate serving girl and changed his first name to Roslyn.

Author Melvin Harris believes that Mrs D'Onston Stephenson, who disappeared in 1887, was butchered by her husband. From wife murder,

Contemporary illustration of the discovery of one of 'Jack the Ripper's victims.

it was but a short step to the killing of the five Whitechapel prostitutes the following year. The devious Stephenson then became a self-professed expert on the crimes and persuaded the Pall Mall magazine to publish his articles, which examined the slayings with a strange authority and detail.

In his later years, Stephenson experienced a religious conversion and, seemingly by way of atonement, wrote a tortuous study of the earliest translations of the Gospels. He completed his book in 1904 and immediately thereafter vanished without trace. No death certificate for him has ever been found — leaving yet another mystery for the 20th century 'detectives' seeking the true identity of 'Jack the Ripper'.

'JACK THE STRIPPER'

NAME: Never established

A.K.A.: The Hammersmith Nudes Murders

PREFERRED MURDER METHOD: Asphixiation of prostitutes with corpses dumped naked and outdoors

NUMBER OF VICTIMS: 6

NAMES OF VICTIMS: Hannah Tailford, Irene Lockwood, Helen Barthelemy, Mary Fleming, Margaret McGowan, Bridie O'Hara

MURDER LOCALE: West London

SPAN OF MURDER CAREER: February 1964 to February 1965

DATE OF CONVICTION: Never caught or charged

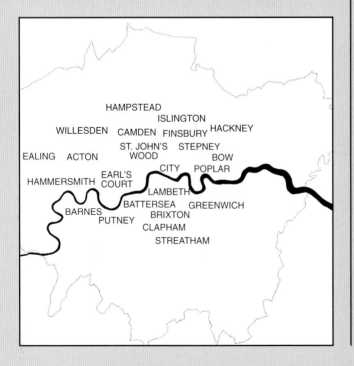

'Jack the Ripper' may well have been the first and most notorious murderer who we would now brand as a serial killer. But although the activities of his near-namesake 'Jack the Stripper' are less well known, the latter was equally adept at bringing terror and hysteria to the streets of London.

The first possible 'Stripper' victim was prostitute Elizabeth Figg, dragged out of the Thames on 17 June 1959. Another probable victim was Hannah Tailford, aged 30, who also appeared to have died from drowning in the Thames on 2 February 1964. The recovery of 26-year-old Irene Lockwood's nude corpse from the Thames on 8 April began to sound alarm bells with Scotland Yard, but as yet there was no obvious link between the victims.

On the morning of 24 April, however, police attitudes hardened when the naked body of a 22-year-old Helene Barthelemy was found lying amid rubbish at a sports ground in Acton, West London. She had been choked to death. Her skin showed up microscopic traces of industrial paint and there were heat marks on one side of the body suggesting it had been stored close to machinery. Perhaps the killer had kept the corpse in a garage or warehouse to await disposal.

There were other, sinister forensic discoveries. Four teeth had been knocked out of Barthelemy's mouth with considerable force, one of which had remained lodged in her throat. And one of her last acts on earth had clearly been to perform fellatio on a man; traces of sperm were recovered from the back of her mouth. Over the following months, the clues from this woman's death surfaced again in the murders of three more prostitutes . . .

The next victim was found early in the morning of 14 July, her nude body bizarrely arranged on a garage forecourt with legs crossed and chest slumped forward. Mary Fleming, from Notting Hill, had been asphyxiated; in other words, her killer had not put his hands around her neck to choke her but had stopped her air supply by other means. Detective Superintendent John Du Rose of Scotland Yard likened it to the effect of pushing a small apple into the back of the throat. He was being coy. The 'Stripper' murdered his victims during fellatio by thrusting his penis into their mouths, blocking the airways while gripping their hair to prevent escape.

On 25 November the body of prostitute Margaret McGowan, missing for almost a month, turned up on a rubbish dump in fashionable Kensington. Again there were the tell-tale clues — but McGowan's death attracted additional media interest because of her links with high-class procurers in the London sex market. Through them, the press uncovered a connection with characters on the edge of the John Profumo-Christine Keeler political sex scandal, which had almost brought down the British government.

The last victim was discovered on 16 February 1965 on an industrial estate in Acton. This time the body had been kept so close to heat that it was almost mummified. Forensic examination confirmed that Bridget O'Hara had lost several teeth, had sperm in her throat and metallic paint on her skin. She bore all the terrible trademarks of the murderer.

As public hysteria mounted, Du Rose decided on a ploy to try to flush out the killer. He called a press conference at which he announced that the hunt had been narrowed to 20 suspects. Later he said the number had been halved. Finally he bluffed his way through a statement that only three names were left in the frame.

The psychological pressure on the murderer worked — O'Hara's was the last killing in the series. A month after her murder, a night security guard on an Acton industrial estate gassed himself with the exhaust from his own van. The bachelor, in his mid-40s, left a note saying: 'I cannot stand the strain any longer.'

Du Rose said the man had been a prime suspect but added: 'Because he was never arrested or stood trial, he must be considered innocent — and will therefore never be named.'

Du Rose also gave a fascinating insight into the mind of a serial killer. He said that the first of the killings may have been an accident. By choking the prostitute with his penis during a frenzied orgasm, it could have been argued that he was guilty only of manslaughter. But Du Rose added: 'When he continued to indulge in his particular perversion, well knowing that the girls concerned would die, he must have recognised that he was fulfilling himself as a murderer.'

Helene Barthelemy

Margaret McGowan

Bridget O'Hara

Mary Fleming

HELENE JEGADO

NAME: Helene Jegado

BORN: c1820

DIED: Guillotined December 1851

PREFERRED MURDER METHOD: Poison

NUMBER OF VICTIMS: 23

MURDER LOCALE: Rennes, France

SPAN OF MURDER CAREER: 1833-51

DATE OF CONVICTION: December 1851

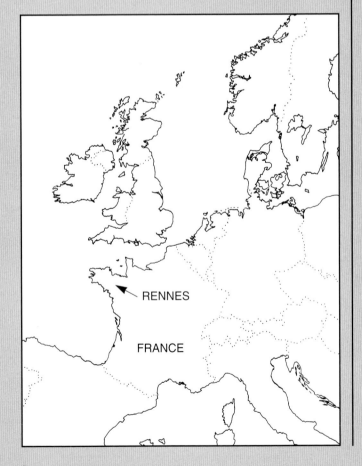

RENNES

FRANCE

An illiterate peasant, Helene Jegado worked as a domestic servant all over France, principally for members of the clergy. But every job she took provided new temptations. She was a kleptomaniac who covered up her petty thieving by the simple expedient of poisoning potential witnesses against her.

Her victims were as likely to be her masters and mistresses as her fellow servants. She would mix arsenic with their food — then, upon their agonising deaths, would go into convincing mourning. 'Wherever I go, people die,' was her constant lament as she moved from job to job.

Between 1833 and 1851, when she was apprehended at Rennes, Jegado murdered at least 23 people, including her own sister. The true total, however, is believed to have been nearer 60. Even when living in a convent, the nuns mysteriously fell sick from her ministrations: Sister Helene was asked to leave, although to protect the good name of the order, no inquiry was ever held.

Jegado's trail of murder ended only after the suspicious death of a fellow servant at the home of a surgeon, Professor Theodore Biddard. Even then, Helene might have escaped detection but for her unwarrented protestation when police arrived on the scene . . . Her first words being: 'I am innocent.' At this stage she had been accused of nothing and simply aroused police interest.

Under interrogation, her medical knowledge raised suspicions. The poisoner, who always used arsenic, was eventually tried for only three murders and three attempted murders. She went to the guillotine in December 1851.

PATRICK KEARNEY

NAME: Patrick Wayne Kearney

A.K.A.: The 'Trash Bag Murderer'

BORN: 1940

DIED: Serving life imprisonment

PREFERRED MURDER METHOD: Shooting

NUMBER OF VICTIMS: At least 32

NAMES OF VICTIMS: Indicted for Albert Riviera, Arturo Marquez, John Le May

MURDER LOCALE: California

SPAN OF MURDER CAREER: 25 December 1972 to 1 July 1977

DATE OF CONVICTION: 13 July 1977

Patrick Wayne Kearney murdered as many as 32 homosexuals and became known as the 'Trash Bag Murderer' because his victims were found scattered along the roadside between Los Angeles and the Mexican border.

The bodies of his first victims were discovered on Christmas Day 1972 when Kearney, himself a declared homosexual, was aged 32. The bearded killer generally preyed on young drifters who haunted the gay areas of Hollywood, dropping their dismembered bodies by the side of the road in rubbish bags. His base was a house at Redondo Beach, where he lived with his best friend David Hill, his room mate for 15 years. It was at their home that police found a bloodstained hacksaw and hairs and fibres from various victims.

Kearney and Hill had fled to Mexico, but on 1 July 1977 they turned themselves in to police. They pointed to a wanted poster and announced: 'We're them!' Hill escaped charges due to lack of evidence, but Kearney pleaded guilty to the murder of 21 men on condition that the prosecution would not press for the death sentence.

EDMUND KEMPER

Like many killers, Edmund Kemper was the product of a broken home. His parents separated when he was seven and he was left in the care of a strict mother in North Fork, California. He practised the art of murder on his pet cats before progressing to shooting his grandmother through the head. Then he slashed her body with a knife. That was in August 1963 when Edmund was 14. Kemper spent five years in a psychiatric hospital and, by the time he was released, he had grown into a 6ft 9in tall, 20-stone giant.

Kemper's next victims were all girl hitchhikers whom he picked up on the freeways. He had the perfect cover to be out cruising, having found work as a flagman for the California Division of Highways. He committed the first of his six hitchhiker murders in May 1972. He stabbed the girls to death, smuggled their bodies into his bedroom and abused them. Using a knife which he nicknamed the 'General', Kemper then cut the bodies into pieces and scattered them in the Santa Cruz mountains.

Because of his penchant for students, Kemper earned a nickname for himself — the 'Co-Ed Killer'. All his victims were stabbed and the bodies abused before being dissected.

Amazingly, throughout, Kemper was being seen regularly by psychiatrists who were pleased at his adjustment to the outside world. Their satisfaction at his progress was greatly shaken, however, when they later learned that Kemper had smashed his mother's skull in as she lay sleeping. He then cut out her larynx 'to stop her nagging' him.

NAME: Edmund Emil Kemper

A.K.A.: The 'Co-ed Killer'

BORN: 18 December 1949

DIED: Serving life imprisonment

PREFERRED MURDER METHOD: Various

NUMBER OF VICTIMS: 10

NAMES OF VICTIMS: Maude Kemper, Edmund Kemper, Mary Pesce, Anita Luchessa, Aiko Koo, Cindy Schall, Rosalind Thorpe, Alice Lui, Clarnell Strandberg (his mother), Sally Hallett

MURDER LOCALE: California

SPAN OF MURDER CAREER: 1963-73

DATE OF CONVICTION: 8 November 1973

Kemper's final victim was his mother's friend, Sally Hallett, whom he invited for tea, hit over the head, strangled and decapitated. After that murder in November 1973, Kemper gave himself up. Teeth, hair and bits of skin were found at his home. Tests revealed that the killer had a tendency towards necrophilia and cannibalism — and an unusually high IQ of 136.

Kemper, who pleaded insanity, was found guilty on eight counts of murder and, despite his plea to be tortured to death, was sentenced to life.

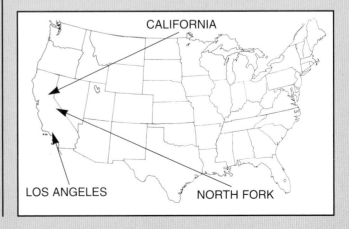

BELA KISS

NAME: Bela Kiss

BORN: 1880

DIED: Disappeared in 1914; final end unknown

PREFERRED MURDER METHOD: Strangulation

NUMBER OF VICTIMS: 24

MURDER LOCALE: Budapest, Hungary

SPAN OF MURDER CAREER: Years leading up to 1914 war

DATE OF CONVICTION: Never tried

When a new tenant moved into a rundown house in the Hungarian town of Czinkota in 1916, he discovered a number of tightly-sealed oil drums in a workshop at the rear. Thinking they contained petrol — in severely short supply during World War 1 — the jubilant tenant prised open the lid of one. Perfectly preserved inside was the naked body of a woman. The contents of a further six drums was the same. Each woman had been garrotted.

The previous tenant of the house, 10 miles from the capital, Budapest, was a plumber and tin smith named Bela Kiss. He had murdered as many as 15 women, his motives being both sex and robbery. Kiss also murdered his wife and her lover, their bodies being discovered in other oil drums found dotted around the countryside.

In 1914, at the age of 34, Kiss was drafted into the Hungarian army, sent to Serbia and reported dead on the battlefield. It was later discovered, however, that he had switched name tags with a dead comrade. Bela Kiss was later spotted back in Hungary in 1919 — and there was even an unconfirmed sighting of him in New York in 1932. He was never caught.

JOACHIM KROLL

NAME: Joachim Kroll

A.K.A.: The 'Ruhr Hunter'

BORN: 1933

DIED: Still serving life

PREFERRED MURDER METHOD: Rape, mutilation, strangulation and cannibalism

NUMBER OF VICTIMS: At least 14

NAMES OF VICTIMS: Manuela Knodt, Petra Giese, Monica Tafel, Ilona Harke, Marion Ketter, Irmgard Strehl, Klara Tesmer, Hermann Schmitz, Ursula Roling, Maria Hettgen, Jutta Rahn, Karin Toepfer, Barbara Bruder, Erika Schuleter

MURDER LOCALE: The Ruhr and all over Germany

SPAN OF MURDER CAREER: July 1959 to July 1976

DATE OF CONVICTION: 1976

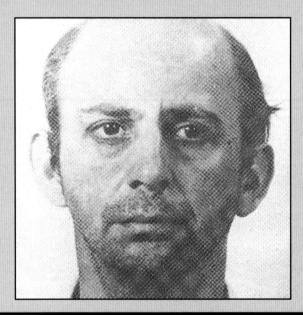

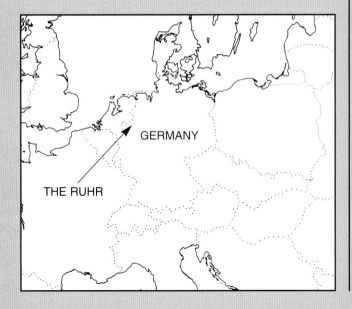

When police searched Joachim Kroll's apartment they found pieces of flesh on plates in the refrigerator. On the stove was a stew of carrots, potatoes — and a tiny human hand.

Kroll, 43, admitted killing at least 14 young women between 1955 and 1976. He told police he only ate victims he considered to be young and tender. He also complained about the price of meat in West German shops. All his murders took place in the Ruhr area and the ages of his victims ranged from 4 to 19. Most had been raped and slices of flesh taken from their bodies.

He was arrested during routine enquiries into the disappearance of a small child. They were told that a lavatory attendant had told a neighbour not to use a particular toilet because it was 'stuffed up with guts'. It was in fact blocked with the remains of four-year-old Marion Ketter. In Kroll's apartment police found plastic bags filled with the flesh of his victims. He confessed to his sickening crimes, telling police that as a young man he had been unable to have sex to a conscious woman. He was officially declared a mental defective.

PETER KÜRTEN

NAME: Peter Kürten

A.K.A.: The 'Vampire of Düsseldorf'

BORN: 26 May 1883

DIED: Guillotined at Klingelputz Prison 2 July 1932

PREFERRED MURDER METHOD: Various

NUMBER OF VICTIMS: Charged with 9; confessed to 68

NAMES OF VICTIMS: Christine Klein, Rosa Ohliger, Rudolf Scheer, Maria Hahn, Gertrude Hamacher, Luise Lenzen, Ida Reuter, Elisabeth Dörrier, Gertrude Albermann

MURDER LOCALE: Düsseldorf

SPAN OF MURDER CAREER: 25 May 1913 to 27 November 1929

DATE OF CONVICTION: 1931

Peter Kürten was labelled the 'Vampire of Düsseldorf', an apt title for one who had relished the taste of blood since childhood. From the age of nine, Kürten thrilled to the most extreme acts of sadism: cutting the heads off swans and holding their dismembered necks to his mouth to drink the pumping blood. He is said to have become a murderer at the age of 10, when he drowned a playmate who couldn't swim by forcing his head under the waters of the River Rhine.

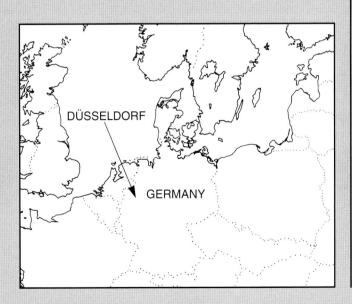

DÜSSELDORF

GERMANY

Kürten slowly discovered that only through atrocities such as these could he get his sexual kicks. And there was little chance of finding much moral guidance at home. His father was a bullying alcoholic who relished any opportunity to beat his 13 children. On occasions he would rape his wife in front of them and commit acts of incest with his daughters. It was one such explosion of brutality that finally put the evil parent behind bars, albeit only for three years.

As Peter Kürten approached adulthood, he had his first brush with the law; he received a two-year jail sentence for theft. Behind bars his resentment against German society festered and so he began passing the time by conjuring up depraved sexual fantasies. He deliberately broke prison rules to obtain solitary confinement because it gave him the peace and quiet he sought to indulge a perverted imagination.

Later, he would tell a court: 'I thought of myself causing accidents affecting thousands of people and invented a number of crazy fantasies such as smashing bridges and boring through bridge piers,' he explained. 'Then I spun a number of fantasies with regard to bacilli which I might be able to introduce into the drinking water and so cause a great calamity.

'I imagined myself using schools or orphanages for the purpose, where I could carry out murders by giving away chocolate samples containing arsenic which I could have obtained through housebreaking. I derived the sort of pleasure from these visions that other people would get from thinking about a naked woman.'

Kürten had made up his mind to murder a young woman. His first attempt, though terrifying for the girl concerned, was a failure. She crawled home battered beyond belief but too terrified to go to the police. The authorities would later hear of this attack from Kürten's own mouth.

On 25 May 1913 Düsseldorf was shaken by the worst murder anyone could remember. Eight-year-old Christine Klein was found in her bed above an inn with her throat cut. She had clearly been raped. The evil deed was perpetrated by the youthful Kürten, although police did not know this at the time. Kürten was later to tell his trial judge:

'I had been stealing, specialising in public bars or inns where the owners lived on the floor above. In a room above an inn at Köln-Mulheim, I discovered a child asleep. Her head was facing the window. I seized it with my left hand and strangled her for about a minute and a half. The child woke up and struggled but lost consciousness.

'I had a small but sharp pocket knife with me and I held the child's head and cut her throat. The whole thing lasted about three minutes. Then I locked the door again and went home to Düsseldorf. Next day I went back to Mulheim. There is a cafe opposite the Klein's place and I sat there and drank a glass of beer, and read all about the murder in the papers. People were talking about it all around me. All this amount of horror and indignation did me good.'

After spending the whole of World War 1 in jail as a deserter, Kürten emerged in 1921 determined to cultivate a new image. On his release, he portrayed himself as a good, hard-working German. He got a shop-floor job in a factory and became a respected trades unionist. He married a prostitute and in 1925 moved to an apartment in the centre of Düsseldorf. To his neighbours, he seemed the epitome of working-class German respectability.

Kürten's bloodlust had not been sated, however. Over the years, a string of mistresses, prostitutes and even complete strangers were brutally murdered with the aid of a knife or scissors. On one occasion Kürten heightened the sexual thrill he obtained from killing by sucking blood from the wound on the side of a young girl's head.

By the summer of 1929, detectives had no doubts that a deviant serial killer was prowling the city streets. Their files suggested 46 crimes of deviancy (including four particularly gruesome murders) were the work of the same, clever fiend. Parents kept their children at home; the elderly never ventured through the door. Talk of a real-life vampire was taken seriously by one and all.

On the night of 23 August, these fears were realised as Kürten carried out the double-killing of two foster sisters: five-year-old Gertrude Hamacher and Louise Lenzen, 14. They were lured onto allotments near the fair in Düsseldorf's Flehe district, where they were strangled, sexually molested and left with their throats sliced open.

The sense of shock and outrage extended well

beyond Germany. But despite the efforts of police, Kürten's attacks grew both more ambitious and depraved. He took to using a hammer on some victims, a cudgel on others. Sometimes it would be his slim, stiletto-like blade or his beloved Bavarian dagger. Detectives found the only common thread was a frenzy in the murders that seemed orgiastic in its nature. One little girl had 36 separate wounds on her tiny frame.

By now the wealthier citizens of Düsseldorf were, quite literally, heading for the hills. Women were packed off to country residences with instructions from their menfolk not to return until the 'Vampire' was caught. Poorer girls had no such advantage. Some, like 21-year-old Maria Budlick, travelled to Düsseldorf in search of work knowing full well of the maniac's atrocities. In her worst nightmare she could not have expected to meet him so soon.

As she stepped off her train on 14 May 1930, a kindly-looking man offered to show her the nearest women's hostel. Maria was at first happy to follow him through the streets but on entering Volksgarten Park fears began to consume her. She was grateful to hear another voice booming out of the darkness: 'Hello, is everything all right?' Maria aired her fears to this second 'Good Samaritan' and, as her original escort disappeared, she happily agreed to accompany her new companion home for a sandwich and glass of milk.

Maria had walked straight into the lair of the 'Vampire of Düsseldorf'. The snack over, Kürten offered to escort her to the hostel she sought but, as they strolled through woods, he grabbed her by the throat and tried to rape her. As she faded into unconsciousness, Maria remembered his last words: 'Do you remember where I live, in case you ever need my help again?' She managed to deny all knowledge of his address and, uniquely, Kürten had mercy on her. It was to be his undoing.

Maria did not contact the police but she wrote of her experience to a friend in Cologne. The letter went astray and was opened at the city's post office. On reading the first few paragraphs, the official concerned realised the importance of her words and called in detectives. Within a few days, they had found her and Maria was showing police the house at No 71, Mettmannerstrasse,

Düsseldorf, and even pointed her vicious attacker out to them.

Kürten had seen her and her police escorts and knew the game was up. Yet rather than panic, he decided first to confess all to his wife. He took her to a favourite restaurant and calmly informed her: 'I am the man sought by the police. I am the monster of Düsseldorf.' Frau Kürten could only stare back numbly as her husband tucked heartily into his own meal and then polished off her own, untouched plate.

On the morning of 24 May 1930 Frau Kürten arrived at the city's police HQ to pass on the horrific information she had been given. When they came to arrest him, Peter Kürten smilingly assured them: 'Come, there is no need to be afraid.'

On the opening day of his trial, 13 April 1931, thousands thronged the surrounding streets to try to catch a glimpse of the 'Vampire of Düsseldorf'.

Peter Kürten surprised them all by looking dapper, immaculately groomed and wearing expensive cologne. It seemed totally incongruous that such a respectable, benign figure should be in the dock confessing to 68 of the most appalling crimes imaginable, including nine murders and seven attempted murders.

When Kürten at last walked to the guillotine on the evening of 2 July 1932, he seemed to regard execution as just another form of sexual fantasy. His last words to the prison psychiatrist were: 'Tell me, after my head has been chopped off, will I still be able to hear, at least for a moment, the sound of my own blood gushing from the stump of my neck? That would be the pleasure to end all pleasures.'

ILLSHAT KUSIKOV

For some reason the Soviet Union bred a high proportion of serial killers with a gruesome penchant for cannibalism. One of the most enthusiastic of recent times was Ilshat Kusikov, a St Petersburg street sweeper.

Neighbours in Ordzhonikidze Street recalled him as a cheery, likable man who was always ready to help his elderly neighbours with jobs around the house. He was devoted to his cat, Dasha, but appeared to have few human friends. He was also on the register at his local psychiatric hospital.

In November 1992 a piece of human torso turned up in the basement of a house close to Kusikov's home. Police failed to link him to the crime, just as they failed to make the connection two years later when the severed head of a vagrant was found in a communal rubbish dump on Ordzhonikidze Street.

NAME: Illshat Kusikov

BORN: 1960

PREFERRED MURDER METHOD: Various followed by cannibalism

NUMBER OF VICTIMS: Unknown

NAMES OF VICTIMS: Edik Vassilevski

MURDER LOCALE: St Petersburg

SPAN OF MURDER CAREER: 1992-95

But in August 1995 another severed head was found, this time belonging to one of Kusikov's fellow psychiatric patients, Edik Vassilevski. Police realised the two men were friends and made 35-year-old Kusikov their main suspect.

When they broke into his house, they found a fizzy drink bottle full of blood, an old gherkin jar used to store dried skin and ears and an aluminium cooking pot containing Edik's last remains. He had been cut up for Russian-style kebabs.

Psychologists said Illshat Kusikov was a sexual sadist for whom cannibalism was the ultimate way of controlling his victims. As he put it himself in interviews with police: 'You know, I always wanted to be a surgeon, but it's better to be a cannibal. If you're a surgeon you have to put the body back together and you stop having control over it. But a cannibal kills and then he can do what he wants with the body. After he kills, he owns it forever.'

LEONARD LAKE AND CHARLES NG

NAME: Leonard Lake (top right) and Charles Chitag Ng (below right)

A.K.A.: Robin Stapley, Paul Cosner

BORN: Lake — 20 July 1946; Ng — 1961

DIED: Lake — took poison 1985; Ng — on death row

PREFERRED MURDER METHOD: Various after torture

NUMBER OF VICTIMS: At least 30

NAMES OF VICTIMS: Include Kathy Allen, Brenda O"Connor, Scott Stapley, Lonnie Bond, Paul Cosner, Charles Gunnar, Michael Carrol, Donald Lake

MURDER LOCALE: California

SPAN OF MURDER CAREER: c1981-85

DATE OF CONVICTION: Ng 1995 (Lake committed suicide prior to conviction).

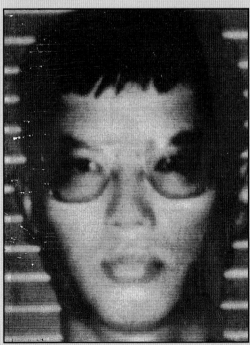

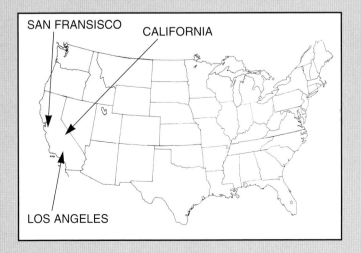

As American serial killers go, Leonard Lake was not a record breaker. The toll of his victims numbered probably between 30 and 40, but at no time did he hold a community in the grip of terror as did Albert De Salvo, the 'Boston Strangler', or Wayne B. Williams, convicted of the Atlanta child slayings. Neither did he earn an exotic sobriquet of the kind handed out by the press and police to other mass killers such as the 'Vampire Rapist' or the 'Moon Maniac'. No such fame could be his . . . for his murders were never even suspected until after his death.

What makes Leonard Lake unique in the annals of serial killer crime is the way he turned the blood-lust that drove him to kill neighbours, friends — even his own brother — into an efficient and well-organised business.

Even the sequence of events leading up to the exposure of Leonard Lake as California's most perverted and brutal killer were largely accidental. They began in June 1985 when police officer David Wright got a radio call to go to a San Francisco hardware store where a young oriental was refusing to pay for a $75 vice. When the policeman arrived, he found that the oriental had run away but that his friend, a burly, bearded Caucasian, was desperately offering to settle the bill. The store manager was ready to accept the cash, but the policeman became suspicious when the man refused to give his name.

His driving licence gave his name as Robin Scott Stapley. When a check call was made to the station, the computer revealed that Stapley was a 26-year-old who had disappeared without trace some months previously. A check on the mystery man's car licence plate revealed that it belonged to a local businessman, Paul Cosner, another missing person, who had last been seen by his girlfriend some weeks previously when he went out to sell the car to a 'weird-looking' man prepared to pay cash on delivery.

Wright arrested the stranger and searched the car. He found a small handgun and a quantity of pornographic pictures. Back at headquarters, the man asked for a pencil, paper and a glass of water. On the paper he wrote a note to his ex-wife, a dubious character called Cricket Balazs. It read: 'I love you. Please forgive me. I forgive you. Tell Mama, Fern and Patty I'm sorry.'

Then he called the detectives back, revealed that his real name was Leonard Lake — and fell forward unconscious. He had swallowed a cyanide capsule he always kept with him. He never came round and died four days later.

With their prisoner dead, mystified police followed up the only clue they had — an electricity bill discovered in Lake's pocket for an address in Wisleyville, Calaveras County, 150 miles east of San Francisco. What they were to find there would turn the stomachs of the toughest of cops, who, until then, had thought they had seen it all.

Lake's remote cabin was a chamber of horrors; a den of lust, torture and agonising death. Leonard Lake, who had died a few days short of his 39th birthday, had kidnapped, raped, tortured, killed and mutilated at least 30 people. And he had faithfully recorded the gruesome details of most of them in diaries, photographs and on film.

The police soon found grim pointers to further horrors. Military camouflage suits hung beside women's clothes in the wardrobes; chains and manacles were attached to brackets on the walls; a blood-stained chainsaw was found in an outhouse.

Outside, a searcher discovered bones. They had been burned but were still recognisably human. As the hunt continued, graves were unearthed and more charred bones and decomposing human remains were carted away in bin liners. As the men toiled in the summer heat, they became covered in a film of dust that stuck to their sweating faces. They were sickened to realise it was human ashes. Officer Wright's shoplifter had turned into the most prolific serial killer of recent history.

Leonard Lake and his former wife, Cricket. She appeared in some of his earliest vile videos.

It was a day or so before police pushed aside a stack of barrels and found the hidden dungeon. A trapdoor gave on to an underground bunker in which were found all the paraphernalia of a modern torture chamber. Lake, it turned out, was a 'survivalist' — he believed the holocaust was coming and had stocked a bunker with guns and food with which he would survive a nuclear war. In his twisted mind, he saw himself as a future saviour of a world peopled by his sex-slave women. To this end, his bunker doubled as a prison. The walls of the bunker's living quarters were decorated with pictures of young women, many of them naked, some of them obviously newly dead. But even worse was to come.

The police had long since realised they were dealing with a monster. But still they were unprepared for what they found next. His bunker was also a film studio. Films in a macabre video cassette library showed Lake taunting, raping and killing his victims. Not only was he satisfying his craving

to kill, he was making snuff videos for sale to the sicker elements of American society.

One video showed a terrified young woman tied to a chair being taunted by Lake and being told she would be his sex slave, doing whatever he ordered until he released her. An oriental accomplice came into vision to cut away the girl's clothes and hold a pistol to her head before leading her away.

The hunt was already under way for the oriental involved in the shoplifting in San Francisco. Now he was identified as the man in the video — Charles Ng, the 24-year-old, English-educated son of a wealthy Hong Kong businessman. Ng, it transpired, had been expelled from his Lancashire boarding school for theft, and later, after being sent to America to complete his education, had joined the army to escape a driving charge. He had been dishonourably discharged, again for theft.

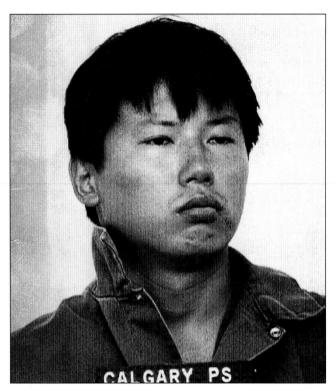

Charles Ng was an avid participant in Lake's murderous fantasies.

Now Ng was suddenly at the very top of the FBI's 'Most Wanted' list.

Ironically, it was Ng's kleptomania that had brought about the capture in San Francisco of Leonard Lake. Lake had been born in San Francisco on 20 July 1946 into a poor family with a history of mental disorders and alcoholism. Thrown out of the Marines, where he had met Ng, he found work as a grade school teacher and circus showman. He had finally settled in Wisleyville, where no one suspected him of his new occupation — drug dealing — and certainly not with various mystery disappearances in the area. On the contrary, Lake had gained a certain respect in Wisleyville for his voluntary work with old people and as a part-time fireman.

Now at last the file could be closed on a number of missing person reports. Harvey Dubbs, his wife Deborah and their baby son Sean were among the victims dug up from shallow graves. A hitch-hiker who had disappeared was also found; he had been tortured so badly he could be identified only through dental records. Some of the victims had apparently been lured to Lake's death ranch through small ads for photographic models, or for cars or furniture either wanted or for sale. The evil pair had even kidnapped their neighbours.

A particularly sick sequence of one of Lake's more gruesome films shows him torturing and photographing local girl Brenda O'Connor. He even told her he had given her baby away, though the remains of both Brenda and her son Lonnie were later discovered in the grim search.

Not all the victims — one of whom was Lake's own younger brother Donald, an epileptic — died in the dungeon. Some were set free in the woods and then hunted down and shot with rifles. Ng was to testify later that two furniture removal men had been doused with petrol and burned alive.

The painstaking search in Wisleyville had taken a little over a week, by which time the authorities had declared Ng was wanted dead or alive. It was another three weeks, however, before Ng was heard of again. And once again it was theft that had brought about his downfall. He had fled to Canada, where he was spotted stealing food from a Calgary store. Challenged by security staff, he pulled a gun and shot one of them before he was finally overpowered.

A Canadian court sentenced Ng to four and a half years for armed robbery, although it at first refused to agree to extradition proceedings, on the grounds that California still maintained the death penalty. However, after completing part of his sentence, Ng was eventually extradited to the US where he was found guilty of 11 counts of murder and sent to Death Row, from where he has pursued a string of appeals.

HENRI LANDRU

NAME: Henri Desiré Landru

A.K.A.: The 'French Bluebeard'

BORN: 12 April 1869

DIED: Guillotined 25 February 1922

PREFERRED MURDER METHOD: Various followed by burning on stove

NUMBER OF VICTIMS: Charged with 11

NAMES OF VICTIMS: Jeanne Cuchet, André Cuchet, Thérèse Laborde-Line, Miss Guillin, Miss Heon, Anna Collomb, Andrée Babelay, Celestine Buisson, Louise Jaume, Anne Pascal, Maria Marchadier

MURDER LOCALE: Paris and environs

SPAN OF MURDER CAREER: April 1915 to 13 January 1919

DATE OF CONVICTION: November 1921

Landru with a probable victim, Mme Izoré.

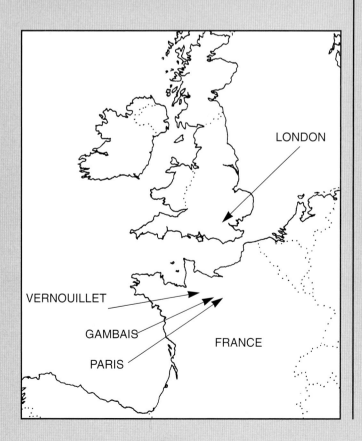

On the battle lines of World War 1 soldiers were cut down in their thousands. There were almost equal numbers of widows and fiancees, grief-stricken, lonely and vulnerable. Paris was full of women like this, desperate to cling to a rock as the terrible tides of war washed around them. It was here that Henri Landru, the 'French Bluebeard' as he became known, found a fertile hunting ground.

113

Landru was dapper, intense and utterly charming and became a magnet for wealthy, middle-aged women. He lured them with small advertisements in newspaper 'lonely hearts' columns.

The man who went on to murder at least 10 women came from humble yet honest beginnings. His father worked as a stoker in a Paris foundry while his mother was a dressmaker. Together they had a daughter but yearned for a son. When Landru was born on 12 April 1869 he was given the name Henri Desiré (meaning much-desired).

It was a hard-working, God-fearing close family unit. Landru's father graduated from the foundry to become a salesman in a bookshop. Little Henri went to a school run by monks where he displayed a sharp mind. In 1888 he left school to work in an architect's office, and three years later fathered a baby girl by a laundry assistant. After completing his military service, Landru married her in 1893.

Landru went on to have three more children with his wife, Marie. But if she had hoped for a respectable family man for a husband in the mould of his father, then she was bitterly disappointed. There were a string of short-lived jobs, most of them peppered with petty crime. His dishonesty became more ambitious down the years and landed him in court on several occasions.

Police reports at the time maintain that he was suffering from diminished responsibility. It was a kindly diagnosis. For Landru was rubbing shoulders with the city's low-life and was as pin-sharp as ever. He numbered pimps, thieves and brawlers among his friends. His existence became increasingly nomadic as the threat of transportation hung over him. His father was so distraught at the wayward behaviour of his son that he hanged himself.

Against this backdrop, Landru advertised for a new wife, writing: 'Widower with two children, aged 43, with comfortable income, affectionate, serious and moving in good society, desires to meet widow of similar status, with a view to matrimony.'

Widow Jeanne Cuchet answered the published plea. She found the advertiser, posing as Raymond Diard, all she had hoped for. He wined and dined her, showered her with flowers and showed a touching interest in the welfare of her 17-year-old son André. Despite dire warnings from her anxious sister, Mme Cuchet gave up her flat and moved with

'Diard' to a house outside Paris in the small town of Vernouillet. When all her wealth and goods were signed over to him, Landru killed her and her son and burned their bodies on the house fire.

In that same year, 1915, there were two other murders at Vernouillet. Landru then moved to at Gambais, where a further seven women were dispatched. Landru was captured on 12 April 1919 after the mayor of Gambais began to probe the mystery resident and his numerous lady friends.

The mayor had been asked by a concerned relative to trace Celestine Buisson who had gone to live at the Villa Ermitage and had never been seen again. Suddenly, the choking smoke that was occasionally emitted from the villa's chimney seemed rather more than just a nuisance. Police found 290 fragments of bones and teeth in the stove as well as clothes and personal possessions around the house. A question mark has long remained on the exact number of his victims.

His trial took place at the Seine-et-Oise Assize Court in November 1921. During interrogations by police, he never admitted his guilt and he continued to maintain his innocence. Nevertheless, he was found guilty and executed by guillotine on 25 February 1922. From his cell, Landru penned a picture and presented it to his defence council. In 1963 the daughter of the attorney had the picture cleaned and there, on the back, appeared a confession written in Landru's own hand.

BOBBY JOE LONG

NAME: Bobby Joe Long

A.K.A.: The 'Classified Ad Rapist'

BORN: 14 October 1953

DIED: On Death Row at Starke Prison, Florida

PREFERRED MURDER METHOD: Strangulation

NUMBER OF VICTIMS: 9

NAMES OF VICTIMS: Include Ngeon Thi Long, Michelle Simms, Virginia Johnson, Kim Swann

MURDER LOCALE: Tampa, Florida

SPAN OF MURDER CAREER: May 1983 to November 1983

DATE OF CONVICTION: 1989

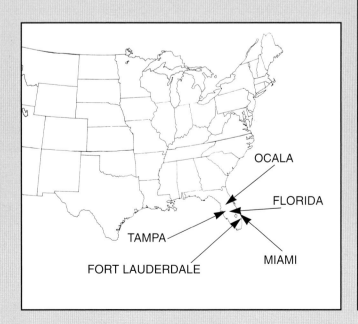

Who knows what goes on in a brain as severely traumatised as that of Bobby Joe Long? A mass rapist and serial killer, he ended up on Florida's Death Row protesting that he was as much a victim as any of the 50 or more women that he raped and the nine that he strangled to death.

The compulsion for sex and the lust to kill both came upon him, he claimed, after a motorcycle crash that fractured his skull and left him semi-conscious for weeks. Even before the motorcycle accident, he had suffered four other severe injuries to his head resulting from falls from horses and bicycles. His problems, however, can be clearly seen to have begun a good deal earlier.

Born in October 1953 in Kenova, West Virginia, Long was a lonely infant. His parents split in 1956 and from that date he and his mother were always on the move as they wandered from town to town, job to job and — worst of all from the small boy's point of view — relationship to relationship. There was always poverty as his mother, although good-looking, was unqualified and able to scrape only a subsistence wage in menial jobs.

So the young Bobby Joe had no stable home, was completely dominated by his mother — and even appeared to be turning into a girl. At the age of 11, he was struck by a congenital illness, a dysfunction of the endocrine system that caused him to grow breasts and made his figure change. A doctor prescribed surgery and more than 6lb of tissue was removed from his chest. The physical problem was solved but throughout his life he continued to experience a proto-menstrual cycle that is said to coincide with the full moon.

115

At the age of 13, he met the girl later was to become his wife. Cindy Jean Guthrie was, in appearance, very like his mother. It may even have been that which attracted him. At any rate, he moved from one woman's dominance to another's. The couple married six months after he had enlisted in the Army to learn an electrician's trade and six months before his fateful motorcycle crash.

Even while still in hospital, Long discovered that sex dominated every waking thought. He fantasised about bedding every girl he met. In addition, he started to become violent at the least annoyance, and every sudden noise seemed like the explosion of a hand grenade. He worked as an X-ray technician, but lost job after job for making advances to the women patients. At one hospital it was discovered that he was making women undress before taking their X-rays.

The compulsion for sex also ruled his home life. He had sex with his wife at least twice a day and masturbated often. In 1976, by now a father of two and going through divorce procedures, he began a succession of rapes that earned him the sobriquet the 'Classified Ad Rapist'. He terrorised the Florida communities of Fort Lauderdale, Miami and Ocala by ringing numbers listed in the classified columns of local papers and making appointments for daytime, when he was most likely to meet unaccompanied housewives.

Apart from this frenzy, he lived a normal life and escaped detection for eight years, even though he was once accused of rape by a vengeful ex-girlfriend. The case went to court but the charges were dropped when he produced witnesses who testified she had specifically invited him to have sex with her. This experience appears to have triggered a bloodlust within Long's warped psyche. As the 'Classified Ad Rapist', he had never been excessively violent to his victims. However, he was shocked by the vindictiveness, as he saw it, of the ex-girlfriend and some part of his brain began to hate women, whom he saw as manipulative.

The first woman he killed was Ngeon Thi Long, a stripper who picked him up in a Tampa bar. He was revolted by her. 'She picked me up,' he said. 'I didn't go after her. She was a whore. She manipulated men and she wanted to manipulate me. Once I had her in the car, I tied her up and raped her.

Then I dumped her body along the highway. Next morning I couldn't believe what I had done. Then I met another girl , and it happened all over again.'

Six more women were to pick Long up in bars, and six more bodies were to be found later along the highway. But the end of the terrifying spree of murder was in sight. As Long said in an interview from his cell on Death Row in Starke, Florida, he wanted to be caught. He knew he could not stop himself, so he made an unconscious decision to help the police. Long raped but did not kill victim number eight. It was to be her testimony that earned him the death sentence.

In November 1983, he saw a 17-year-old girl cycling home from her job on the night shift at a doughnut factory. She was the first of his victims who had not made the first move. He leapt out and knocked her off her bicycle, tied and blindfolded her and put her in his car. He drove around for a while, during which time she confided to him that she had been sexually abused by her stepfather, whom she now had to work to support.

Long drove the girl around for hours, stopping at a bank machine to get cash and at his apartment. On both occasions she was able to peek from behind the blindfold and later gave police exact descriptions of where she had been. Long then raped her and finally released her at the spot he had kidnapped her. He knew deep down that he would be quickly caught.

Yet two days later he was still free to murder his ninth victim. He followed a woman driving a car erratically, guessing she'd be drunk. She pulled over when she realised she was being followed and quickly agreed to get into his car, believing he would return her to her own when she sobered up.

Kim Swann was a big-framed young woman and Long hated her instantly. He attacked her, but she fought back grimly, kicking a hole in his dashboard and screamed without stopping. Long finally overpowered her and undressed her, but even as he looked at her naked body, the raging need for sex had dried up. She woke up again and screamed and this time he strangled her to death. He drove around for a while and dumped her on the outskirts of Tampa. He had not bothered to rape her.

Four days later he was arrested for the rape of the 17-year-old and was sentenced to death.

PEDRO LOPEZ

Even if 31-year-old Pedro Lopez's frightening boast that he had raped and murdered over 300 girls was a twisted exaggeration, he nevertheless well deserved the epithet 'Monster of the Andes'.

NAME: Pedro Armando Lopez

A.K.A.: The 'Monster of the Andes'

BORN: 1949

DIED: Serving life sentence in Ecuador

PREFERRED MURDER METHOD: Strangulation

NUMBER OF VICTIMS: He claims over 300

MURDER LOCALE: Peru, Colombia and Ecuador

SPAN OF MURDER CAREER: 1967-80

DATE OF CONVICTION: 1980

Lopez, the son of a prostitute from a Colombian village, was raped by a man after being abandoned by his mother when he was just eight years old. At 18, he was imprisoned for car theft. While in jail, he killed three of four men who had attacked him.

After his release, Lopez began killing young girls of to the Ayachucos indian tribe in Peru. When he was caught trying to abduct a nine-year-old girl, the indians linked Lopez with the murders and tried to bury him alive. He was rescued by an American missionary who insisted Lopez was handed over to the police. But the authorities simply had him deported, and he continued his killing spree throughout Columbia and Ecuador.

Lopez preferred young girls with 'a certain look of innocence and beauty'. Piecing together information about girls having disappeared from three countries, police at first thought they were on the trail of white slavery. Then, in April 1980, a flash flood near the Andes town of Ambato, in Ecuador, washed away the river bank and exposed the remains of four of the missing girls.

Lopez was arrested in April 1980 when he was spotted leading a young girl by the hand through a market square. At first he denied murder, but a priest managed to coax his sickening secrets from him and passed details to the police.

Lopez then confessed to raping and killing 110 girls in Ecuador, 100 in Columbia and more than 100 in Peru. This total could not be substantiated, but horrified police began to give it credence when, in Ambato alone, they found the remains of 53 girls, all aged between 8 and 12. Other bodies were found buried in concrete at construction sites throughout Ecuador.

It was no wonder that, while in custody, Lopez was segregated in the women's cell of Ambato prison, following threats to castrate him and burn him alive. Prison director Major Victor Lascano said: 'We may never know how many young girls Lopez killed. His estimate of 300 may even be too low.'

Lopez himself simply admitted that he had a lust for killing girls in daylight rather than at night so that he could see their faces clearly. But after confessing to his crimes, he made a telling statement: 'I lost my innocence at the age of eight. So I decided to do the same to as many young girls as I could.'

Found guilty of multiple murders, Lopez was sentenced to life imprisonment. Had he been tried in Columbia, he would have been executed by firing squad.

HENRY LEE LUCAS

NAME: Henry Lee Lucas

ACCOMPLICE: Ottis Toole

BORN: 23 August 1936

DIED: On Death Row in Huntsville Prison, Texas

PREFERRED MURDER METHOD: Various

NUMBER OF VICTIMS: At least 150; he has claimed between 360 and 600

MURDER LOCALE: All over the USA

SPAN OF MURDER CAREER: 1960-83

DATE OF CONVICTION: Arrested 1983

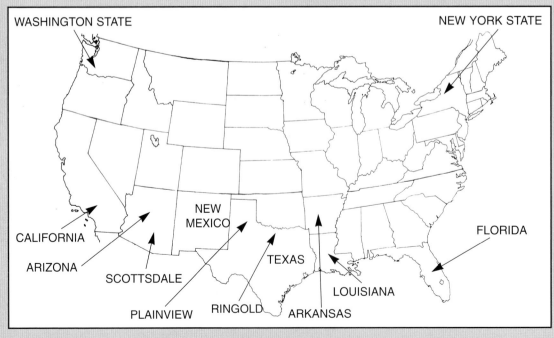

It began with the discovery of an empty purse. Two birdwatchers had come across it while strolling along a riverbank at Stoneburg, Texas, in October 1982. Inside was an ID card in the name of Kate Rich, an 80-year-old widow who lived 10 miles away in Ringgold. Police knew her house had recently burned down but believed she was away staying with relatives.

Fresh checks failed to uncover the old lady's whereabouts but forensic examination of the ashes of her home failed to reveal any sign of human remains. The Texas Rangers were called in and house-to-house inquiries elicited the interesting fact that a middle-aged vagrant, Henry Lucas, and his young woman had rented a trailer-home in Ringgold that summer — and that the man had done a few odd jobs for Mrs Rich.

Detectives tracked Lucas to his squalid hut near Stoneburg, dubbed the 'Chicken Shack' by locals. With his tatty clothes, straggly hair, scruffy beard and glass eye, he looked like the baddie from some poorly-made horror B-movie. Yet when questioned he seemed cool enough. He admitted carrying out odd jobs for Mrs Rich. He had teamed up for the summer with a girl drifter named Becky but she had become homesick and left him.

Police went away unconvinced. They checked him out further by interviewing each one of Stoneburg's 52 residents. To a man and woman, they all had a good word for the tatty tramp. Apparently he had an excellent reputation as a handyman. However, a check on Lucas's record revealed a very different picture from the harmless 'gentleman of the road' they had been told about.

As a child, Henry Lucas had been severely beaten and abused by his mother, a Chippewa Indian who earned her living as a prostitute. The woman had frozen his crippled father to death by turning him out of the house in the middle of winter. And she had once beaten the young Henry so badly that he had ended up with brain damage. It got worse. In 1960, at the age of 23, Lucas had taken revenge on his mother by raping her and stabbing her to death. A judge gave him 40 years and he was taken into a mental institution. Released briefly on parole in 1970, he served another four years after he was caught for an attempted rape and kidnapping.

Armed with this disturbing background, Texas Ranger Phil Ryan returned to the Chicken Shack. He questioned Lucas about a couple of rings the vagrant had been hawking around. Again Lucas

Sheriff Bill Conway points to the spot where Kate Rich had been buried.

stayed cool, claiming he had been given the rings by Becky, who had been worried about getting mugged.

The Ranger noticed a newly-packed suitcase and asked Lucas where he was going. 'Dunno,' he replied. 'I just been in one place too long.'

Phil Ryan demanded to look inside, and Lucas reluctantly agreed. Hidden beneath some clothes, Ryan found a lethal, razor-sharp two-foot dagger. 'It's for self-defence,' Lucas assured him. 'There's a lot of mean people out there.' The detective booked him for concealing an illegal weapon and marched him down to Montague County Gaol for more questioning.

Ryan's team were ready for a long and exhaustive interrogation session. So they were staggered when Lucas sneered: 'You guys aren't interested in that dagger. What you really want to know is about Kate Rich and my wife Becky. I'll tell you one thing. You guys are up a creek without a paddle. You ain't ever going to know what happened to them unless I tell you.'

And then out it came . . . a catalogue of sex-murders over 13 bloody years.

Lucas told dozens of stories of torture, rape and mutilation. Some were carried out by him alone, some with his bisexual lover Ottis Toole (Becky's uncle) who had a particular preference for children. He told how the killing started before the stabbing of his mother when, at the tender age of 15, he killed a 17-year-old girl because she refused to have sex. He revealed how the orgy of death continued the day he was first released on parole, when his victim was a woman who had refused his advances. 'I told them (the prison psychiatrists) not to let me loose,' he said. 'I told them I would do it again. They wouldn't listen.'

Detectives considered the whole confession could be an act of fantasy — until Lucas got tired of what he called 'mind games'. He took them back to the Chicken Shack and showed them the stove in which lay the charred remains of Kate Rich. In an isolated field not far away, he pointed out chunks of rotting flesh. This, he claimed, was where he had scattered the dismembered body of his erstwhile lover Becky.

Why had he killed them? Lucas offered only vague ramblings. He had wanted money from

A smirking Lucas returns to Montague Jail, Texas following a court appearance.

Kate Rich. As for Becky, he was mad that she wanted to leave after he'd looked after her.

When Lucas appeared in court, the judge began to reprimand him for his smirking expression. Murder, he was told, was no laughing matter. 'I know that your honour,' Lucas replied. 'I've done it a hundred times.'

The judge paused, scarcely believing what he had heard. 'What did you say?' he asked.

'I've killed about a hundred women,' Lucas told him. 'Maybe it's more than that if I get to counting. I know it's not normal for a person to kill a woman because she won't have sex with him but that's what I've done, lots of times.'

The judge summoned the prosecutor and asked

whether he really believed the defendant was mentally fit to stand trial. Lucas quickly interrupted: 'Judge, if you think I'm crazy, there's a hundred or more women out there who says different. Yes, I'd say I'm mentally competent — and I'm guilty.

Pictured with Texas Rangers, Henry Lee Lucas is accompanied to the site of an unsolved killing. He admitted to so many killings that it was difficult to tell what was fact and what was fantasy.

121

I'd just like to get this damn thing over with once and for all.'

Soon afterwards, Lucas began taking detectives through the crimes he claimed were down to him — as well as incriminating as his accomplice Ottis Toole, who was serving a 20-year sentence in Florida for arson. One officer accused Lucas of inventing his confession in an attempt to get off with an insanity plea. Lucas turned on him: 'You think I'm lying? OK, you ask them down at Plainview if they found a body without a head. And then you ask them out in Scottsdale, Arizona, if they found a head and no body.'

Ten months later campers near Scottsdale, Arizona, found a skull in the desert. It was matched to a torso found outside Plainview in December 1981.

Often Lucas could produce irrefutable evidence of his involvement. He told how he had once scattered pillow feathers over the body of a 76-year-old lady he had bludgeoned to death in Jacksonville. This information had never been released to the media. It was a detail only the murderer could have known.

Out came more than 100 names; names of women Lucas claimed to have killed the length and breadth of the nation. New York State, Washington State, California, Florida — all featured on his list. Later the total would rise to 360, some of which he later retracted, giving rise to claims that the whole confession was a sham.

But while several of the murders clearly could not have been down to Lucas (because eye-witness accounts placed him in other parts of the country at the crucial times) a majority undoubtedly were. In too many cases, his recollections enabled the bodies of missing persons to be recovered. Most had been raped. He also claimed to have had sex with some of them after death.

By the time he started his first jail sentence of 75 years, Lucas had settled on a figure of 157 murders. He had been sentenced for only five of them but a further 21 murder charges were pending in Texas, Arkansas, Louisiana, New Mexico and Texas. As attorneys from those states queued to bring him to court, Lucas languished on Death Row in Texas.

Asked to explain his actions, Henry Lee Lucas

Lucas being led into the Georgetown Courthouse.

gave Americans perhaps their most chilling-ever insight into the twisted mind of the serial killer:

'I was bitter at the world. I had nothing but pure hatred. Killing someone is just like walking outdoors. If I wanted a victim I'd just go out and get one.'

MICHAEL LUPO

Michael Lupo's reign as a serial killer of homosexuals in the mid-1980s sent tremors through of London society.

NAME: Michael Lupo

BORN: 1953

DIED: Serving life sentence

PREFERRED MURDER METHOD: Strangulation

NUMBER OF VICTIMS: 4

NAMES OF VICTIMS: Tony Connolly, James Burns, Damien McClusky, unidentified man

MURDER LOCALE: London

SPAN OF MURDER CAREER: March-April 1986

DATE OF CONVICTION: July 1987

killer, 24-year-old Tony Connelly, was found in a railway workman's hut at Brixton on 6 April 1986. He had been strangled with his own scarf. A month later Lupo was arrested and charged with a total of four murders and two attempted murders. He pleaded guilty and in July 1987 was sentenced to life imprisonment.

First in line was the gay community, aware that its people were targets. Later, after Lupo was caught, it emerged that his job as a fashion shop manager and make-up artist had brought him close to a number of well-known high-society names. Now it was their turn to worry. Would they be dragged into a grubby Old Bailey trial? The fears were largely groundless but for months Fleet Street was buzzing with gossip.

Lupo was a gay killer who claimed to have had 4,000 homosexual lovers. He indulged in sado-masochistic activities of the weirdest kind — including slitting the scrotum of his partners so that he could massage their testicles. The victim that confirmed to police the existence of a serial

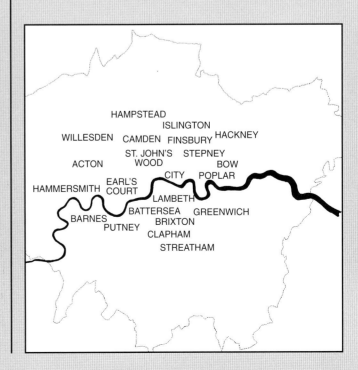

CHARLES MANSON

NAME: Charles Manson

A.K.A.: Killings performed by the 'Manson Family'

BORN: 1934

DIED: Serving life sentence in San Quentin

PREFERRED MURDER METHOD: None

NUMBER OF VICTIMS: 7 (Manson himself claims to have killed over 35)

NAMES OF VICTIMS: Steven Parent, Abigail Folger, Voytek Frykowski, Jay Sebring, Sharon Tate, Leno LaBianca, Rosemary LaBianca

MURDER LOCALE: California

SPAN OF MURDER CAREER: 1969

DATE OF CONVICTION: 29 March 1971

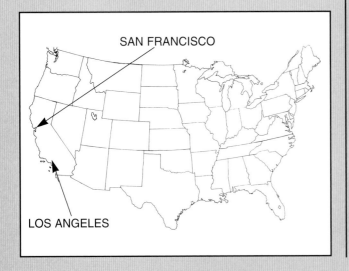

Charles Manson was a serial killer who caused others to do his dirty work — his twisted 'Devil's Children' sect.

Manson, the self-styled Messiah, was born illegitimately to a hardened prostitute in Cincinnati, Ohio, in 1934. He 'graduated' from foster homes to juvenile detention centres. In one vicious act revealing his latent, twisted tendencies, he grabbed a boy from behind and held a razor blade to his throat as he carried out a violent rape. Manson's file was marked 'Dangerous' and 'Not to be trusted' and he was transferred to the Federal Reformatory in Virginia.

Manson's sexual preferences veered towards other men. But shortly after his release on parole in 1954, he married a 17-year-old waitress. They had a son but, after travelling to California in a stolen car, Manson again ended up in jail and his wife left him. One last attempt at 'normality' came when Manson remarried between prison stays and sired another son, but that marriage also collapsed.

Manson was now firmly set on a life of crime and imprisonment. So institutionalised was he that, when parole came up, he asked to remain within the prison. His request was refused.

Back on the road, the criminal drifter latched onto the new era of 1960s music and became obsessed with the Beatles. It was no surprise that Manson gravitated towards the flower-power cult, with its heart in San Francisco. With a guitar on his back and drugs becoming a bigger part of his life, Manson had found his niche. His strange magnetism drew drop-outs and drug addicts to him. Manson discovered he had his own strange following — and a deadly power over a growing rag-taggle of young women who adored Manson, even giving up their stable, often middle-class lives to be with him.

By 1969 the Manson sect was already taking root, settling into Spahn Ranch outside Los

ABOVE: Sharon Tate.

BELOW: Victims Voytek Frykowski, Sharon Tate, Steven Parent, Jay Sebring, Abigail Folger.

Angeles. This assortment of the lost, the weak and the potentially evil called themselves the 'Family'. Attracting wayward youngsters, bikers and small-time criminals, Manson gathered a hard core of 25 devotees with over 60 other 'associates'.

One day, a drug-fuddled Manson announced that now was the time for 'Helter Skelter', Manson's ultimate mission, named after the title of a Beatles album track. He told of Armageddon, which he would launch through a race and class war which only his supporters would be certain of surviving. They would change the world by striking out at the white establishment, he told them. They would kill. Thus the first stage of 'Helter Skelter' got underway one fateful day in 1969.

Shortly before dawn on 9 August, four of Manson's disciples — Atkins, Krenwinkel, Kasabian and Watson — entered the grounds of a mansion rented by film producer Roman Polanski and his beautiful actress wife Sharon Tate. Polanski was away filming but Tate had invited a group of friends round for a party.

The living room in which Sharon Tate and Jay Sebring died on 9 August 1969.

Susan Atkins and Charles Manson arrive in court, Los Angeles 17 April 1970.

The gathering of Hollywood glitterati had just minutes to live. With strange war cries, the knife-wielding killers set upon them and, in a short explosion of mind-numbing violence, five people were butchered. The scene these angels of death left behind them turned the stomachs of even the most hardened of Los Angeles cops.

They found the body of Steven Parent, the 18-year-old guest of the caretaker, slumped in his car in the driveway. Parent had met the raiders as he drove from the house and had been shot. Next was the body of Abigail Folger on the lawn. She had been cut to pieces as she tried to flee.

The other bodies were found in the house. Polish film director Voytek Frykowski had been battered with a club by Watson — all the while whispering: 'I am the devil come to do the devil's work.' He had then been finished off by Atkins, who stabbed him six times with a knife. Hollywood hair stylist Jay Sebring had been stabbed then finished off with a gunshot.

But the most sickening sight in this drug-crazed

Charles Manson as he appeared before a Parole Board, 1986. Parole was refused!

Charles Manson at his trial, the duration of which can be judged by the growth of his hair!

orgy was the body of Sharon Tate. The 26-year-old actress begged to be spared for the sake of the child she was carrying. Her pleas for mercy were greeted with derision. She suffered 16 stab wounds. Her unborn baby died along with her.

A nylon rope had then been knotted around the dead woman's neck, slung over a ceiling beam and the other end tied around the hooded head of Sebring. The word 'Pigs' was scrawled in blood on the door of the mansion.

Even after this, as America reeled in the hor-

ror of it all, Charles Manson felt he had not achieved his aim: a macabre belief that such murders would spark off a race war. There was more bloody work to be done. And this time Manson wanted to be in on the action himself.

The night after the Polanski mansion slaughter, Manson, accompanied by Watson, Krenwinkel and Leslie Van Houten, broke into the home of Leno and Rosemary LaBianca, owners of a small supermarket chain. Manson tied up the couple, then left them to the mercy of his

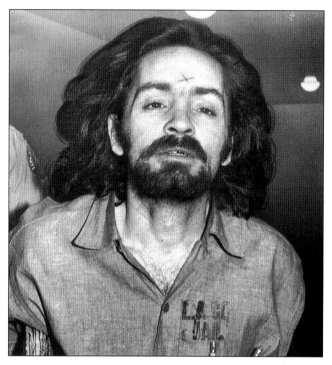

LEFT and ABOVE: More views of Manson during the protracted trial.

BELOW: Heavy security after Manson has been found guity of first degree murder on seven counts.

three loyal cult slaves. A sword, knives and forks were used in the slaying. Police found a fork protruding from Leno LaBianca's body — and 'War' carved in his stomach.

Ludicrously, Los Angeles police did not initially connect the raids on the Tate and LaBianca mansions. It was Susan Atkins, one of Manson's strongest devotees, who was to bring the evil group to justice. She had been picked up in connection with the murder of drug dealer Gary Hinman, killed 10 days before the mass murders. His blood had been used to scrawl a message on a nearby wall. It read: 'Political Piggy'.

Atkins, still revelling in her involvement with headline-making butchery, could not keep her mouth shut. She bragged about her role, sickening cellmates with her claims of drinking Sharon Tate's blood. She boasted:

'It felt so good the first time I stabbed her. When she screamed at me, it did something to me,

Manson raises an eyebrow for the camera during a prison interview.

sent a rush through me, and I stabbed her again. I just kept stabbing her until she stopped screaming. It was like a sexual release, especially when you see the blood. It's better than a climax.'

The Manson tribe was rounded up and the incredible story flashed around the world. Charles Manson, the short, scraggy ex-con who had spent more than half his life behind bars, was charged with nine murders in all (the Tate and LaBianca massacres and two other slayings) but was suspected of orchestrating as many as 25 more from his desert ranch.

At his trial, Manson spoke of his weird band of disciples: 'These children who come at you with knives, they are your children. I didn't teach them. You did. You made your children what they are . . . I am only what lives inside each and every one of you.'

On 29 March 1971, after what was then the longest (nine months) criminal trial in American history, the jury returned guilty verdicts on all counts against the Manson gang. They were sentenced to death but this was commuted to life imprisonment in 1972 when California's death penalty was banned.

Another Manson hair style.

PETER MANUEL

NAME: Peter Thomas Anthony Manuel

BORN: 15 March 1927

DIED: Hanged at Barlinnie on 11 July 1958

PREFERRED MURDER METHOD: Various

NUMBER OF VICTIMS: 9

NAMES OF VICTIMS: Annie Knielands, Marion Watt, Vivienne Watt, Margaret Brown, Isabelle Cooke, Peter Smart, Doris Smart, Michael Smart, Sydney Dunn

MURDER LOCALE: Lowland Scotland and Newcastle-on-Tyne

SPAN OF MURDER CAREER: 2 September to 1 January 1958

DATE OF CONVICTION: 26 May 1958

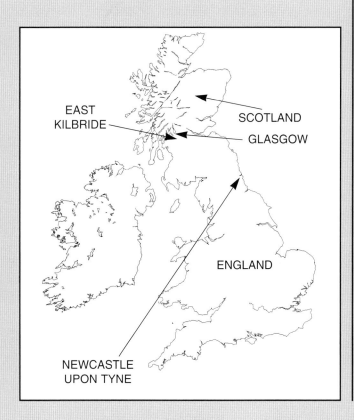

If it could be said of anyone that he was destined to end his days on the scaffold, that man was Peter Manuel. A thug and a troublemaker from the age of 11, he spent most of his short life in approved schools, Borstal institutions and jails before taking his final walk to the gallows at the age of 31.

Manuel was born on 15 March 1927 in Manhattan to Scottish parents who had emigrated to New York in search of a better life. It seems they failed to find it, for the family returned to Scotland after five years and moved to Coventry in 1937. A year later, the 11-year-old Manuel was in trouble with the law after being caught breaking into shops. A spell in an approved school helped make him a hardened little villain ready to turn to violence to obtain either money or sexual satisfaction.

In 1941, after the family home had been destroyed in a German bombing raid, the family went back to Glasgow. Manuel was unable to join them until 1946 because he was in Borstal, where he had been sent for assaulting a woman with a hammer in 1942 at the tender age of 15.

Short but strong, dark-haired Manuel had piercing eyes and was a convincing liar. Within weeks of his return to Scotland, he was arrested for housebreaking. While awaiting trial, he raped an expectant mother and indecently assaulted two other women. At his subsequent trial, in which he conducted his own defence, he was sentenced to eight years in jail. He was released in 1953.

Manuel began courting a girl, and even set the wedding date, for 30 July 1955. When his fiancée discovered his criminal background, however, she dropped him. The end of the affair obviously weighed heavily on the young man's psyche because, on what would have been his wedding night, he attacked a woman in a field. Her screams alerted neighbours who called the police, but as they searched the area he managed to hide, keeping the woman quiet at knife point. Eventually the woman talked him into letting her go, after which he was arrested and charged with sexual assault. Oddly, he was acquitted.

Six months later the brutal young thug had graduated to murder. His first victim was 17-year-old Annie Knielands. He was alleged to have killed her on 2 January 1956 and dumped her body on a golf course at East Kilbride, near Glasgow. She had been badly beaten around the head and, although not raped or sexually molested, semen stains on her clothing showed he had obtained sexual gratification through the act of murder.

Two days later, a horrified golfer came across the corpse and ran to tell the police. On his way he met a group of people to whom he gabbled out his story. Ironically, one of the group was Manuel who, as a result, was interviewed by police. Detectives were immediately suspicious of him because his face was freshly scratched. When his home was searched, items of clothing were missing that he had been known to have worn recently. However, his father gave him an alibi, swearing that he had been indoors on the evening in question.

In March that year, police received a tip-off that a burglary was to take place and Manuel was caught in the act. While still awaiting trial in September, there were burglaries on successive nights, both of which the police linked to Manuel. On the morning after the second break-in, a domestic help discovered three bodies in a neighbouring house. They were Mrs Marion Watt, her daughter Vivienne and her sister Margaret Brown. All had been shot at close range, the older ladies dying in their beds.

Manuel was the prime suspect. He was interviewed but no incriminating evidence was found. Instead, police attention switched to the murdered woman's husband, William Watt, who had been on a fishing trip in Argyll at the time of the slayings. Detectives nevertheless deemed it possible that he had had time to return home, kill the women and get back to Argyll. He was charged and held in Barlinnie prison — where Manuel was also sent to serve 18 months for the first attempted burglary.

Manuel wrote to Mr Watt's solicitor asking him to represent him in an appeal against the burglary sentence. He hinted that in return he could help disprove the case against Watt, and gave details that convinced the solicitor that Manuel must have been present at the murders. After 67 days in custody, the innocent Mr Watt was released. Manuel did nothing to help him, merely offering the name of a known criminal who was quickly eliminated from inquiries.

Manuel came out of jail in November 1957. Less than a month later, another 17-year-old girl, Isabelle Cooke, was reported missing. A shoe and a handbag were discovered in a disused colliery shaft. But even while police searched for the girl, another three bodies were found in a house just 10 minutes' walk away from Manuel's home.

Isabelle Cooke,17, disappeared on 28 December 1957. Her body was not found.

Margaret Brown (above), was staying at her sister Marion Watts' house when Manuel broke in . . .

. . . she died with her sister Marion (above) and her daughter,16-year-old Vivienne Brown.

Peter Smart, an engineering manager, had been shot through the head at close range, as had his wife Doris and their 11-year-old son Michael. They had been killed on New Year's Day 1958 and between then and their discovery on 6 January, neighbours had reported that lights in their home had been switched on and off, suggesting either that the killer had stayed at the house or else had returned to the scene of the crime. On 4 January, another local couple had disturbed an intruder in their bedroom but he had fled when the husband pretended he had a gun.

Peter Manuel was arrested on 14 January and charged with the murder of the Smarts and the recent, thwarted break-in. His father was charged with receiving stolen goods — a camera and gloves that had been taken from a house near Isabelle Cooke's home. In an misguided attempt to shield his son, Manuel senior claimed to have bought them at a nearby market.

Now, possibly for the first time in his evil life, Manuel began to show remorse. He offered a full confession in return for his father's release. He led police to the spot where he had buried Isabelle Cooke and showed them where he had thrown two guns into a river.

Manuel's trial on eight counts of murder began on 12 May 1958. Ten days later he sacked his counsel and conducted his own defence. In it, he renounced his confession and accused William Watt of murdering his own family — forcing the unfortunate man to face cross-examination by the killer of his loved ones.

Manuel was found guilty of seven murders, as there was insufficient evidence in the case of Annie Knielands. After the case, it was also ascertained that the monster had killed a taxi driver, Sydney Dunn, shot the previous December in Newcastle upon Tyne, where Manuel had gone for a job interview.

On 11 July 1958 Peter Manuel took his final, short walk to keep his date with the hangman.

THE 'MONSTER OF FLORENCE'

NAME: Unknown

PREFERRED MURDER METHOD: Shooting couples seated in parked cars

NUMBER OF VICTIMS: 16 (?)

MURDER LOCALE: Florence

SPAN OF MURDER CAREER: August 1968 to 8 September 1985

CONVICTION: Still at large

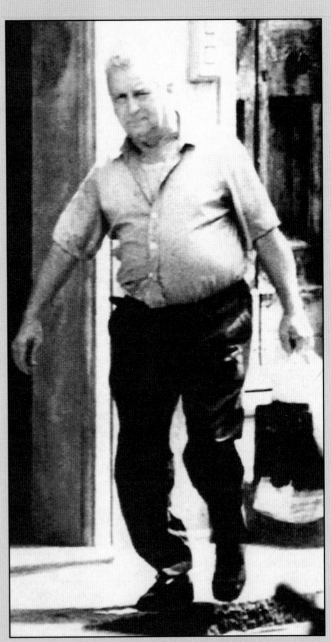

Pietro Pacciani, accused of being the 'Monster of Florence', but freed in 1996 after a judicial review.

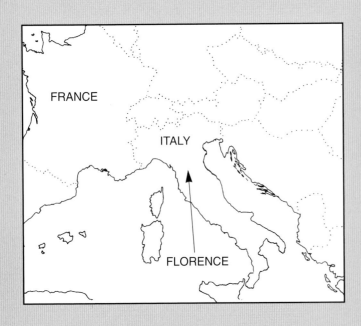

In 1968 Barbara Locci and her lover Antonio Io Bianci were shot dead as they lay together on the front seat of their car. The woman's cuckolded husband was arrested and convicted of the murder.

It was the first blunder in a catalogue of errors in the law's hunt for the so-called 'Monster of Florence'. For in 1974 Signor Locci's innocence was at last proved and he was released — as a series of similar, merciless killings of courting couples began occurring in the picturesque Tuscany.

The next victims were another courting couple killed in their car. Forensic tests showed the same .22 calibre Beretta pistol had been used as in the first murder. The female victim had been mutilated. The following year two more were killed, and in 1983 a homosexual German pair were murdered, probably in error. Neither was mutilated.

The 'Monster of Florence' did not strike again until 1981. His female victim in June that year was stabbed 300 times. Four months later, another woman was murdered and mutilated.

The murderer was now killing every year, and all the murders bore the same hallmarks. The men were shot through the driver's window. The same gun was then turned on the girl, whose body was dragged from the vehicle and mutilated with a scalpel. Most of the women, although not all, had their left breast hacked off. All 67 bullets fired in the 16 murders were from the same gun and bore the letter 'H'.

The monster's last victims were a French couple slaughtered in their tent in 1985. An envelope sent to Florence police contained part of the woman's genitalia.

In all, five men were wrongly imprisoned during the hunt for the perverted serial killer and another man named by gossips as the killer cut his own throat. Three were released when more killings occurred while they were behind bars. The fourth was released by order of a judge because there was no evidence against him. And the fifth is still the subject of fierce debate.

His name is Pietro Pacciani, a peasant farmer who in 1951 was charged with secretly tailing his 16-year-old fiancée and another man into the woods. During the course of her seduction, the girl's left breast became exposed — and the stalker could stand the sight no longer. He stormed up to the couple, stabbed the man 19 times and forced the terrified girl to make love next to the corpse. Pacciani served 13 years in jail for the killing.

It should have been the end of the episode. In fact it was the start of a horror story that paralysed the Tuscan countryside for years as the 'Monster of Florence' held the region in bloody terror. As is common in such cases scores of anonymous notes were sent to police headquarters and the name Pietro Pacciani began cropping up continuously. Detectives speculated that, embittered by the betrayal of his girlfriend, Pacciani had sought to avenge himself on other couples.

A profile of the unsavoury farmer — who had again been jailed briefly in 1987 for the molestation of his two daughters — was fed into a computer along with the names of more than 100,000 people who had had the opportunity of carrying out the crime. The name-crunching machine whittled it down to one: Pacciani.

Police were convinced the monster had been snared but they had only the flimsiest of evidence. Pacciani's smallholding was taken apart minutely but nothing was found — until a bullet was spotted in a freshly excavated hole. It conveniently matched the other 67 bullets fired in the 16 murders.

It seemed too good to be true. Had a wily policeman planted the evidence? However, even in the absence of the murder weapon, a jury was convinced of Pacciani's guilt. After a six-month trial in 1994, he was jailed for life. However a judicial review later tested the evidence and found it wanting — and in 1996 Pacciani again walked free.

HERMAN MUDGETT

NAME: Hermann Webster Mudgett

A.K.A.: Dr H. H. Holmes

BORN: May 1860

DIED: Hanged on 27 May 1896 at Moyamensing Prison, Philadelphia

PREFERRED MURDER METHOD: Various

NUMBER OF VICTIMS: Admitted to 27 but could have reached 200

MURDER LOCALE: Chicago

SPAN OF MURDER CAREER: 1891-94

DATE OF CONVICTION: 30 November 1895

Contemporary portrayal of how Herman Mudgett put paid to his female victims deep within his Chicago 'Torture Castle'.

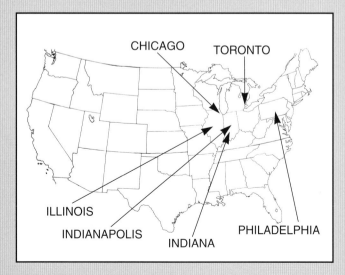

To his neighbours, he was Dr H. H. Holmes, a smart, respectable, even handsome young man with a certificate proving him to be a graduate of the prestigious Ann Arbor Medical School in Michigan. So impressive was his qualification that nobody thought to run a routine check on him. If they had once done so, they would have discovered that Dr Holmes was an invention. In reality, he was Herman Webster Mudgett — destined to become one of the most notorious serial killers in American history.

Nobody knows where Herman Mudgett came from. He arrived in Chicago in the 1880s with two wives and no money but with a mission: to get rich quick. He realised that, in this city preparing to host the prestigious World's Fair, he had found an ideal environment for his criminal ambitions. Chicago was bustling with new trade, commerce, wealth and expectation. He found eager young women, keen to make their names, find fame, fortune and fine husbands in the wake of the fair. Since he had charm, style, wit and a way about him that women found irresistible, Mudgett was ever ready to 'help' them — more often than not to their ultimate cost.

Mudgett also discovered the other side of Chicago: a city which attracted the down side of newly-found prosperity. Chicago contained an army of thieves, ruffians, swindlers and rum-runners; ghettos beset by racketeers; gangs eking their evil way into hitherto respectable neighbourhoods; small-time chisellers carving crafty fortunes before making a swift exit. Mudgett had found his twisted, spiritual home.

Dapper, moustachioed Mudgett quickly and easily found a job in the boom city as a prescription clerk at a drug store on the junction of 63rd and South Wallace Streets in a conurbation known as Englewood. His employer at the pharmacy was a widow called Mrs E. S. Holton, who found him wise, charming, courteous and forever helpful to her many customers. Indeed, business had never flourished so much before 'Dr Holmes' arrived. Mrs Holton, clearly delighted with her learned employee, took a back seat in the business.

No one noticed when, after only a few months, Mrs Holton and her young daughter were no longer seen in the drug store. Mudgett, in his guise as Holmes, told those very few customers who were interested that his former boss and her child had moved to California after selling him the controlling interest in the shop. Mrs Holton and her daughter were never seen again.

Mudgett had what he had wanted for a long time: a base upon which to build an empire he had decided was rightfully his. As the drug store continued to prosper, the 'good doctor' cast his eyes on a huge, double-plot of land across the road at 701 and 703 Sixty-third Street. It was to be the site of what later became known infamously as Holmes Castle.

To finance this enormous purchase of land and the three-storey property built on the site, Mudgett launched a series of daredevil scams, many of which, astoundingly, paid off. He marketed a 'sure-fire cure for alcoholism' at $50 a bottle. He sold ordinary tap-water as an all-purpose 'miracle cure'. And, in his most audacious, money-making wheeze, he 'invented' a device for turning water into domestic gas that almost won him a $25,000 contract from Chicago's Gas Company.

Holmes Castle was speedily erected, via a series of elaborate frauds, bogus deeds and false promises to builders. This edifice of evil contained about 100 rooms of various sizes, with a series of false partitions, staircases leading nowhere, long, dark corridors, trap-doors and secret passageways.

By 1888, Mudgett, aged 28, had completed his 'command centre', the centre of his empire of bent deals, from where, as Dr Holmes, he travelled across the United States carrying out crime after crime. Then a single act of greed prefaced his downfall.

Mudgett befriended a small-time Philadelphia hoodlum, Benjamin Pitezel, and hatched a plot to fake the latter's death by murdering a vagrant, and then cash-in on a huge insurance policy in Pitezel's name. But when a body was found in Callowhill

Street, Philadelphia, on 3 September 1894, it was not that of a vagrant but of Pitezel himself — murdered by his partner-in-crime. Mudgett almost got away with it, but an eagle-eyed insurance operator cast doubt upon Pitezel's death and alerted police in Philadelphia, who in turn contacted their already-suspicious counterparts in Chicago.

Detectives raided Holmes Castle. And what they found defied belief. Over the years, a string of young women had been lured to Holmes Castle with the promise of jobs, working on sundry spurious projects masterminded by their boss. Few of them, it appeared, had ever left.

In virtually all rooms, there were gas pipes with fake valves, so that 'guests' had no way of stopping the poison fumes which eventually took their lives. In the evil doctor's huge bed-chamber was an electric bell which rang whenever a door was opened in the chilling, labyrinthian mansion. In his office was a giant, six-foot wide stove, in the grate of which lay part of a bone and a human rib.

The basement hid the grizzliest murder secrets of all. Scattered or buried everywhere were human bones, among them the ribs and pelvis of a 14-year old child. A hooped barrel was found containing acid, along with a surgical table on which lay knives. Underneath the table were several women's skeletons; one macabre theory was that Mudgett first acid-burned off the flesh of his victims then sold the skeletons for medical research.

A nearby storeroom revealed a blood-spattered noose, beneath which were two brick vaults filled with quicklime. Also in the basement was a medieval-style torture rack on which, it was alleged, Mudgett tested his sick belief that a human body could be stretched to twice its normal length.

A contemporary report of the findings within Mudgett's 'castle' reads: 'The second floor contained 35 rooms. Half a dozen were fitted up as ordinary sleeping chambers and there were indications that they had been occupied by various women who worked for the monster, or to whom he had made love while waiting to kill them.

'Other rooms were without windows and could be made airtight by closing the doors. One was completely filled by a huge safe, almost large enough for a bank vault, into which a gas pipe had been introduced. Another was lined with sheet iron covered by asbestos and showed traces of fire. Some had been sound-proofed while others had extremely low ceilings and trapdoors in the floors from which ladders led to smaller rooms beneath.

'In all of the rooms were gas pipes with cut-off valves. But the valves were fakes. The flow of gas was actually controlled by a series of cut-offs concealed in the closet of Holmes' bedrooms. Apparently, one of his favourite methods of murder was to lock a victim in one of the rooms and then turn on the gas. Police believed that in the asbestos-lined chamber he had devised a means of introducing fire, so that the gas pipe became a terrible blow-torch from which there was no escape.'

Although no final count could ever have been made, for much of the evidence had long since been disposed of, police estimated that Mudgett murdered no fewer than 150 people. In addition, the bogus doctor killed at least two of the three wives he led to the altar, their deaths following a torture routine the fiend took to his grave.

Even at his trial, Mudgett insisted on being called Holmes, the alter-ego he had adopted to staggering financial success and had used to charm then slay countless victims. In late October 1895 he stood before a jury in Philadelphia, after a row between police there and in Chicago over who should try him first. After a hearing lasting five days, the jury of 12 men returned a verdict of guilty of the murder of Benjamin Pitezel.

It was not until six months later that Mudgett signed a death-cell confession to 27 further murders and six attempted murders in Chicago, Indianapolis and Toronto. A wheeler-dealer to the end, he actually sold his confession for $10,000 to newspaper tycoon William Randolph Hearst.

It was a sum Mudgett would never receive. On the morning of 7 May 1896 he was led along Death Row by two warders at the Philadelphia County Prison. To the very end, the liar, cheat, conman — and possibly the worst serial killer the world has ever known — refused to acknowledge his own name. 'Ready, Dr Holmes?' the hooded hangman asked him.

'Yes,' Mudgett replied to his executioner, adding the instruction: 'Don't bungle.' His instruction was not followed as he would have wished: Mudgett took an agonising 15 minutes to die on the gallows.

HERBERT MULLIN

NAME: Herbert William Mullin

BORN: 18 April 1947

DIED: Life imprisonment

PREFERRED MURDER METHOD: Various

NUMBER OF VICTIMS: 13

NAMES OF VICTIMS: Lawrence White, Mary Guilfoyle, Father Henri Tomi, James Gianera, Joan Gianera, Kathy Francis, Daemon Francis, David Hughes, David Oliker, Robert Spector, Brian Card, Mark Dreibelbis, Fred Perez

MURDER LOCALE: Santa Cruz

SPAN OF MURDER CAREER: 13 October 1972 to 13 February 1973

DATE OF CONVICTION: July 1973

Herbert Mullin seemed a perfectly normal American male, brought up in a strict Roman Catholic household, and voted 'most likely to achieve' by his fellow high school classmates. At 17, he was engaged. Life promised a golden future for the boy from Felton, California.

Then came the death of his friend Dean Richardson, killed in a road accident in 1965. Mullin set up a shrine to him in his bedroom — and began to fear that he may be homosexual. His fiancée broke off the engagement and Mullin became even stranger. He gradually drifted into a private world of his own making and became hooked on hallucinogenic drugs. He was a classic paranoid schizophrenic.

In 1972 the voices began. Mullin believed that Satan was addressing him. This was his excuse for murdering a tramp whom he hit over the head with a baseball bat in October 1972. His second victim was a girl student, whose body he cut open and whose innards were found strewn on the ground. He confessed these murders to a priest but later stabbed him to death. The slayings continued, Mullin randomly picking his victims.

On 13 February 1973 Mullin once more heard the voices and shot dead his last victim, an elderly man. Hearing the gunshot, a neighbour looked out of his window and wrote down Mullin's car registration number. When arrested, he confessed to 13 murders, all carried out in the Santa Cruz mountain country, and in July 1973 he was sentenced to life imprisonment.

EARLE NELSON

NAME: Earle Leonard Nelson

A.K.A.: The 'Gorilla Murderer'; the 'Dark Strangler'

BORN: 1897

DIED: Hanged on13 January 1928 in Winnipeg Prison

PREFERRED MURDER METHOD: Various

NUMBER OF VICTIMS: 22

NAMES OF VICTIMS: Clara Newman, Laura Beale, Lillian St Mary, Anna Russell, Mary Nesbit, Beatrice Withers, Virginia Grant, Mable Fluke, Blanche Myers, Wilhelmina Edmunds, Florence Monks, Elizabeth Beard, Bonnie Paice, Germania Harpin and baby, Mary McConnell, Jenny Randolph, Minnie May, Mrs Atworthy, Mary Sietsema, Lola Cowan, Emily Patterson

MURDER LOCALE: All over USA and Canada

SPAN OF MURDER CAREER: 20 February 1926-9 June 1927

DATE OF CONVICTION: November 1927

Earle Leonard Nelson, born in Philadelphia in 1897, was orphaned and brought up by an obsessively religious aunt. Shunning normal childhood pastimes, he spent much of his early years with his head in the Bible. As family acquaintances said, the boy was 'too good to be true'. And they were right . . .

He became a Peeping Tom and, at the age of 21, was jailed for two years for trying to rape a neighbour's daughter. Upon his release in 1919, he changed his name to Roger Wilson, married a teacher and apparently settled down. That all changed in 1926 when he went on an evangelical tour through the United States and Canada, brandishing a Bible, staying in a string of boarding houses — and murdering their owners.

Nelson claimed 22 victims, all of them landladies who had fallen for his moralistic but charming approaches. He would strangle, then rape his victims before moving on to the next town. He became known as the 'Gorilla Murderer' because of his simian jaw, dark complexion and broad, throttling hands. He was also labelled the 'Dark Strangler' and the 'Phantom'.

Captured in Winnipeg, he went to the gallows begging for forgiveness on 13 January 1928.

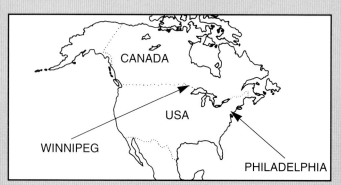

DENNIS NILSEN

NAME: Dennis Andrew Nilsen

BORN: 1945

DIED: Serving life imprisonment

PREFERRED MURDER METHOD: Strangulation

NUMBER OF VICTIMS: 15

NAMES OF VICTIMS: Kenneth Ockendon, Malcolm Barlow, Martyn Duffey, John Howlett, Billy Sutherland, Stephen Sinclair, Archibald Allen,

MURDER LOCALE: London

SPAN OF MURDER CAREER: 31 December 1978 to 27 January 1983

DATE OF CONVICTION: 4 November 1983

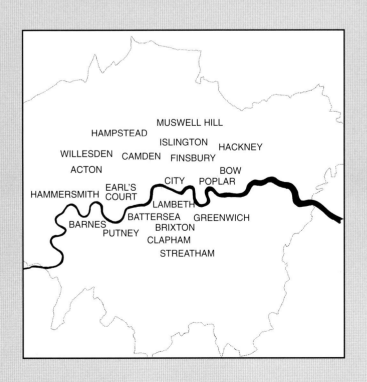

A metropolitan police poster produced following the disappearance of Canadian, Kenneth Ockenden.

Nilsen was the killer who chilled a nation, Britain's biggest mass-murderer. He claimed some 15 lives — he later disputed the number — in just over four years. Only one of his victims was missed, a Canadian tourist called Kenneth Ockendon, for whom TV and press appeals were made following his disappearance. The rest came from the shady world of single young men drifting in and out of homosexual circles looking for love or money or simply a place to spend the night.

Maniac in the making: Dennis Nilsen in Army uniform. He was to spend 12 years as a soldier.

The bespectacled clerk, who considered himself something of an intellectual, waited until his victims were soundly sleeping or deeply distracted before he made his deadly move. Armed with a tie, he lassoed their necks and squeezed the life out of them. Even today, not all the victims have been identified.

At one stage, his compulsion to kill led to a line of bodies taking up every inch of gloomy room under his floorboards. He eventually disposed of them by chopping them up and putting them in a garden bonfire which flared into a furnace as the flesh sizzled and spat.

After he moved house, he no longer had access to a garden, so he was forced to dissect corpses more fully, removing maggoty innards to dump on wasteground, while flushing much of the remaining skin and bone down the toilet.

This charnel house was 23 Cranley Gardens, Muswell Hill, North London, an address that has since gone into the archives of horror. It was there that, due to the inadequacies of the drainage system, Nilsen's crimes were finally uncovered on 9 February 1983.

Dennis Nilsen had been born 38 years earlier, far north in Fraserburgh, Scotland, the son of a local girl and a Norwegian serviceman who desert-

ed his family after World War 2. Never knowing his father, Dennis became close to his fisherman grandfather, until the kindly old man died of a heart attack. Nilsen later recalled one of his most striking childhood memories as seeing his grandfather lying in his coffin. It was the start of a lifelong obsession with death.

At the age of 15, Dennis joined the Army, fulfilling a long-term ambition. He loved the comradeship and orderliness of service life and trained as a butcher. It was in the Army that he first became aware of his attraction to men. He hid his feelings, for fear of being ostracised, indulging only by obsessively studying his naked body in a full-length mirror. Soon he discovered that he reached a peak of excitement when his body resembled a corpse with the aid of make-up and imagination. His fantasies ran wild at the grotesque images he created with the help of white face paint, blue lip colouring and vivid red dye resembling blood trickling down his T-shirt.

When he left the Army at the age of 27, Nilsen joined the Metropolitan Police. Just a year later he

Nilsen told police that he never went out looking for a victim to murder. He sought only company . . .

quit, disillusioned with life on the thin blue line. In 1974 he found himself a job as a clerical officer for the Department of Employment at a central London branch. He joined the union and wrangled tirelessly on behalf of less eloquent workers.

After a series of one-night stands, he found a young man with whom he made a home. David Gallichan whom Nilsen met in a London pub, was also lonely. They lived together in Melrose Avenue, Willesden, West London, using cash bequeathed to Nilsen by his natural father, and their relationship lasted two years although Gallichan pursued other affairs.

When Gallichan decided to move on, Nilsen was haughty on the outside and outraged on the inside that someone so clearly inferior to himself should walk out on him. He resolved that such treachery would never happen again.

At the end of 1978 Nilsen celebrated the New Year with a stranger picked up at a pub. They slept together, although apparently without having sex. As dawn broke, Nilsen realised that he could not bear this new-found bedfellow to leave. He used a tie to strangle the sleeping man, then finished him

off by plunging his head into a bucket of water.

Nilsen embarked on the ritualistic behaviour which went hand-in-hand with his horrible killings. He washed the body of his victim in the bath, dressed it in new clothes and kept it beside him for the rest of the day, making conversation as he busied himself in the flat. Affectionately, he snuggled up to the corpse, whispering sweet nothings. At night, he wrapped the body in a curtain and put it under the floorboards.

This unknown victim was the first of some 15 young men to be slaughtered by Nilsen in his grim quest for companionship. The exact number has been disputed by the killer since he was put behind bars. At first, he was shocked by his own barbarity, but it wasn't long before he accepted himself as a man compelled to kill. His targets were always the same — young homeless drifters who would not be missed. He flattered himself that he was showing more care for them after death than they ever knew in life.

The disappearance of only one of the men killed during a four-year spree sparked concern. Canadian tourist Kenneth Ockendon spent a

The peace of a suburban street London street was the perfect front for mass-murderer Nilsen.

When interviewed by a psychologist, Nilsen described his grisly work as 'like being in a butcher's shop'. It was the disposal of the bodies that led to his capture.

pleasant evening talking and drinking with Nilsen before returning to the Melrose Avenue flat, where his host used the flex of his stereo headphones to kill the friendly foreigner. Nilsen watched impassively as a poster and TV campaign was launched by Ockendon's family, appealing for information.

Soon decomposing bodies were lining up under the floorboards of the ground-floor flat. Nilsen decided to rid himself of the problem by having a bonfire in the garden. As morning broke over London, he dragged the bodies of his victims out from their dank graves and hauled them into the middle of a specially-prepared bonfire which fizzed and spluttered for hours.

When he moved to Cranley Gardens, in Muswell Hill, North London, there was no garden in which to dispose of the evidence. Instead, he butchered the bodies of the men he killed. He stewed some of the flesh, dumped more on waste land and flushed still more down the toilet. It was only a matter of time before the sewers blocked.

Nilsen lived at the top of a converted six-bedroom house which had four other occupants. They tried everything to clear a blocked downstairs toilet before calling the plumber. He failed to cure the problem and passed the job over to a larger firm. An engineer who was called in to sort out the pipework was struck by the unusual stench beneath the manhole cover. He was unable to identify the curious waste matter which he saw before him and promised to return the following day with his boss.

Alerted by the general concern, Nilsen knew that he had to so something to prevent discovery. After dark, he crept downstairs clasping a torch, dropped into the manhole and collected bucket-loads of rotting flesh. His appalling task was in vain, however. When the engineer returned, he was astonished to see that the pipes, which only hours before had been splattered with the unidentifiable mess, were now clean.

But Nilsen had not been thorough enough — and further probing by the engineer uncovered further evidence. The police were called and soon established that the material from the sewer was human flesh. Detectives were waiting for Nilsen when he returned home from work that night. When told that human remains had been found in

the drain, Nilsen replied: 'Good grief, how awful.' Only moments later, though, he confessed and took police into his flat where the grisly evidence of his last murder remained stashed in a wardrobe.

During the wave of publicity following Nilsen's arrest, model and dancer Carl Stotter told police that he had narrowly escaped death at the hands of the mass-murderer after meeting Nilsen in a pub and returning with him to the attic room in Cranley Gardens.

Stotter had later awoken gasping for breath, with a swollen tongue and burn marks around his neck. Nilsen had not only tried to strangle him but had also thrust his head into a bucket of water. For three days, Stotter was unable to move. Nilsen nursed him, tending his injuries, after convincing him he had suffered a bad dream. Stotter was one of at least seven young men attacked by Nilsen who lived to tell the tale.

In court, Nilsen's defence counsel tried to persuade the jury that the killer was mad. Thanks in part to Stotter's evidence, the panel at the Old Bailey did not believe it. He was found guilty of six murders and two attempted murders. On 4 November 1983, still showing not a shred of remorse, Dennis Nilsen was jailed for life.

Ten years later, a psychologist's interview with Nilsen was shown on television. With eerie lack of emotion, the killer said: 'The most exciting part of the little conundrum was when I lifted the body and carried it. It was an expression of my power to lift and carry him and have control. The dangling elements of his limp limbs were an expression of his passivity. The more passive he could be, the more powerful I was.'

He spoke about the dissection of bodies and how he removed people's innards when the smell was too putrid to bear. 'There isn't a lot of blood. If I stab you right now or you stab me your heart is beating. There would be blood spurting and splashing all over the place. In a dead body there is no splashing at all. The blood congeals and becomes part of the flesh. It is like a butcher's shop.'

And he expounded his astonishing theory that the dead were now a part of him: 'The bodies are all gone, everything's gone. But I still feel spiritual communion with these people.'

DR WILLIAM PALMER

NAME: Dr William Palmer

BORN: 1824

DIED: Hanged on 14 June 1856 in Stafford Gaol

PREFERRED MURDER METHOD: Poison

NUMBER OF VICTIMS: c14

MURDER LOCALE: Rugeley

SPAN OF MURDER CAREER: 1850 to 21 November 1855

DATE OF CONVICTION: May 1856

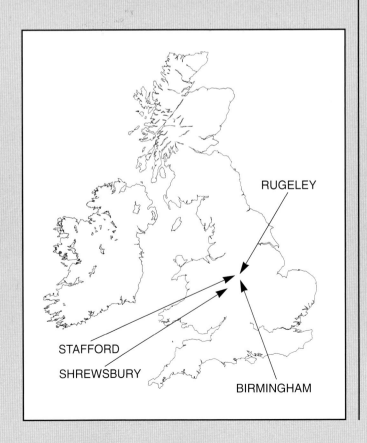

Evil Dr William Palmer had one motive for murder: plain, simple greed. He had a fondness for good living and a weakness for betting heavily on horses. Yet no matter how often he staked money on a nag's nose, he never developed a talent for this costly pastime. Sadly, his greater 'talents' were as a serial killer — he was brought to justice only after a string of mysterious deaths among his family.

William Palmer was born in 1824 in Rugeley, Staffordshire, in the English Midlands. His first attempts to join the medical profession were disgracefully blighted. By the time he was 17, he had already been dismissed from two pharmacy apprenticeships, once for taking cash and then for running an illegal abortion service.

He finally qualified as a doctor at St Bartholomew's Hospital, London, in 1846. The following year he married Anne Brookes, the heiress daughter of a wealthy widow. The harmony of his home life was shattered when a servant gave birth to his illegitimate baby. But he paid little heed to his family or, indeed, to his doctor's practice, preferring to while away his time at racecourses. He even signed over his business to an assistant to give himself more time for the turf. The inveterate gambler spent hundreds of pounds and his debts mounted.

It was then that a string of deaths occurred in

his family. First, Palmer's rich mother-in-law died while staying at his house. Then his wife, who had been heavily insured, mysteriously gave up her hold on life. His brother Walter, four children, an uncle and several of his more vocal creditors met similar ends. Palmer, it seems, regularly got away with murder.

He benefited from his wife and brother's death to the tune of some £26,000 in cash. It still was not enough to pay off the huge sums he owed. He became embroiled with money-lenders who pressed him for cash.

In November 1855, at the height of his financial woes, Palmer accompanied a gambling friend, 28-year-old John Parsons Cooke, to the races at Shrewsbury and saw him win more than £2,000. Afterwards, Cooke drained a celebratory brandy and gasped: 'Good God, there's something in it — it burns my throat.' Palmer himself nonchalantly knocked back the few remaining drops in the bottom of the glass. In front of a witness he declared: 'Nonsense, there is nothing in it.'

Cooke was taken back to Rugeley, where he stayed at an inn opposite Palmer's house. The doctor prepared for him all kinds of food and medication and was regularly at his bedside, administering broths, pills and drinks to his violently vomiting friend. A maid who sipped some of the soup also fell ill with vomiting. Palmer claimed to other visiting medics that Cooke was suffering from biliousness. In fact, he displayed not a single symptom.

Palmer waited until the bookmakers had paid out Cooke's winnings — using the money to settle some of his own gambling debts — before finally finishing him off. Poor Cooke suffered convulsions for several days before finally succumbing. His terrible death, in which he went rigid in spasms and finally suffocated, bore all the symptoms of strychnine poisoning. Afterwards, Cooke's father-in-law arrived and demanded a post mortem. During analysis of his body, no trace of strychnine was found. There was evidence, however, of antimony, a lesser drug which induces sickness.

The court case which followed at London's Old Bailey drew crowds of spectators who squeezed into the public gallery of the Central Criminal Court to witness this sensational trial. They heard the prosecution assert that only strychnine poisoning could have produced such horrible symptoms in a victim. The day before his friend's demise, Palmer had been seen buying strychnine from a local druggist. And the doctor kept a medical manual in which he had written on the first page: 'Strychnine kills by causing tetanic fixing of the respiratory muscles.'

The jury heard how Palmer stood to benefit from Cooke's death. He was found rifling through the personal belongings of his friend soon after he died. The court was told that some cash, papers and documents relating to cash matters were never found by Cooke's family. Palmer was also said to have attempted to sabotage the post mortem by hampering the surgeons carrying it out. If the jury had any doubts about Palmer's guilt, the summing up by Lord Chief Justice Campbell dismissed them. He succinctly demolished every argument put forward by the defence.

It took the jury just 100 minutes to find Palmer guilty of murder. In the dock, the evil doctor was silent. His only response to the damning verdict was a twitching around his mouth which gradually turned into a sneer.

Palmer was sentenced to be executed at Stafford Jail at eight o'clock on the morning of 14 June 1856. An estimated 25,000 people flocked to the town by road, rail, on horseback and on foot.

To the very end, Palmer refused to confess. He insisted he had been unjustly convicted of the murder of Cooke by strychnine. Most interpreted this protestation as meaning that he had killed his friend by some other means. In fact, his last remark made to the priest who visited him before his execution was: 'Cooke did not die from strychninia.'

When the governor of the jail pointed out the mode of death was secondary and that the important fact was whether or not Palmer had killed him, the condemned doctor replied: 'I have nothing more to say than this — that I am quite easy in my conscience and happy in my mind.' The murdering doctor uttered not another word, moan or groan, as the death sentence was carried out.

CARL PANZRAM

NAME: Carl Panzram

AKA: Jeff Rhoades, John O'Leary

BORN: 1891

DIED: Hanged at Leavenworth on 5 September 1930

PREFERRED MURDER METHOD: Shooting, strangulation

NUMBER OF VICTIMS: Admitted to 21

MURDER LOCALE: Worldwide

SPAN OF MURDER CAREER: 1920-1929

DATE OF CONVICTION: 1929

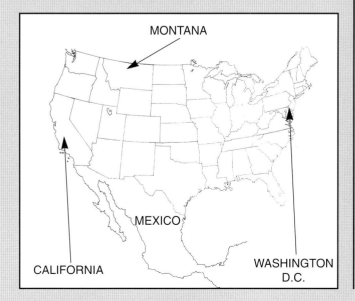

From his cell on Death Row in America's Leavenworth Prison, Carl Panzram wrote: 'In my lifetime I have murdered 21 human beings, I have committed thousands of burglaries, robberies, larcenies, arsons and last but not least I have committed sodomy on more than 100 male human beings. For all these things I am not in the least bit sorry.'

Born of Prussian immigrant parents in Warren, Minnesota, in 1891, Panzram had been in trouble with police from the age of eight. He spent several terms in prison. Historians have only his word for the tally of his crimes, since he murdered indiscriminately all over the world, but his principal areas of operation were West Africa, Mexico, California, Montana and Washington DC.

'I was the spirit of meanness personified,' he said this after a period in the army to which he had volunteered while drunk and in which he had spent three years in military prisons.

Freed in 1910, he killed indiscriminately during his travels round the world, sexually assaulting many of his victims. In 1920 he bought a yacht called *John O'Leary* and hired ten crewmen, whom he got drunk at a shipboard party and sexually abused before throwing them overboard.

In 1928 he was jailed at Leavenworth for 20 years for murder and a string of robberies. He told the warden: 'I'll kill the first man who crosses me.' He carried out his threat by battering a civilian employee with an iron bar. He went to the gallows, having spurned attempts at a reprieve by telling liberal campaigners: 'I wish the whole world had but a single throat and I had my hands around it.'

LESZEK PEKALSKI

The school trip was in full swing. No one paid any attention to the shambling figure of 16-year-old Leszek Pekalski as he lurked on the periphery. When he decided to slip away, he found it surprisingly easy.

NAME: Leszek Pekalski

BORN: 1966

REFERRED MURDER METHOD: Various

NUMBER OF VICTIMS: Admitted to 70

MURDER LOCALE: All over Poland

SPAN OF MURDER CAREER: 1982-94

DATE OF CONVICTION: 1994

It was with remarkable ease too that he happened across a girl and struck up a conversation. Nobody knows what was said. She probably felt sorry for him. Tragically, he did not extend the same feelings to her. Now was the point that a misfit turned into a murderer and began a reign of terror lasting a dozen years. By the time he was 28, Pekalski had claimed the lives of at least 70 women — to become Poland's most notorious mass-murderer.

Pekalski had a tough start to life, abused by his mother and deserted by his father. When his mother abandoned him, he was brought up by nuns and, later, was cared for by Jehovah's Witnesses. The trauma of his unhappy home life left him unable to form a loving relationship with a woman.

On the fateful day of the school trip, he discovered that a dead girl or woman could be easily controlled. After beating, stabbing or strangling his victims, he would have sex them.

Pekalski became a wanderer, travelling his homeland and killing as he went. Frequently, those he encountered took pity on him, not realising the threat. Even the police were lenient with him. In 1990 he was arrested on suspicion of rape and identified by the victim. The investigating officers merely ordered that he attend a psychiatric examination. He was finally given a two-year suspended sentence — and the killing spree continued.

After strangling and beating a 17-year-old girl to death with a metal post in woods near her home, Pekalski watched from a hideout as the girl's devastated father discovered the body. Eighteen months later a shop girl noticed Pekalski was still talking about the murder when the file on it was all but closed. At last the police pieced together the clues that led to him. He was arrested and talked to police freely about his exploits.

In a handwritten confession, Pekalski admitted carrying out 70 murders.

MARCEL PETIOT

NAME: Dr Marcel Petiot

A.K.A.: Henri Valery

BORN: 1897

DIED: Guillotined on 26 May 1946

PREFERRED MURDER METHOD: Lethal injections

NUMBER OF VICTIMS: Confessed to 63: tried for 27 and found guilty for 24

MURDER LOCALE: Auxerre

SPAN OF MURDER CAREER: 1941-3

DATE OF CONVICTION: 1946

When Doctor Marcel Petiot became mayor of Auxerre, he seemed a paragon of respectability. In 1928 his pregnant housekeeper vanished without trace. Two years later a woman patient was murdered. A friend who pointed the finger of blame at the doctor also mysteriously fell ill and died. Petiot signed the death certificate.

During World War 2, Dr Petiot pretended to be a member of the French Resistance and offered to aid refugees, mainly Jewish. Instead he robbed and murdered 27 of them. Their bodies were found in his cellar when his house burned down in 1944. Petiot fled and really did join the Resistance, using the name Henri Valery. Finally arrested in 1944, he put up an outraged defence, passing himself off as a hero of La Liberation.

The jury was sympathetic — until they heard how the doctor had injected an entire Jewish family 'for typhoid' then watched through a peephole as they died in agony. Petiot was guillotined on 26 May 1946.

Marcel Petiot thought that the smoke of war would cover his tracks but justice finally caught up with him.

JESSE POMEROY

When a number of children were abducted and sadistically tortured in the backstreets of Boston, Massachusetts, in 1872, few could believe that the foul sexual assaults could have been committed by a 12-year-old boy. Yet the culprit was indeed found to be Jesse Pomeroy, a gangling child with a hare lip, one completely white eye and extremely low intelligence.

NAME: Jesse Pomeroy

BORN: 1860

DIED: 1932 after 58 years in solitary confinement

PREFERRED MURDER METHOD: Torture and mutilation

NUMBER OF VICTIMS: Confessed to 28

MURDER LOCALE: Boston

SPAN OF MURDER CAREER: 1872-March 1874

DATE OF CONVICTION: 1874

Between December 1871 and September 1872 several boys were discovered unconscious in the backstreets of Boston after being attacked, beaten and tortured with knives, whips and even pins. Sent to a reform school, he was handed back into the care of his mother two years later and embarked on a youthful pursuit of fresh victims, both male and female. His juvenile reign of terror was finally ended in April 1874 when the hideously mutilated corpse of four-year-old Horace Mullen was found dumped in a Boston suburb.

When his mother moved house, the new owners found 12 corpses buried in the rubbish tip. Pomeroy was arrested and confessed to torturing to death 27 youngsters.

Although aged only 14, he received a death sentence, in 1876 commuted to solitary confinement for life. He served 58 years alone, making many attempts on his own life before being removed to an asylum, where he died in 1932.

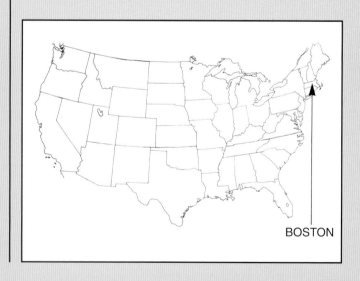

BOSTON

HEINRICH POMMERENCKE

NAME: Heinrich Pommerencke

A.K.A.: The 'Beast of the Black Forest'

BORN: 1937

DEATH: Sentenced to life imprisonment

PREFERRED MURDER METHOD: Stabbing

NUMBER OF VICTIMS: At least 10

MURDER LOCALE: Hamburg, the Black Forest and Austria

SPAN OF MURDER CAREER: 1959-60

DATE OF CONVICTION: October 1960

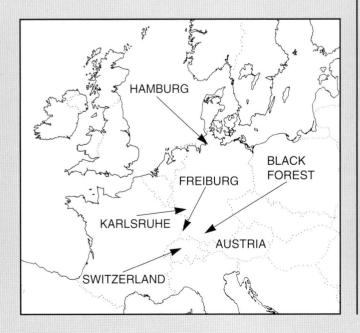

Born in East Germany in 1937, Heinrich Pommerencke became known as the 'Beast of the Black Forest'. Between 1955 and 1960 his reign of terror included at least 10 rapes and murders, 20 rapes and 35 other assaults and burglaries. His killing fields were Hamburg, the Black Forest and Austria.

Pommerencke's worst excesses were in 1959 when southern Germany lived in fear of the 'Beast of the Black Forest'. That was the year that 18-year-old Hilda Knothe was abducted in a Karlsruhe park, had her clothes ripped from her body, was brutally raped and had her throat slashed with a razor. One month later, beautician Karen Walde, 18, was raped and bludgeoned to death with a rock. And 21-year-old teacher Dagmar Klimek, sleeping in an empty railway carriage, was hurled onto the track and stabbed to death.

Although the hunt for the serial killer reached fever pitch, Pommerencke claimed two more victims before being arrested in 1960. Even then his capture was accidental — he having left a suspicious parcel in a tailor's shop. The shopkeeper called the police who discovered that the package contained a handgun. Under questioning, Pommerencke confessed to the killings.

At Freiburg, he told his trial judge that his need to kill was because 'sex films made me tense'. He was sentenced to 140 years' imprisonment.

RICHARD RAMIREZ

NAME: Richard Leyva Ramirez

A.K.A.: The 'Night Stalker'

BORN: 28 February 1960

DIED: Currently on Death Row in San Quentin

PREFERRED MURDER METHOD: Various

NUMBER OF VICTIMS: At least 19

NAMES OF VICTIMS: Included Jennie Vincow, Dayle Okazaki, Tsai-Lian Yu, Vincent and Maxine Zazzara, Harold Wu, Malvia Keller, Patty Higgins, Mary Cannon, Joyce Nelson, Maxson and Lela Kneiding, Chitat Assawahem, Ahmed Zia, Peter and Barbara Pan

MURDER LOCALE: Los Angeles and San Fransisco

SPAN OF MURDER CAREER: June 1984 to 31 August 1985

DATE OF CONVICTION: 1989

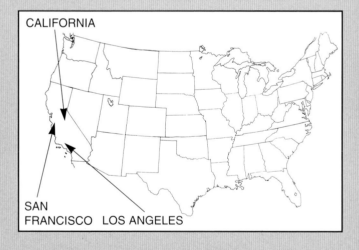

CALIFORNIA

SAN
FRANCISCO LOS ANGELES

Richard Ramirez, or the 'Night Stalker' as he was dubbed by the media, was an avowed satanist who terrorised the streets of Los Angeles between June 1984 and August 1985. His favoured method was to creep into a house at night, shoot or strangle any adult males and then subject women and children to sadistic rape and mutilation. Occasionally he would leave his mark as the 'devil's disciple' — an inverted pentagram scrawled on a mirror or wall. He also used to draw occult signs on the victims' bodies.

Ramirez, born in El Paso, Texas, in 1960, turned to crime at an early age. A police profile described him as 'a confused, angry loner who sought refuge in thievery, drugs, the dark side of rock music, and finally murder and rape.'

As the 'Night Stalker', he was responsible for at least 19 victims, whose ages ranged from the early 30s to the 70s. The ways he dispensed with his victims were varied but included shooting, bludgeoning, throat cutting or battering to death. Although the attacks satisfied Ramirez's sadistic sexual urges, he also stole from those he killed. For many of his younger victims the terror would be heightened as he drove them out of the city miles from home, dumping them in open country to fend for themselves.

Many citizens of the Los Angeles environs began to believe that the 'Stalker' had a demonic power that made him unstoppable . . . until the FBI got lucky. They found a fingerprint in a getaway car used after one of the attacks and matched it to those of a known petty criminal called Richard Ramirez. His photograph was circulated to the press, though detectives could have had little idea of the instant reaction it would bring.

One August Saturday in an LA suburb, a man tried to drag a woman out of her car. He was attacked by her husband and the gathering crowd suddenly recognised the face they had seen in that morning's newspapers. Ramirez, for so long the monster who thrived on instilling fear into others, now knew how it felt. He was attacked by the mob and turned over to the cops bruised and bleeding.

Ramirez, then aged 25, was duly convicted and received 19 death sentences. He knew he was unlikely to be executed, however, as California had not carried out an execution since 1967. Before leaving the courtroom for San Quentin's death row, he snarled: 'You maggots make me sick. I will be avenged. Lucifer dwells within all of us.' Of the death sentence he joked: 'Big deal. Death comes with the territory. See you in Disneyland.'

Ramirez was convicted of 19 murders and sentenced to death. He still awaits execution in San Quentin.

'Night Stalker' Richard Ramirez's murderous trademark was an inverted pentagram.

CHARLES SCHMID

NAME: Charles Howard Schmid

ACCOMPLICES: Mary French, John Saunders

BORN: 8 July 1942

DIED: Died in prison while serving life imprisonment.

PREFERRED MURDER METHOD: Various

NUMBER OF VICTIMS: 3

NAMES OF VICTIMS: Alleen Rowe, Gretchen and Wendy Fritz

MURDER LOCALE: Arizona

SPAN OF MURDER CAREER: 31 May 1964 to 16 August 1965

DATE OF CONVICTION: 1966

Charles Schmid (left) and accomplice John Saunders.

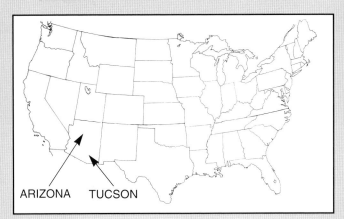

ARIZONA   TUCSON

Born on 8 July 1942, Charles became the adopted son of Charles and Katharine Schmid, of Tucson, Arizona. He was pampered and seemed to be a perfectly normal child. But Schmid had a problem that obsessed him — his height. As a teenager, he was only 5ft 3in and felt he needed to compensate for this by telling tall tales and 'buying' friends with drink and drugs.

Schmid's wealthy parents gave him everything, including a house, and it was there that he became leader of a pack of druggies. He seduced several female followers — but once the novelty of sex wore off his thoughts turned to murder. On 31 May 1964 Schmid, his girlfriend Mary Rae French and John Saunders murdered Alleen Rowe, battering her to death with a rock.

On 16 August 1965 Schmid killed again, this time on his own. He strangled two sisters, Gretchen and Wendy Fritz. His friend Richard Bruns helped him dispose of the bodies in the Arizona desert but later turned Schmid in.

All three were arrested on 11 November and at the ensuing trial American parents were horrified by what many saw as the moral decline of the nation's youth. Saunders was sentenced to life imprisonment, and Mary French received four to five years. With capital punishment abolished in Arizona, Schmid was sentenced to two terms of life imprisonment.

In November 1972, however, Schmid and a triple murderer escaped from the Arizona State Penitentiary. They hid on a ranch where they held the owners hostage for two days before splitting up, mercifully without committing further homicides. They were recaptured shortly afterwards.

JOHN SCRIPPS

NAME: John Scripps

A.K.A.: The 'Tourist from Hell'

BORN: 1961

DIED: Hanged 19 April 1996

PREFERRED MURDER METHOD: Various followed by dismemberment to dispose of bodies

NUMBER OF VICTIMS: 4

NAMES OF VICTIMS: Timothy MacDowall, Gerald Lowe, Daren and Sheila Dalmude

MURDER LOCALE: Far East

SPAN OF MURDER CAREER: October 1994 to March 1995

DATE OF CONVICTION: 11 November 1995

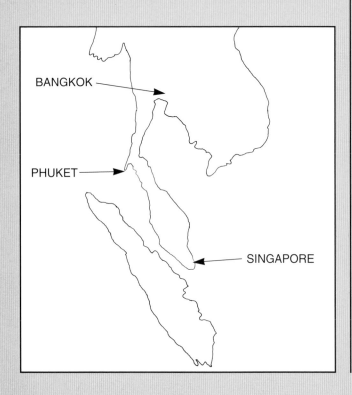

John Martin Scripps earned his nickname the 'Tourist From Hell' through his habit of killing holiday-makers he befriended as he travelled around the world.

Scripps, son of a London lorry driver and a bar-maid, was an accomplished thief while still in his teens. At the age of 19 he stole enough money to fund a trip to Canada where he met and fell in love with a 17-year-old Mexican schoolgirl. He later traced her to her home in Mexico and brought her back to Britain to marry her.

His bride left him when, at 23, he was jailed for three years for a string of 40 burglaries. Scripps never got over the loss. He turned to drugs and in 1988 was jailed for 13 years for heroin trafficking. He absconded in 1994 while on weekend leave from his Hertfordshire prison.

Scripps travelled to Spain, linked up with some old cellmates and obtained enough money to fly to Mexico. There he took out a new British passport in the name of John Martin and used it to travel to Singapore, Bangkok, Hong Kong, Los Angeles, San Francisco and Miami.

In 1995 he returned to Mexico via Belize and met a 28-year-old Cambridge graduate, Timothy MacDowall, who was on a backpacking holiday. When MacDowall's family reported him missing the following month, it was found that more than £13,000 had been transferred from his British bank to various accounts opened by Scripps in America. Detectives believe Scripps killed MacDowall and scattered parts of his body around Belize.

On 8 March, Scripps arrived in Singapore and checked into the River View Hotel. At the reception desk he met chemical engineer Gerard Lowe and talked him into sharing a room to cut costs. That night he killed Lowe, cut up his body, wrapped the pieces in bin liners and dumped them in a nearby waterway. They later resurfaced in Singapore harbour.

Scripps flew on to Bangkok and then to the Thai island of Phuket. On the plane he met Canadian Sheila Damude, 48, who was travelling with her 21-year-old son Daren. They and Scripps booked into adjoining rooms at a Phuket hotel. The Damudes were seen having breakfast there the following morning — the last time they were seen alive. Scripps murdered them later in the day, placed a 'Do Not Disturb' sign outside their hotel room and went off the dump their bodies.

He was finally arrested as he arrived back in Singapore on 19 March. Police suspected him of

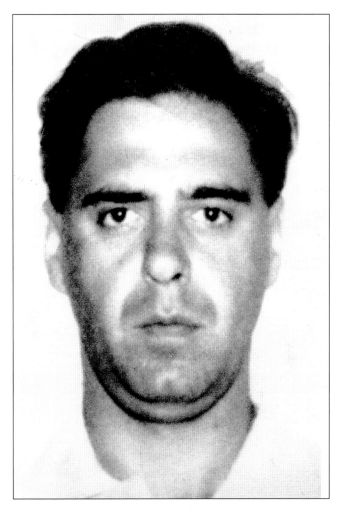

Scripps' was executed in Singapore's notorious Changi Prison on 19 April 1996.

fraud, but a search of his bags uncovered valuables belonging to the Damudes and Gerard Lowe. Also in his backpack were a hammer, two serrated knives, a mace spray, two sets of handcuffs, a set of thumb cuffs, and a 10,000-volt stun-gun. Scripps confessed to killing Lowe but would not comment about the other deaths. He was put on trial for murder and on 11 November 1995 received the sentence of death.

Scripps at first sought clemency from the Singapore government. But as the prospect of a prolonged incarceration in the notorious Changi Prison dawned on him, he withdrew his plea.

On 19 April 1996, as dawn broke over the Straits of Singapore, he was led to a wooden scaffold. Hooded and with his hands and feet bound, a rope was put around his neck and, at 6am, the trap door opened.

JOSEPH SMITH

NAME: George Joseph Smith

A.K.A.: The 'Brides in the Bath Murderer'

BORN: 11 January 1872

DIED: Hanged in Maidstone Prison on 13 August 1915

PREFERRED MURDER METHOD: Drowning

NUMBER OF VICTIMS: 3

NAMES OF VICTIMS: Beatrice Mundy, Alice Burnham, Margaret Lofty

MURDER LOCALE: Herne Bay, Blackpool, London

SPAN OF MURDER CAREER: 13 July 1912 to 18 December 1914

DATE OF CONVICTION: 1 July 1915

Joseph Smith (above) and seen posing with one of his unfortunate 'wives', Beatrice Mundy (above right).

Joseph Smith, born 1872, became known as the 'Brides In The Bath Murderer' because he killed three of his five bigamously-wed wives after the first, Caroline Thornhill, whom he married in 1898, left him and emigrated to Canada.

Smith, of Bethnal Green, London, then used a series of pseudonyms for his subsequent, bigamous marriages. Beatrice Mundy died by drowning in July 1912 still clutching a piece of soap in her hand. Alice Burnham left a large clump of hair in her death bath. But the murder of Smith's final victim, Margaret Lofty, proved literally a fatal mistake for him. A newspaper reported her drowning in London, revealing suspicious similarities with the previous deaths.

Smith was tried at the Old Bailey and hanged at Maidstone Prison on 13 August 1915.

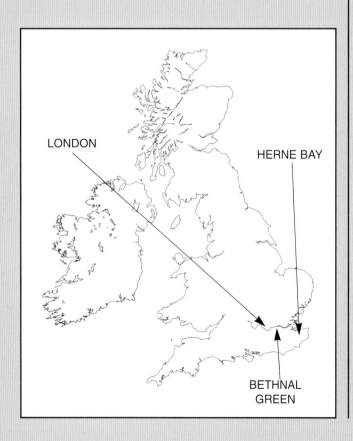

LONDON

HERNE BAY

BETHNAL GREEN

RICHARD SPECK

A nurse opened the door of her Chicago hostel quarters on 14 July 1966 and heard the frightening words: 'I'm not going to hurt you.' At the door was Richard Speck, a tall, gangling 25-year-old with blonde hair and a pockmarked face.

NAME: Richard Franklin Speck

BORN: 6 December 1941

DIED: Sentenced to death, commuted to life imprisonment

PREFERRED MURDER METHOD: Strangulation or stabbing

NUMBER OF VICTIMS: 8

NAMES OF VICTIMS: Gloria Davy, Suzanne Farris, Merlita Gargullo, Mary Jordan, Patricia Matusek, Valentina Pasion, Nina Schmale, Pamela Wilkening

MURDER LOCALE: Chicago

DATE OF CONVICTION: 6 June 1969

He forced three nurses upstairs into another room and tied them up, telling them that he needed money to get to New Orleans. Downstairs he found three more and bound them too. The intruder had been there for a half hour collecting money and jewellery when three more girls arrived home and were also tied up.

It was then that Speck began to take the girls one by one into a separate room at intervals of approximately 25-30 minutes. The first was Pamela Wilkening. She never returned.

Speck continued taking the girls out individually and, as the number of nurses decreased, panic set in. One of the girls, Curazon Amurao, managed to wriggle under the bed and was overlooked by Speck as he proceeded to lead her friends into the other room. From under the bed, Curazon managed to get a good look at Speck, later enabling her to give police a full description. The hidden witness choked her sobs as Speck's last vic-

tim, Gloria Davy, was subjected to an horrific sexual assault. She was raped for about 25 minutes before finally being led to the other room. Curazon stayed in hiding under the bed for hours, even after Speck left.

When the police arrived, they found one of the bloodiest crime scenes ever. After the girls had been led into the other room, they has been either strangled or stabbed, or both.

Curazon told the police that the man who murdered the nurses had a tattoo — 'Born To Raise Hell' — tattooed on his arm and had spoken in a Southern accent. With this information, and the knowledge that the knots binding the nurses' wrists had almost certainly been tied by a seaman, detectives questioned officials of the Seamen's Union who speedily identified Speck. Conclusive proof that he was the sadistic killer was gained by matching fingerprints from the nurses' home with those on a form that he had recently filled out.

Speck had a history of robbery and burglary. Married at the age of 20, he had begun to suffer bouts of uncontrollable violence after discovering that his wife was having affairs.

ILLINOIS   CHICAGO

LUCIAN STANIAK

NAME: Lucian Staniak

A.K.A.: The 'Red Spider'

BORN: 1941

DIED: Committed to asylum 1967

PREFERRED MURDER METHOD: Rape mutilation and disembowellment

NUMBER OF VICTIMS: At least 20

NAMES OF VICTIMS: Include Janina and Aniella Kozielska, Bozena Raczkiewicz

MURDER LOCALE: Poland

SPAN OF MURDER CAREER: 1964-67

DATE OF CONVICTION: 1967

Nicknamed the 'Red Spider', Lucian Staniak murdered some 20 Polish girls between 1964 and 1967. Travelling the country in search of his victims, he would rape them before mutilating and often disembowelling them. His mode of operation drew likenesses with the infamous 'Jack the Ripper'.

He sent a series of crowing, taunting letters, all written in a distinctive spidery red script, to Polish newspapers. The first read: 'There is no happiness without tears, no life without death. Beware, I am going to make you cry.'

He certainly made detectives weep with frustration as he stalked young blondes, usually striking on public holidays. His first victim, a 17-year-old girl, was raped and murdered at Olsztyn on the anniversary of Poland's liberation from Nazi occupation. The 'Spider' followed up his vile deed with a sinister threat to police: 'I picked a juicy flower in Olsztyn and I shall do it again elsewhere, for there is no holiday without a funeral.'

In 1967 police narrowed their suspects to 26-year-old Lucian Staniak, a translator whose job with a Krakow publishing firm took him to all parts of the country. He said he had begun his killing spree after a woman driver, who had mown down and killed his sister and parents, was let off by a court. His first victim was chosen for her likeness to the woman. Staniak admitted 20 murders and was tried for six of them. He was ordered to be incarcerated for life at Katowice asylum.

JOHN STRAFFEN

NAME: John Straffen

BORN: 1930

DIED: In prison

PREFERRED MURDER METHOD: Strangulation

NUMBER OF VICTIMS: 3

NAMES OF VICTIMS: Brenda Goddard, Cicely Batstone, Linda Bowyer

MURDER LOCALE: Bath

SPAN OF MURDER CAREER: 15 July 1951 to July 1952

DATE OF CONVICTION: Sentenced to death July 1952, later commuted to life imprisonment

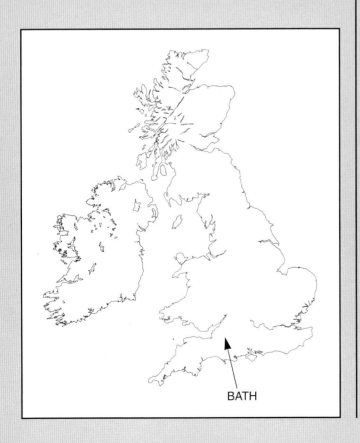

BATH

Child killer John Straffen spent his childhood at a school for the mentally retarded. As a youth he was sent to an institution for assaulting a 13-year-old girl. At the age of 22, he strangled two small girls — a crime he said he committed simply 'to annoy the police' because he hated them so much.

Straffen's problem was that he had the mind of an eight-year-old but the rage and sexual urges of an adult. The courts simply did not know what to do with him. After assaulting the 13-year-old girl, they sent him to an institution. But his inevitable release at the age of 21 resulted in the deaths of his next two victims, in the town of Bath where he lived.

This time Straffen was sent to Broadmoor asylum for the criminally insane — but he escaped back into the English countryside within six months, as a result of extraordinarily lax security when he was allowed to sweep a yard beside an unlocked gate. Within a bare three hours he had struck again, murdering five-year-old Linda Bowyer before being recaptured.

The case of John Straffen created a furore in Britain around the timeless dilemma over how to treat or incarcerate dangerous mental defectives. In July 1952 he was found guilty of his third murder and sentenced to death, later commuted to life imprisonment.

PETER STUMP

NAME: Peter Stump

ACCOMPLICES: Katherine Trompin, Beell Stump

PREFERRED MURDER METHOD: Various followed by cannibalism

NUMBER OF VICTIMS: 15

MURDER LOCALE: Bedburg, Germany

SPAN OF MURDER CAREER: 1564-89

DATE OF CONVICTION: 1589

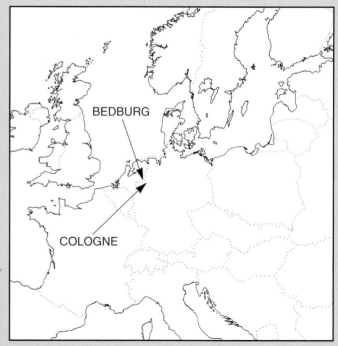

In 1589 Germany hosted one of the most sensational trials in history — that of Peter Stump, accused of selling his soul to the Devil for the ability to transform himself into a wolf. Aided and abetted by his daughter and mistress, Stump had roamed the countryside inflicting his atrocities upon the innocent. Whether or not anyone thought of him as a 'werewolf' hardly matters. No servant of Satan could have contrived a more devilish, stomach-churning existence.

The tortures and punishment finally endured by Stump following his capture near Cologne are horrible to record. Yet they represent barely a tenth of the suffering he meted out to the unfortunates who crossed his path.

For 25 years Stump roamed the countryside around the village of Bedburg tearing innocent victims to shreds to satisfy his bloodlust. According to a contemporary assessment of his foul deeds, once he had tasted human flesh, 'he took such pleasure and delight in the shedding of blood that he would night and day walk the fields and perform extreme cruelties.'

His favoured victims were young girls, whom he captured and raped before 'changing into a wolf' to tear them apart. In just five years, according to his German biographer, he murdered 15 women and children, including two girls who were pregnant. In some cases, he tore out their hearts and ate them 'panting hot and raw'.

Stump was aided and abetted in his savagery by his mistress, Katherine Trompin, and by his daughter, Beell, with whom he was committing incest. Beell bore him a son but such was his stomach-churning depravity that he ate the infant — and declared the brains as 'a most savoury and dainty delicious' meal.

Until his capture, limbs of his victims were found almost weekly in the fields around Bedburg, whose villagers dared not leave their homes unless armed or protected. Stump's atrocities upon the innocent finally ended when, ironically, a pack of hunting dogs led their masters to him in their search for what they believed to be a real wolf.

When tracked down, he is said to have still been in the guise of a werewolf. According to the superstitious witnesses, he made a desperate last attempt to resume his human shape as he hid behind a bush. But he was spotted removing his 'Devil's Girdl' (a supposedly false skin) and seized.

In court in Cologne, he was predictably found guilty, and his fate matched in horror that of his victims. The judge ordered: 'His body shall be laid on a wheel and, with red hot burning pincers, in several places to have the flesh pulled off him from the bones. After that his legs and arms to be broken with a wooden hatchet, afterwards to have his head struck from his body, then to have his carcass burned to ashes.'

After being forced to watch the burning of Stump's headless corpse, his mistress and daughter were also burned at the stake.

Peter Stump was accused of selling his soul to the Devil for the ability to transform himself into a werewolf.

PETER SUTCLIFFE

NAME: Peter William Sutcliffe

A.K.A.: The 'Yorkshire Ripper'

BORN: 2 June 1942

DIED: Sentenced to life; sent to Broadmoor 1984

PREFERRED MURDER METHOD: Hammer blows

NUMBER OF VICTIMS: 13

NAMES OF VICTIMS: Wilma McCann, Emily Jackson, Irene Richardson, Tina Atkinson, Jayne MacDonald, Jean Jordan, Yvonne Pearson, Helen Rytka, Vera Millward, Josephine Whitaker, Barbara Leach, Marguerite Walls, Jacqueline Hill

MURDER LOCALE: Leeds, Bradford, Huddersfield, Halifax, Manchester

SPAN OF MURDER CAREER: 30 October 1975 to 17 November 1980

DATE OF CONVICTION: 22 May 1981

Peter Sutcliffe on his wedding day

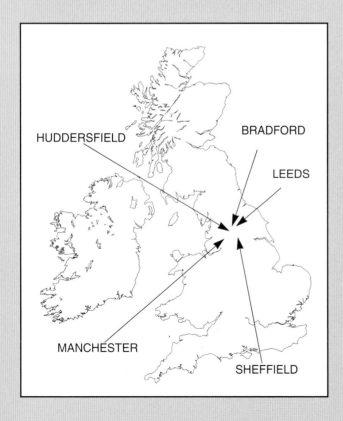

It could have been just another routine murder — the fatal attack upon a prostitute by one of her sick 'tricks'. But the stabbing to death of Wilma McCann was to be the start of a series of murders which has gone down in 20th century criminal history.

Newly married Peter Sutcliffe and wife Sonia.

The 28-year-old prostitute, whose half-naked body was found on a playing field in Leeds on 30 October 1975, was the very first victim of the 'Yorkshire Ripper'.

It was almost three months before the killer struck again, on 20 January 1976. This time the target was 42-year-old prostitute Emily Jackson, found dead with horrific injuries in the Chapeltown red-light area of Leeds.

The post-mortem examination found more than 50 stab wounds inflicted with a heavy-duty Phillips screwdriver, which left a distinctive star shaped penetration mark. There was also the imprint of size-seven Dunlop boot on her thigh, as though the murderer had stamped on her. But the injuries which killed Emily Jackson, and presented the police with crucial clues, were the two crushing hammer blows delivered to her head.

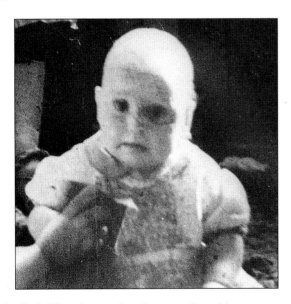

Peter Sutcliffe when only a few months old.

On 9 May a prostitute who picked up a 'trick' in Roundhay, Leeds, was attacked with a hammer. Through the fog and pain of semi-consciousness, she was later able to tell police how her assailant masturbated nearby and then slipped a £5 note into her hand warning her not to tell anyone what had happened. She also gave what would later be recognised as an excellent description of the 'Ripper' but because she had been diagnosed as educationally sub-normal, little heed was paid to her words.

On 6 February 1977 a jogger discovered 28-year-old Irene Richardson's body open ground at Roundhay, Leeds. It bore the typical, sickening hallmarks of a 'Ripper' killing: body face down, death caused by hammer blows to the skull, stab wounds to the stomach. Bizarrely, her boots had been arranged carefully between her open thighs.

Within the next year, five more women would be dispatched in similarly horrific circumstances. There was Patricia Atkinson, found dead on 23 April, a 33-year-old Bradford prostitute who would be the only one of the 13 victims killed indoors. Her bedsheets bore the distinctive size seven boot mark and she died from four heavy blows to the

LEFT: Peter Sutcliffe leaves Newport Court, Isle of Wight.

ABOVE: The Press watch a blanket-covered Sutcliffe in police custody.

head. There were six chisel marks found on her abdomen.

On 26 June the 'Ripper' murdered his youngest victim, 16-year-old Jayne MacDonald. She was on a night out with friends but was found dead the following morning in a playground near Chapeltown. Heavy blows to the head had probably killed her but the murderer had again inflicted numerous stab wounds.

The next attack came on 10 July in Bradford. But although the 42-year-old victim was slashed from her breasts to her navel and bore four chest stab wounds, she survived an emergency operation. Her description of her attacker turned out to be inaccurate — hardly surprising under the circumstances.

By now undercover police were so widespread in the Leeds and Bradford red light districts that the 'Ripper' struck west into the heart of Manchester. There, on the night of 1 October, he murdered prostitute Jean Jordan, 20, with 11 blows to the head and 28 separate stab wounds.

Her body lay for more that a week in a cemetery at Moss Side. But when it was at last discovered, charred from burning, it yielded a vital clue. Her murderer had foolishly paid her with a new £5 note, serial number AW 51 121565. It was one of a batch distributed to a particular bank and distributed through various employers to less than 6,000 people. One of those was a lorry driver called Peter William Sutcliffe, aged 31, the man who would one day be unmasked to the world as the 'Yorkshire Ripper'.

Sutcliffe was among those interviewed. Police learned that the former gravedigger was holding down a well-paid job as a long-distance lorry driver and owned a house in Bradford where he lived with his Czech-born wife, schoolteacher Sonia Szurma. But it was Sutcliffe's criminal past which should have alerted detectives. In 1969 he had been arrested for 'going equipped for theft', officers having found him in possession of a hammer.

With hindsight, it seems incredible that this incident, taken alongside the £5 note clue, failed to ring alarm bells with detectives. The 'Ripper' himself recognised that he had made a stupid mistake in paying Jordan with a new £5 note. Before her body was found, he had returned to Moss Side to

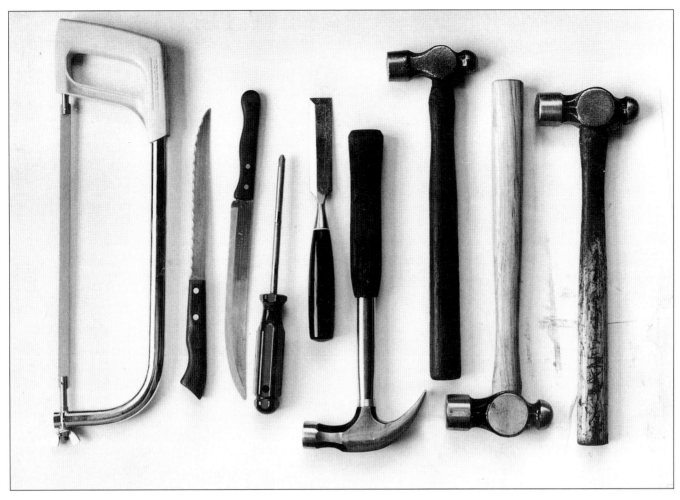

The tools of the 'Yorkshire Ripper'.

try to recover it. He failed, and in a fury slashed the body open with a knife. In a clumsy attempt to disguise the attack as a 'Ripper' killing, he had then burned the body on a bonfire in a nearby allotment.

The scare did little to deter Sutcliffe. In December he attacked a woman in Leeds. Miraculously, she survived and was able to tell detectives that her assailant hit her over the head, screaming: 'You dirty prostitute.'

Soon after New Year 1978, the 'Ripper' carried out two murders in 10 days, a sign that his confidence was sky high. Yvonne Pearson, aged 22, was battered and stabbed to death on 21 January in Bradford. Her body was not found until 26 March, by which time the killer had clearly returned to inflict fresh wounds. On 31 January his victim was 18-year-old Helen Rytka from Huddersfield — the only one of his victims with whom Sutcliffe had sex.

Then on 8 March police received a communication they regarded as one of their best clues to date — the first of three letters signed 'Jack the Ripper' and posted from Sunderland. Detectives took them seriously but tragically they were a cruel hoax.

And so the killings continued. Vera Millward, murdered on 16 May in the car park of Manchester's Royal Infirmary, was smashed over the head and had her stomach slashed open. Josephine Whitaker, a 19-year-old building society worker, was the subject of frenzied stabbing and died on 4 April 1979. Barbara Leach, a 20-year-old Leeds University student, was killed by a blow to her head and eight stab wounds to the stomach. Her body was found in Bradford on 2 September.

It was almost a year before Sutcliffe claimed his 12th victim, 47-year-old executive officer Marguerite Walls. She was found covered with grass clippings near her home in Farsley, between Leeds and Bradford, on 18 August 1980. The 'Ripper' had switched from his usual techniques,

Sutcliffe being led away after a hearing.

perhaps in a bid to confuse police, and had strangled her with a ligature. A few weeks later a 34-year-old Singapore doctor studying at Leeds University was also attacked with a noose. But she was luckier, saved by a passing police car which scared Sutcliffe off.

By now more than 250 officers were working full-time on the biggest manhunt in British criminal history. Nearly 200,000 people had been interviewed, over 160,000 vehicles checked, 23,000 households contacted and £5 million spent.

A (now infamous) tape recording had been sent to Yorkshire police purporting to come from the 'Ripper'. The Geordie accent further convinced the squad that the man they sought was from the north-east. This too proved to be a hoax, however.

Sutcliffe was interviewed by the police five times — twice in November 1977 about the £5 note, in August 1978 because his car had been seen in a red light district, in November 1978 when his tyres were checked and on 29 July again about his red light jaunts. During the July interview, the officer concerned even urged his superi-

ors to regard Sutcliffe as a prime suspect. His report went unheeded. Sutcliffe, it was pointed out, didn't have a Geordie accent.

It was a routine police enquiry that finally ended the carnage. The 'Ripper' was stopped with a prostitute in Sheffield, the city he had targeted as his new stalking ground. He was arrested on suspicion of theft (his car had false number plates) but the discovery of the ball-peen hammer and Phillips screwdriver nearby rang alarm bells with the officers. Later at Dewsbury police station, Sutcliffe told his interrogators: 'I am the "Yorkshire Ripper".' His full confession took 16 hours to dictate.

On 22 May 1981 Peter Sutcliffe was found guilty of 13 murders and seven attempted murders. He was given a life sentence with a recommendation that he should serve at least 30 years. Later psychiatrists declared him mad, and he was sent to serve his time in Broadmoor hospital for the criminally insane.

JACK UNTERWEGER

When Jack Unterweger was arrested for the murder of a teenage girl, he seemed to be just another killer.

But, though sentenced to life imprisonment, Unterweger was determined to prove he was no common criminal. At every opportunity he pored over books. He acquainted himself with the great writers. He edited a prison newspaper and literary review. He wrote a book — semi-autobiography called *Fegefeuer* (Purgatory) — which became a best-seller. In it, Unterweger tried to explain his violent past — by the age of 24, when he committed the murder, he had 15 convictions including burglary, rape and pimping.

There followed a play and a clutch of literary awards. Unterweger's infamy turned into fame. He became beloved of the free-thinking society and was held up as a paragon, the criminal who reinvented himself as one of the good. His early release from prison, in October 1990 after serving 15 years, was heralded as a great social reform.

He was feted in society and appeared on TV chat shows. He favoured white suits and red bow ties and drove expensive cars with the licence plate 'KACK 1'. Yet behind the facade of a writer, he had the soul of a serial killer. Despite his spell behind bars, the urge to kill did not leave him.

In public he was a hero, while in private he embarked on a orgy of murder. And yet during his 20 months of freedom, he was constantly under suspicion from the police. Prostitute murders normally averaging one a year in Austria suddenly grew. The bodies of four women were found during April and May 1991 alone.

Unterweger's killing spree spread across Austria where he killed six women in the spring of 1991 and into Czechoslovakia. Three murders were committed in Los Angeles between June and July

NAME: Jack Unterweger

BORN: 1950

DIED: Hanged himself in prison in June 1994

PREFERRED MURDER METHOD: Strangulation with item of clothing

NUMBER OF VICTIMS: At least 11

NAMES OF VICTIMS: Included Margaret Schäfer, Brunhilde Masser, Heide Hammerer, Elfriede Schrempf, Sylvia Zagler, Sabine Moitzi, Marica Harvat and Karin Sladky.

MURDER LOCALE: Austria, Czechoslovakia and Los Angeles

SPAN OF MURDER CAREER: 1974-1991

DATE OF CONVICTION: June 1994

1991 — exactly the same period Unterweger was there. Each had been strangled with her own bra.

By now, the police had a growing file of the murders and their stark similarities. The victims were picked up in red-light districts; strangled with articles of their own clothing; they were naked; they had been subjected to bondage rituals; some attempt had been made to bury them; their clothing was scattered and although their jewelry was left, personal effects such as letters were missing. It was obvious the killer wanted to exercise power over his victims and inflict pain and humiliation.

Unterweger was arrested in Florida in 1992. He was extradited to Austria where he was held on remand, standing trial only in April 1994. In March he was convicted of nine murders and he was sentenced to life without parole.

After the verdict, he was taken to Graz prison where, 12 hours later, he hanged himself.

THE 'WEREWOLF OF CHÂLONS'

A case unique in the annals of serial killers is that of the nameless 'Werewolf of Châlons', arraigned in Paris in 1598 on murder charges so sickening that all documents were destroyed after the case. Referred to in court records only as the 'Demon Tailor', even his real name has become lost in history.

NAME: Unknown

A.K.A.: The 'Demon Tailor'

DIED: 1598

PREFERRED MURDER METHOD: Throat-slitting followed by cannibalism

NUMBER OF VICTIMS: Unknown

MURDER LOCALE: Châlons, Paris, France

DATE OF CONVICTION: 14 December 1598

Medieval France was the centre of spate of witch-hunts which reached their most bizarre in the pursuit of 'werewolves'. In a span of 100 years, no fewer than 30,000 cases were reported to the authorities. Some of these could be attributed to rabies, prevalent at the time, and which turns its victims into aggressive madmen. Others might nowadays be diagnosed as cases of lycanthropy.

The term tends to be used to describe someone who is assumed to be mentally sick and believes he has assumed wolf-like characteristics. The study of lycanthropy is the only way in which medical science can today come to terms with the long-held beliefs in werewolf delusions, which predate the birth of Christ by 1,000 years. In France 400 years ago, for instance, church and state believed literally that such a metamorphosis could take place. It was just as the terror of werewolves reached fever pitch that the 'Demon Tailor', from Châlons, was dragged into the dock on 14 December 1598.

The Paris court was told that the tailor lured into his shop a string of unsuspecting victims — the younger the better. There he would subject them to gory perversions before slitting their throats and dressing the flesh, almost as if he were a professional butcher. He would then eat them.

The monster's despicable habits also took him to woods around the city where he would 'assume the form of a wolf' and prey on innocent walkers. The total number of his victims was never properly established but it ran into dozens. When his house was raided, barrels of bones immersed in bleach were found in the cellar.

When he was sent to the stake the day after his trial, a huge crowd gathered. Unlike many another convicted werewolf who repented of his sins as the first flames licked around his legs, the 'Demon Tailor' betrayed no hint of remorse. He could be heard cursing and blaspheming to the very end.

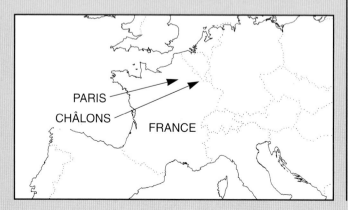

PARIS

CHÂLONS

FRANCE

FRED AND ROSE WEST

NAME: Frederick and Rosemary Pauline West

BORN: Fred — 29 September 1941
Rose — 29 November 1953

DIED: Fred — Hanged himself in Winson Green Jail,
1 January 1995
Rose — Still serving life imprisonment

PREFERRED MURDER METHOD: Various

NUMBER OF VICTIMS: 12

NAMES OF VICTIMS: Anne McFall, Rena West,
Charmaine West, Lynda Gough, Carol Cooper, Lucy
Partington, Therese Siegenthaler, Shirley Hubbard,
Juanita Mott, Shirley Robinson, Alison Chambers,
Heather West

MURDER LOCALE: Gloucester

SPAN OF MURDER CAREER: 1967-92 (Rose from
1969)

DATE OF CONVICTION: Rose — 1996

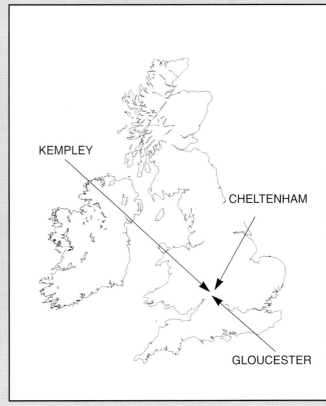

The address was No 25 Cromwell Street — an ordinary semi-detached house in an ordinary terrace. An anonymous, grime-streaked place, the kind of functional home you might find in any British city. Few passers-by ever gave it a look — certainly not a second glance.

The occupants, Fred and Rose West, were generally well-liked by their neighbours. Most considered him a cheery, hard-working type and her a busy, lively mother. There were a few mutterings about the surprising number of night-time male visitors, and some concern that the children were occasionally disciplined too harshly. But it didn't amount to much. Certainly nothing to tell the police or social services about. In privacy-obsessed Britain it was no one else's business.

And so, for more than two decades, Fred and Rose's secret life flourished unchecked. Like an all-consuming cancer, their career as sadistic sexual torturers and murderers of young girls became the very focus of their existence, their whole reason for being. In a world where the word 'evil' has become something of a cliche, the Wests' crimes could have been crafted by the devil himself. To describe them merely as 'evil' is a little like describing Stalin as misguided.

Only their pathetic victims discovered the whole, sickening truth. These victims it was who were dragged down to the dark cellar, their faces sheathed in sticky brown parcel tape, plastic breathing tubes stuffed inadequately into their nostrils, limbs bound tightly. Only they glimpsed the depths of the Wests' depravity in those last agonising moments.

Even after the sweet release of death, the girls were denied any dignity. Mutilated — some say cannibalised — by their tormentors, the bodies would be heaved unceremoniously into pits dug in the cellar or the back garden. No one thought it odd that Fred carried out a lot of do-it-yourself work around the house. After all, he was a builder.

The terrible secrets of 25 Cromwell Street were unfolded to an incredulous world during Rose West's trial in November 1995. Soon everyone was asking the same questions. Why did it happen? How could fate have thrown together two of the most devilish minds in the history of crime and allowed them to feed off each other's sordid desires. Part of the answer, say the psychologists, lies in their past.

Rosemary Pauline Letts was born on 29 November 1953 in a maternity hospital at Barnstaple, North Devon. She grew up in the

Three of the Wests' victims, from left to right: Alison Chambers, Anne Mcfall, Shirley Robinson.

nearby seaside village of Northam and went to infant school there. Teachers remember her as an ordinary little girl. As one put it: 'She didn't excel at anything, neither was she a troublemaker.'

But at home, life for the young Rose was anything but ordinary. Her father William Letts, a steward in the Royal Navy, battered and bullied his wife Daisy and treated the seven children with appalling severity. As the third youngest, Rose escaped the worst of his attentions. But her brothers lived in fear of a man later diagnosed as a schizophrenic psychopath.

When Rose was 11, the family left Northam for Plymouth, later moving to Bishop's Cleeve near Gloucester. But by 1969 Daisy decided she could no longer hold the marriage together. She walked out, taking Rose and her two younger brothers with her. That same year, as Rose waited at a bus stop in Cheltenham, she met the man who would help shape her terrible destiny. She was chatted up by Fred West, then 27, and began to go steady with him. At the time, police now believe, he had already committed two murders. For her part, the busty, 15-year-old Rose had begun dabbling in prostitution. It was truly a match made in hell.

Heather West.

Fred's past had been equally traumatic. Born on 29 September 1941, he grew up with no guidelines to acceptable sexual behaviour. His mother (coincidentally also called Daisy) regarded him as her favourite, and there were rumours that she seduced him at the age of 12. His father, Gloucestershire farm labourer Walter West, was equally fond of incestuous relationships. Fred, who had two younger brothers and three sisters, would later tell how his father regarded the children as sexual playthings, saying that it was natural for him to have sex with them and that he had a right to do so. No wonder Fred began to follow the same route.

In June 1961 Fred was hauled down to the local police station and accused of making a 13-year-old girl pregnant. To the amazement of the officers, he seemed unabashed and openly admitted molesting young girls. 'Doesn't everyone do it?' he asked.

It was a turning point in Fred's life. Although he escaped on the child abuse charge (his terrified victim collapsed and refused to give evidence in court) his close relationship with his mother was over. She banished him from her house and he went to live with his Aunt Violet in nearby Much Marcle.

Fred West killed his daughter Heather in 1987.

The Wests' back garden is covered over as police search for bodies.

By the time Fred met Rose on that summer day in Cheltenham, he was already a family man. His first wife, Rena, had been five months pregnant by another lover when she married Fred on 17 November 1962. Fred gave baby Charmaine his name and he and Rena then had a child of their own, Anne-Marie.

The marriage soon ran into trouble. Fred wanted her to enact sadistic sex games with him, a prospect she loathed. When they split up, he took his two girls with him and Rose became their stand-in mother.

For little Charmaine, it was a tortuous childhood. The Wests abused her terribly on the grounds she was 'not one of theirs'. Years later, during Rose's trial, witnesses told of watching Charmaine being forced to stand on a wooden chair, her hands tied behind her with a leather belt, while Rose raised a wooden spoon to beat her.

Police believe that at some point Fred West killed Charmaine. And when Rena came looking for her little girl, he dispatched her in the same dispassionate manner. Neither of them was ever reported missing and Charmaine's absence was easily explained by Rose: 'She's gone off with her mother,' she told friends.

On 17 October 1970 Rose and Fred had their first child, Heather. Two years later they were married and moved into their first proper home, 25

Cromwell Street. Now they could create their own fantasy world, a world in which Rose not only freely indulged Fred's desire for sadistic sex but actively embraced it herself.

The house became filled with whips and chains, manacles and bondage gear. There would be the home-made pornographic films, the attempts at bestiality, the string of punters who paid for Rose's servicers as a prostitute. And all the time, the couple were on the lookout for young girls whom they could lure home as sexual playthings. In this, Rose played a key role. Fred later admitted that it was a lot easier to pick up girls when he had Rose in the car with him. The hapless victims felt more secure when they saw a woman present. Once they found out their mistake, it would be too late.

However, Fred West claimed his first victim long before he met Rose. Eighteen-year-old Anne McFall, from Sandhurst, Gloucestershire, began an affair with Fred while she was working as a nanny for him and Rena, and she was soon pregnant by him. Police believe he murdered her because she

Policeman in the Wests' garden.

started putting pressure on him to end his relationship with Rena. She was buried in a field at Kempley, Gloucestershire, in 1967 next to the body of her unborn child. Police recovered her remains in June 1994, the year most of the victims' bodies were uncovered.

The next two to die were Rena and little Charmaine. Police believe Fred killed his wife when she came looking for her child in 1971 and that Charmaine was strangled a few hours later. Charmaine was buried at the Wests' first home — 25 Midland Road, Gloucester — and was found on 4 May 1994. Rena was buried next to Anne McFall at Kempley. Her body was also dug up by police in 1994.

Murder number four was carried out on a 19-year-old Gloucester girl called Lynda Gough. She had become friendly with some of Fred and Rose's lodgers at the Cromwell Street house and in

Police dig for bodies at Much Marcle.

March 1973 she moved in herself. She was dead within a matter of weeks, the victim of a twisted sex 'game' in which she was an unwilling player. Her dismembered body was found beneath the bathroom floor. Tape had been wound thickly around her head and her limbs were piled on top of each other.

The fifth victim was 15-year-old Carol Cooper, the resident of a children's home in Worcester. She was last seen on the night of 10 November 1973 as she boarded a bus to visit her grandmother. West admitted killing her, although he claimed Rose wasn't involved. Carol was found under the cellar floor at 25 Cromwell Street.

Sixth to die was Lucy Partington, a devoutly religious 21-year-old from Gretton, Gloucestershire, who was studying medieval English at Exeter University. She vanished in Cheltenham on the night of 27 December 1973 as she walked to a bus stop. The Wests picked her up as they drove back from a Christmas visit to Rose's parents in Bishop's Cleeve, and over the next week

they subjected her to a horrendous ordeal of torture and rape, ending with her dismemberment by Fred. On 3 January 1974 he checked into a hospital casualty department suffering from a deep cut to his hand — an injury now thought to have been caused as he hacked up his helpless victim.

Next of the known victims was Swiss-born Therese Siegenthaler, aged 21, from London. She had been hitch-hiking to Ireland for a holiday when Fred West picked her up in his lorry near Chepstow. She was taken to Cromwell Street where she was imprisoned and subjected to a sado-masochistic orgy. Police found her remains under a floor at Cromwell Street. Like many of the other victims, she had limbs and bones missing — possibly hacked out by Fred as gruesome souvenirs.

The eighth to be murdered was another school-girl, 15-year-old Shirley Hubbard, from Droitwich, Worcestershire. She vanished on 14 November 1974 as she travelled from Worcester by bus back

25 Cromwell Street, Gloucester.

to her foster parents' home. Fred wound one of his 'mummy'-style masks around her face and pushed breathing tubes into her nostrils. Then he repeatedly raped her. Her body was found under the cellar floor at Cromwell Street.

Juanita Mott was next to die in the Wests' torture chamber. Picked up as she hitch-hiked into Gloucester from her home in Newent on 11 April

1975, Juanita Mott was lured home by the Wests, tied with 17ft of grey plastic clothes line and endured ligatures made from her own stockings. The 18-year-old was killed by a blow from a ball hammer, after which Fred decapitated her and buried her in his cellar.

The tenth victim, Shirley Robinson, was a bisexual 18-year-old who shared three-in-a-bed sex sessions with the Wests. Her fate was sealed after she became pregnant with Fred's child and fell in love with him. During the spring of 1978 Rose, who was pregnant with the child of a West Indian man, began to feel jealous and put pressure on her husband to get rid of Shirley. Fred later told his brother-in-law Jimmy Tyler: 'Shirley is mooning about and hanging round me all the time. Rose just won't stand for it. She'll have to go.' Shirley vanished on 11 May 1978. Her body was found next to that of her unborn child in the garden of 25 Cromwell Street.

A few months after Shirley's death, Fred and Rose latched on to 16-year-old Alison Chambers, who was exactly the kind of vulnerable girl they liked so much. She was a resident at a children's care home in Gloucester but visited Cromwell Street regularly to see a friend lodging there. The Wests asked her to become their nanny but soon after she moved in she became embroiled in their sadistic sex play. She was last seen on 5 August 1979 and was found by detectives underneath Fred's lawn.

The last known victim, Heather West, was also the one who first roused police suspicions about Fred and Rose's family life. Born in 1970, Heather is thought to have been the result of an incestuous relationship between Bill Letts and his daughter. Fred made her life hell, administering vicious beatings when she refused to let him molest her. She feared her parents so much that by the time she was a teenager she avoided talking in their presence. Heather disappeared on 17 June 1987 and the Wests told friends and neighbours that she had run away from home. The explanation was generally accepted . . . but this was one killing too far. Like many a murderer before them, over-confidence was their downfall.

In the summer of 1992 Police Constable Steve Burnside was walking his Gloucester beat when he was approached by a group of children who claimed that youngsters were being abused at a house in Cromwell Street. They thought the family's name was Quest, and their warning was convincing enough to warrant further police interest.

That same year, all five remaining West children aged under 16 were taken into care by the local social services and Fred and Rose were charged with a series of sexual offences, including rape and buggery.

Yet still they eluded justice. The case against them was dropped after two prosecution witnesses refused to testify. The couple hugged each other in the dock. Their ordeal, as they saw it, was over.

Detective-Constable Hazel Savage, of Gloucestershire Police, had other ideas. She had investigated the allegations and was convinced something terrible was going on behind the doors of Cromwell Street. In quiet chats with the West children, she first won their trust and then began to coax information from them.

The subject often came back to Heather's disappearance. Fred, said the children, would often make jokey remarks about her being 'under the patio'. To Savage's mind, the 'jokes' were made a little too often to be simply the product of one man's poor taste. Early in 1994, she approached senior officers for guidance. At first they were sceptical and advised that much more evidence was needed. But Savage persisted. On 23 February 1994 she obtained a search warrant and the following day police began digging in the garden. On 25 February, Fred and Rose West were arrested. The secrets of the 'House of Horror' were at last being laid bare.

At exactly 12.55pm on Wednesday 23 November 1995 the jury foreman at Winchester Crown Court announced that Rose West had been found guilty of the murders of all 10 victims whose deaths had been linked to her. She was sentenced to life imprisonment and the judge, Mr Justice Mantell, told her: 'If attention is paid to what I think, you will never be released.'

Soon afterwards, police announced they were continuing investigations into the deaths of nine other girls who disappeared after visiting Cromwell Street.

Fred West never stood trial for his appalling crimes. On New Year's Day 1995 he hanged himself in his cell at Winson Green jail, Birmingham — a humane death by his standards. In one of those odd twists of fate, he was found by prison staff at 12.55pm, exactly the same time of day that his wife would later hear her fate in court. He had cheated justice but, in the eyes of many people, his final act was the only decent thing he ever did.

WAYNE WILLIAMS

NAME: Wayne Bertram Williams

A.K.A.: The 'Atlanta Child Murderer'

BORN: May 1958

DIED: Still serving life imprisonment

PREFERRED MURDER METHOD: Strangulation

NUMBER OF VICTIMS: Convicted of 2; official list gives 28

NAMES OF VICTIMS: Convicted for Ray Payne and Nathaniel Cater; others include Yusuf Bell, Milton Hervey, Angel Laner, Eric Middlebrooks, Christopher Richardson, Lubie Gater

MURDER LOCALE: Atlanta, Georgia

SPAN OF MURDER CAREER: July 1979 and 21 May 1981

DATE OF CONVICTION: February 1982

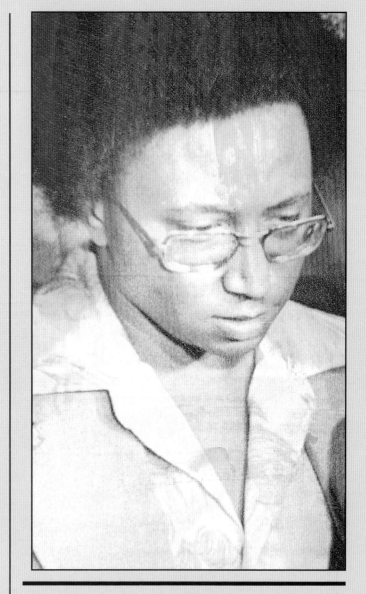

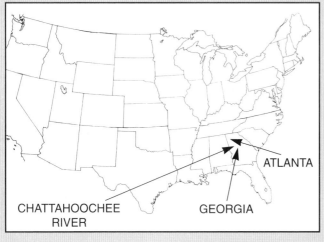

The killings started in July 1979 when two black children were strangled in the heart of America's deep south. Within a year, the number of victims notched up was seven . . . but that was only the start.

Corpses began to turn up in and around Atlanta, Georgia, at the rate of one a month. All of them were young — not nearly strong enough to fight off an adult attacker. Their bodies were dumped in rivers or on waste ground. A pattern emerged. The dead were aged between 7 and 14, and all but two were boys. There was evidence of sexual assault.

Yet none of this helped the manhunt. Families began keeping their children behind bolted doors to save them from the fiend. When the number of unsolved deaths reached 26, the public were baying for justice. President Ronald Reagan was so shocked that he pledged a special grant towards the hunt for the killer. Yet months after the slaughter of the innocents started, there was hardly any evidence to lead detectives to the perpetrator.

Determined officers interviewed 20,000 people trying pin down the killer. A further 150,000 were quizzed on the telephone. A task force of 35 FBI officers were installed in Atlanta to flush out who-

ever was responsible but it was all to no avail. Dozens of bounty hunters descended on Atlanta, attracted by the bonanza of $100,000 reward money. Despite their eagerness to cash in no fresh clues were turned up. Desperate parents formed vigilante groups to protect their families. They armed themselves with baseball bats and patrolled the streets — but failed to find the elusive killer.

Police chief Lee Brown was left scratching his head and wondering at the audacity of the mystery killer. He ruled out the possibility of a white man with a racist grudge — a white man would be unable to mingle with black children in playgrounds without attracting attention to himself. Serial killers also prey on their own kind, so a white killer would target white children. No, it seemed a black serial killer was on the loose.

Wayne Williams is led into court in Atlanta, where he called the prosecutor a 'fool'.

Finally, the breakthrough the police craved for occurred as a team of officers kept watch on South Drive Bridge spanning the Chattahoochee River. Their idle chatter was silenced by the sound of a splash only feet away from the spot where they were standing. The team, comprising two policemen and two FBI officers, sprang into action. Two men plunged into the river, although they failed to find the cause of the splash. The others ran to the road and helped seal off the bridge.

For the first time, lawmen came face to face with serial killer Wayne Bertram Williams — if only they had known it. He was one of the drivers stopped, questioned and released that night. It was two days before frogmen turned up the body of Nathaniel Cater, a 27-year-old black who had been strangled. A few days later, the body of 21-year-old Ray Payne, likewise black and choked, was also hauled from the river. Both had been thrown into the water from the bridge at the same time. It seemed the killer had broken his pattern and turned his deadly attentions to adults, too. Police once again scrutinised the list of drivers stopped on the bridge that fateful night in May 1981. Williams, a 23-year-old who lived with his parents in a suburb of Atlanta, was brought into the police station and held overnight.

Wayne Williams was a curious figure. Ostensibly, he was a radio ham who ran an advertising agency. But he was no traditional ad-man, spending much of his time tuning into short wave radio to monitor police and ambulance activity. When an incident occurred, he would speed to the scene, photograph the action and sell the result to local newspapers and television stations. He was well-versed with the ways of the media. After being pulled in for questioning for a second time, he himself hosted a news conference at which he declared his innocence. 'One cop told me, "You killed Nathaniel Cater. It's just a matter of time before we get you." I never killed anybody and I never threw anything from the bridge.'

He remained under round-the-clock surveillance while police desperately sought the evidence they needed to nail him. The vital link finally came from the forensic laboratories, where scientists discovered that dog hairs taken from Nathaniel Cater's clothes matched those in

Williams protested his innocence — but the killings ceased once he was locked up.

Williams's car. They further linked him with 10 other victims.

Now the prosecution case literally hung by a hair. Williams continued to protest his innocence. At the start of the nine-week trial, in which he was accused of murdering Cater and Payne, it didn't take long for Williams's talented lawyer, Alvin Binder, to rip the paltry evidence to pieces, but a crucial ruling by the judge changed everything. He allowed the prosecution to introduce evidence which linked Williams with other victims even though he was not accused of their murders.

A 15-year-old boy testified that he had been fondled by Williams and that he had later seen his abuser with Lubie Geter, 14, a victim of the strangler. More witnesses told how they had seen Williams in the company of other victims.

In the dock, Williams denied being gay, called the prosecutor 'a fool' and accused the police and witnesses of lying. He said: 'I never met any of the victims. I feel just as sorry for them as anybody else in the world.' It took the jury of eight blacks and four whites 12 hours to decide on a verdict. They must have been mindful that while Williams was in custody, the string of killings had stopped. Williams, they declared, was guilty. He was led to the cells, tear-stained and still protesting his innocence.

RANDALL WOODFIELD

NAME: Randall Brent Woodfield

A.K.A.: The 'I-5 Killer'

BORN: 26 December 1950

DIED: Still serving life in Oregon State Penitentiary

PREFERRED MURDER METHOD: Shooting

NUMBER OF VICTIMS: At least 2; probably over 20

NAMES OF VICTIMS: Shari Hull, Julie Reitz, Donna Eckard, Janell Jarvis

MURDER LOCALE: I-5 Freeway from Washington State through Oregon and California

SPAN OF MURDER CAREER: 18 January 1981 to 15 February 1984

DATE OF CONVICTION: June 1981

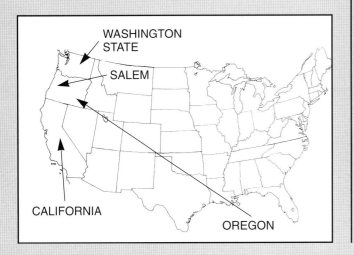

Oregon was a state in fear in 1990; a so-called 'thrill killer' was on the loose. He wore a fake beard that was to become his trademark, and he soon became known as the 'I-5 Killer'. His name was Randall Brent Woodfield.

At first Woodfield attacked and stole from his victims. As he became more unhinged, however, he turned to perversion, rape and murder. One of his most vicious attacks was on two girls aged eight and ten whom he forced to perform oral sex on each other in their own bedroom before allowing them to go free.

In January 1981 two Salem office workers, Lisa Garcia and Shari Hull, were sexually assaulted, striped and finally shot through the head. Neither of the girls was dead, however, and Lisa managed to get to a phone and call for help. Shari Hull died later in hospital and from then the police were looking for a killer.

Woodfield committed more rapes and murders up and down the I-5 freeway. His greatest mistake was murdering Julie Reitz, whom he shot through the head in her house.

There were strong links between the two of them and before long the police had arrested him. Woodfield had a great career ahead of him as an American footballer, but his habit of exposing himself had put an end to it.

Woodfield received 90 years imprisonment, with an additional 35 years for rape.

GRAHAM YOUNG

NAME: Graham Frederick Young

BORN: 7 September 1947

DIED: 1 August 1990 in Parkhurst of a heart attack

PREFERRED MURDER METHOD: Thallium poisoning

NUMBER OF VICTIMS: 3

NAMES OF VICTIMS: Molly Young, Bob Egle, Fred Biggs

MURDER LOCALE: London and Bovingdon, Herts

SPAN OF MURDER CAREER: 21 April 1962 to 19 November 1971

DATE OF CONVICTION: July 1972

Sinister schoolboy Graham Young was different from the rest. While others his age played soccer, climbed trees and scabbed their knees, he preferred to tinker with his chemistry set. His interest was not confined to making smoke bombs or colourful explosions. He had a passion for poisons — and a deadly desire to try them out.
It wasn't long before his childhood games took on a frightening reality which was to lead to murder and life imprisonment.

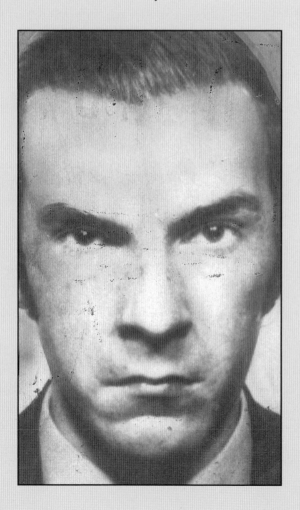

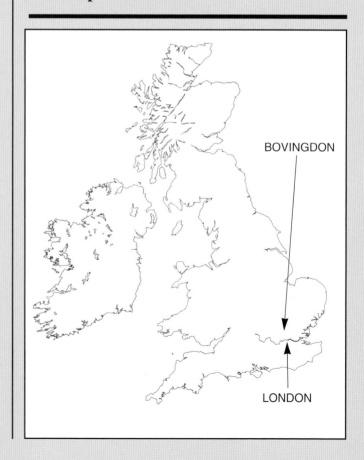

BOVINGDON

LONDON

Born in 1947, Young had a lonely childhood, his mother having died when he was just three months old. Initially cared for by his mother's sister, at the age of two Graham was sent to live with his father, who had since remarried. After being torn from his first, happy home, the child would never trust anyone's affection again. Graham Young developed an eerie coldness towards the human race.

Cutting himself off from the world, the lonely boy chose for his role models a number of infamous villains. He was fascinated by the activities of Victorian criminals Dr Hawley Crippen, the wife killer, and Dr William Palmer, the poisoner. Then at the age of 13 Graham Young read a book that was to change his life and seal his fate: about another Victorian medic, Dr Edward Pritchard, who poisoned his wife and mother with antimony. Young obtained antimony from a local pharmacist by lying about his age — and astonishing the chemist with his knowledge of poisons which he was using in his school 'experiments'. He began carrying a phial of the poison around with him at all times, referring to it as 'my little friend'.

The most obvious guinea pigs for Young's bizarre compulsion were his schoolfriends in the London suburb of Neasden. One of them became seriously ill after his sandwiches were laced with antimony over several days. When Young's stepmother discovered the bottle and confiscated it, the murderous prodigy simply switched to another supplier . . . while at the same time turning his attention to members of his immediate family. In 1961 his sister began to suffer severe stomach cramps. Soon bouts of aches and agonising pains afflicted the entire family. The symptoms continued to worsen throughout that year and the next. In April 1962 his stepmother died after terrible suffering. Her body was cremated, destroying all evidence of her poisoning. At 14, Young had committed the 'perfect crime'.

For some, that shocking event might have served as a stark reminder of the perils of playing with poison. Not for Young, however, who persisted in dosing the food and drink of his father and sister. Anxious experts finally diagnosed that they were suffering the effects of poison. Young's father had taken arsenic, they decided.

The reaction of his teenage son was breathtaking. 'How ridiculous,' snorted Young, 'not being able to tell the difference between arsenic and antimony poisoning.'

It was Young's chemistry teacher who uncovered the boy's murderous intent. Searching his desk, the teacher found drawings of people dying in agony with bottles of poison by their side. There were also charts of what doses of various poisons would kill a human being. The police were called in and, posing as careers guidance officers, interviewed Young.

He was swiftly taken into custody when police found sachets of antimony tartrate in his pockets. They were also aghast to discover that Young, although admitting affection for his family, was far more concerned with the outcome of his experiments than with their welfare. At his subsequent trial, the 15-year-old was found guilty but insane. His destination was the criminal psychiatric institution, Broadmoor.

Nine years later, apparently cured of his fatal fascination, Graham Young was released. He applied for a menial job at the firm of John Hadland, makers of specialist, high-speed optical and photographic instruments in Bovingdon, Hertfordshire. While admitting to knowing something about chemicals, he did not confess his guilty past. Instead, he told how he had suffered a mental breakdown after the death of his mother. A psychiatrist's report produced on his behalf stated that Young had made 'an extremely full recovery' from a 'deep-going personality disorder'. Young would 'fit in well and not draw any attention to himself in any community,' the report added.

Indeed, Young did slot in. His workmates made him welcome in his capacity as storeman. They shared jokes and cigarettes with him. In return, he would be unofficial tea boy, happily furnishing them with hot drinks to repay their kindness.

Suddenly, staff were struck down with a mystery disease, soon nicknamed the 'Bovingdon bug'. Within weeks of Young being employed, in June 1971, about 70 people were affected with symptoms including diarrhoea, cramps, backache, nausea and numbness.

Head storeman Bob Egle, 59, one of Young's closest colleagues, was among the worst hit. After

187

eight days of searing pain, he died in hospital. The doctors blamed broncho-pneumonia and polyneuritis. Meanwhile, other employees were still wracked with pain. By September, 60-year-old Fred Biggs was ill. His condition deteriorated over the weeks and, in November, he died. Another man was in hospital while others were falling sick by the score.

Young seemed genuinely shocked and saddened by the death of Bob Egle. He even went to his victim's funeral. When Fred Biggs passed away, he apparently said: 'Poor old Fred. I wonder what went wrong? He shouldn't have died. I was very fond of old Fred.'

By now there was a general tide of panic in the company. Many employees were terrified the chemicals they were using would cause them serious damage. There was a full inquiry launched by the management, part of which included a head-to-head discussion between investigation chief Dr Arthur Anderson and the workforce.

During the debate, Graham Young could not resist revealing the impressive extent of his expert knowledge of poisons. The humble storeman asked the doctor whether he believed the illnesses were consistent with signs of thallium poisoning.

Arthur Anderson was instantly suspicious. Young's knowledge of chemicals appeared too thorough and detailed for a layman. He wanted to find out more about the background of the young fellow who by now had been employed at Hadland for six months.

Detective Chief Inspector John Kirkland, of Hemel Hempstead Police, was called in and he in turn contacted Scotland Yard. Within hours, the full, sorry story of Young's miserable past caught up with him. He was arrested on suspicion of murder. When police pounced, he was carrying a bottle of thallium — tasteless, odourless and deadly.

Young freely admitted to police his involvement, unable to let the opportunity to prove his skills pass. 'I could have killed them all if I wished . . . but I let them live,' he told detectives.

At his home, police found rows of bottles containing a variety of chemicals. They were stacked beneath the picture portraits of Young's heroes — Adolf Hitler and other odious members of the Nazi high command.

Graham Young was a child prodigy – as a poisoner. The 15-year-old was found guilty of murder but insane.

Young went on trial at St Albans Crown Court accused of two murders, two attempted murders and two cases of administering poison. Despite his confession to police, he denied the charges. His audacity was staggering. When incriminating entries in his diary were produced, he claimed they were no more than notes for the plot of a novel.

A diary entry before the death of Biggs read: 'I have administered a fatal dose of the special compound to F. and anticipate a report on his progress on Monday. I gave him three separate doses.'

It took the jury less than an hour to find Graham Young guilty. He was sentenced to jail for life. Young did indeed spend the remainder of his miserable life in custody. In August 1990, the arch poisoner was found on the floor of his cell at Parkhurst Prison. He had died from a heart attack at the age of 42.

'ZODIAC'

NAME: Unknown

PREFERRED MURDER METHOD: Various

NUMBER OF VICTIMS: 7 although later letter suggested 37

NAMES OF VICTIMS: Included David Faraday, Bettilou Jensen, Darlene Ferrin, Cecilia Shepherd, Paul Stine

MURDER LOCALE: Vallejo and San Fransisco, California

SPAN OF MURDER CAREER: 20 December 1968 to 11 October 1969 (?)

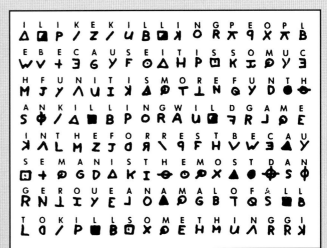

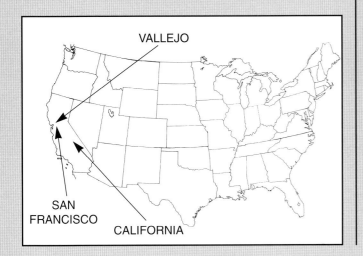

The brief reign of terror of the killer known only as 'Zodiac' lasted for just a year, during which time he slew five people and wounded two more. The killings were followed by letters to San Francisco newspapers — letters so gruesomely detailed that they could only have been written by the murderer himself. Each letter was signed with the symbol of the zodiac: a cross superimposed on a circle.

The first slayings were of a teenage couple in a lovers' lane near Vallejo on 20 December 1968. They had been shot as they apparently fled from their car. They had not been molested or robbed, and there was no obvious motive for the crime. On 5 July 1969 a man with a gruff voice called police to report a double murder in the same area, adding: 'I also killed those kids last year.' This time police found a 22-year-old waitress dead and her 19-year-old boyfriend seriously wounded. Their assailant had driven up alongside their car and opened fire without warning.

A month later, three newspapers received coded messages from the murderer, who threatened to go on a 'kill rampage' if they were not published. Each paper complied, and when the three fragments of code were matched, Zodiac's message was found to read:

'I like killing people because it is more fun than killing wild game in the forest, because man is the most dangerous animal of all. To kill something gives one the most thrilling experience. It is even better than getting your rocks off with a girl. The best part of it is when I die I will be reborn in paradise and all I have killed will become my slaves. I will not give you my name because you will try to slow down or stop me collecting slaves for my afterlife.'

The message ended with further coded letters. Thousands of members of the public claimed to have cracked the clues and proudly sent police the results, but all leads proved fruitless.

On 27 September the gruff telephone voice of the 'Zodiac' told police to search the shores of Lake Berryessa, where they found two students stabbed. The girl had suffered a frenzy of knife thrusts to her front and back and she died in hospital two days later. Her boyfriend, however, survived to describe the attack by a hooded figure with the zodiac sign across his chest. The assailant also daubed the sign on the side of their white car, along with the dates of the previous slayings.

Two weeks later, 'Zodiac' shot a young cab driver dead through the head and fled into the streets of San Francisco. Witnesses described a man in his forties, about 1.7m (5ft 8in) tall, with thick horn-rimmed glasses and crew-cut brown hair.

A shred of bloodstained shirt ripped from the cab driver's back was sent to the San Francisco Chronicle accusing police of incompetence and threatening to wipe out a school bus. A man believed to be the killer rang the police four days later, offering to give himself up if he could talk to a famous lawyer on a live television show. Lawyer Melvin Belli stood by on a morning talk show. A record audience listened at home with bated breath as a man calling himself 'Sam' phoned the show 15 times. But the gruff voice was not apparent and police feared the caller was a hoaxer.

San Francisco police had no strong clues to the identity of the 'Zodiac' when the killings suddenly stopped. In December 1969 they received a further piece of bloodstained shirt, accompanied by a letter that claimed eight murders — causing detectives to search their files in vain for an eighth victim who could be attributed to the 'Zodiac'. Nothing further was heard from the killer until 1974, when a further letter was received claiming a total of 37 victims and threatening that 'something nasty' was about to happen. 'Zodiac' has never been heard of since.

HANS VAN ZON

NAME: Hans van Zon

ACCOMPLICE: Old Nol

BORN: April1942

DIED: Serving life imprisonment

MURDER METHOD: Bludgeoning with lead piping

NUMBER OF VICTIMS: 5

NAMES OF VICTIMS: Elly Hager-Segor, Claude Berkley, Coby van der Voort, Jan Dense, Reyer de Bruin

MURDER LOCALE: Holland

SPAN OF MURDER CAREER: July 1964 to August 1967

DATE OF CONVICTION: 1968

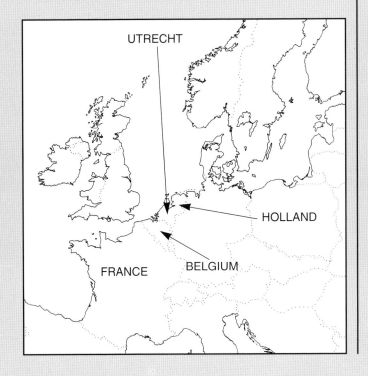

Born in Utrecht, Holland, in April 1942, Hans Von Zon was a compulsive liar and weaver of fantasies at a very early age.

Gradually sliding out of the real world, he built around himself a complete fantasy existence, to the despair of his mother and eventually of his employers. Sacked from all of his teenage jobs, Von Zon began posing as a student, viewing that as more glamorous lifestyle than his own.

In 1958, at the age of 16, he turned to crime. At first he was only a minor confidence trickster but he soon graduated to thieving. Von Zon realised that he had homosexual tendencies but tried to hide them. In 1964 he dated a girl but, after his first attempt at lovemaking, she called off the affair. Spurned, he slit her throat. His next love affair was with a homosexual movie director. For whatever reason, that relationship also turned sour and the man was similarly dispatched by his lover. Von Zon did not kill again for three years.

Shortly after the slaying of his male lover, Von Zon married a chambermaid, who supported both of them on her meagre wages. Gradually becoming fearful that he was plotting to kill her, his wife went to the police, who put him in jail for a month to cool down. But it was not his wife who was to be his next victim; Von Zon was keeping a 37-year-old mistress who, when she tried to end the affair, had her head smashed in with a lead pipe and her throat cut with the familiar bread knife.

Von Zon then teamed up with an ex-convict called Old Nol who blackmailed him into committing a string of other murders. The two were caught when blows from lead piping failed to kill their final victim. Nol was sentenced to seven years. Von Zon was given a minimum of 20 years, and psychiatrists were amazed at the various worlds he had created for himself. He believed he was everything from a CIA agent to a movie star.

ANNA ZWANZIGER

NAME: Anna Zwanziger

BORN: 1760

DIED: Under the headsman's sword 1811

PREFERRED MURDER METHOD: Poison

NUMBER OF VICTIMS: 3

NAMES OF VICTIMS: Frau Glaser, Judge Grebhard, Frau Grebhard

MURDER LOCALE: Nürnberg

SPAN OF MURDER CAREER: Taken into custody October 1809

CONVICTION: 1811

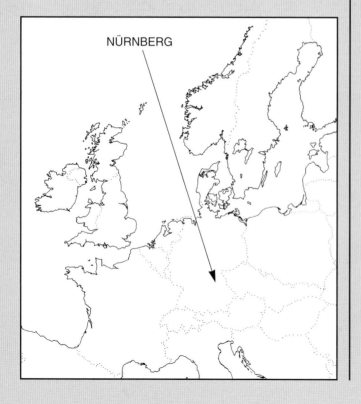

NÜRNBERG

Born Anna Schönleben in Nürnberg, Germany, in 1760, she married a successful lawyer named Zwanziger. But when he became a hopeless alcoholic, his wife was forced onto the streets.

Since her husband was now consuming 10 bottles of wine a day, Anna became a prostitute to support herself and two children. But, always one to assume airs and graces, she insisted to her friends that she only ever slept with 'gentlemen'.

With her coquettish ways, she learned how to win over older men — and put the gift to her advantage. Upon the death of her husband, she advertised herself as a gentlemen's housekeeper and inveigled her way into the service of the lonely and wealthy. She then set about ridding herself of all rivals to her affections.

Her first victim was the wife of an old judge she was working for. The woman died in agony of poison. Anna had hoped to benefit from the aged judge's will. Her next victim was another judge whom Anna killed when she discovered he had wedding plans which did not involve her. She also put arsenic in the drink of three servants, although incredibly they survived.

The third judge she worked for refused to believe his wife's feeling that food tasted strange since their new housekeeper's arrival. It was only when he himself found a white sediment in his brandy glass that he became suspicious. It was too late. His wife and baby died from poisoning.

Anna Zwanziger was arrested in October 1809 after police exhumed her victims' bodies and discovered traces of arsenic. She eventually confessed saying that she trembled with pleasure when she was handling arsenic. She was put to death by the sword in 1811.